BRANDO

BRANDO
A LIFE IN OUR TIMES
RICHARD SCHICKEL

Atheneum
New York 1991
Maxwell Macmillan Canada
Toronto
Maxwell Macmillan International
New York Oxford Singapore Sydney

For
Olympia Dukakis,
Austin Pendleton,
Louis Zorich,
Actors' Actors
and a Critic's Friends

Copyright © 1991 by Richard Schickel

Atheneum   Maxwell Macmillan Canada, Inc.
Macmillan Publishing Company   1200 Eglinton Avenue East
866 Third Avenue   Suite 200
New York, NY 10022   Don Mills, Ontario M3C 3N1

Macmillan Publishing Company is part of the Maxwell
Communication Group of Companies.

Library of Congress Cataloging-in-Publication Data
Schickel, Richard.
     Brando: a life in our times/Richard Schickel.
        p.   cm.
     ISBN 0-689-12108-3
     1. Brando, Marlon.   2. Actors – United States – Biography.
     I. Title.
     PN2287.B683S3   1991
     791.43′028′092 – dc20   91-9735   CIP
     [B]

Macmillan books are available at special discounts for bulk
purchases for sales promotions, premiums, fund-raising, or
educational use. For details, contact:

Special Sales Director
Macmillan Publishing Company
866 Third Avenue
New York, NY 10022

10 9 8 7 6 5 4 3 2 1

Printed in the United States of America

CONTENTS

ICE AGE

March 1, 1991

Dear Marlon Brando:

Even choosing the proper form of address is difficult. 'Mr Brando' is, of course, an absurdity, considering the length of our relationship, which now stretches back over four decades, and 'Marlon' is a presumption, considering the distance and one-sidedness of that relationship, which exists solely in my own mind. Let us, however, adopt your least favorite tactic: let us try to live with a compromise and move along.

Why am I writing to you? Because I seem to have written something *about* you, and I find it difficult to let it go forth into the world without offering an apology for my intrusion on your life and an explanation for the form that intrusion has taken.

That is especially so at this wretched moment, when tragedy has afflicted you and your family, and the gossip press has for some months been in full, distasteful cry, searching out dubious quotations from obscure, if not entirely disreputable, witnesses to your life, purporting to shed light on the awful events of last May 16 when your son Christian shot and killed Dag Drollet who, as all the world now knows, was your daughter Cheyenne's lover and the father of her unborn child is, of course, feckless. I know, as you know, as any reasonably intelligent human being knows (or ought to know), that it is impossible for outsiders to reach the heart of this kind of darkness. And I don't propose to join in this cheap and foredoomed enterprise. Indeed, this work was in progress last May and, aside from this introduction and the epilogue, was completed before the law reached its conclusion in the case of your son who has now pleaded guilty to voluntary manslaughter and been sentenced.

Having acknowledged the incident and vowed not to dwell upon it at length, there is nothing more the discreet author can do – except, perhaps, acknowledge, as well, his sympathy for you. For in the dark of his sleepless nights every father has imagined – dreaded – his children getting into some terrible trouble; has rehearsed, guiltily, the possibility of his unintentional complicity in these vaguely imagined disasters. Curiously, we can

1

understand what you are going through now in a way that we cannot fully understand – not being actors or celebrities – many of the other events of your life. And one can accord you the boon one would most crave in similar circumstances: respect for your privacy in this matter.

Indeed, throughout the writing of this book (which was contracted, I hasten to stipulate, six years ago) the question of privacy has weighed heavily on me for a variety of reasons. For example, one knows (and endorses) the disdain you feel for the writing that has accreted around you. A few years ago, I recall, an intermediary approached you on behalf of a completely respectable (and, as far as you are concerned, respect*ful*) writer, requesting an interview for a book he proposed writing about you. The man was not interested in dishing the dirt. He guaranteed he would not press you about Movita, Tarita or any of the other ladies who had passed through your life over the years, titillating the tabloids. 'If you're rich and famous getting laid a lot isn't that difficult,' you once said, and he agreed with that sentiment – or lack of it.

His concern was solely with your art and its sources, and though he was fully aware of how you felt about recording your reflections on those matters ('picking your navel – AND SMOKING IT'), he – and the intermediary – hoped you might have mellowed somewhat over the passing years. After a decent interval, your opinion of what might result from such an enterprise was communicated to the scrivener, in the form of yet another picturesque metaphor: 'Frozen monkey vomit.'

It made me laugh when I first heard it. It made me laugh again as I typed it out here. For you don't know the half of it. I assume you haven't read any of the many volumes that have been written about you. But I have. Here is something from one of the more recent of them. 'In all, 35,000 documents, 300 books and countless newspaper clippings were read for this work.' Yes, indeedy. And here is a typical example of the kind of insight those prodigies of research produced: 'For him, love and sex are the meaning of life.' Talk about frozen monkey vomit!

Nor is this an isolated instance. We stand, indeed, on the brink of a new Ice Age, for the accumulation of gelid celebrity upchuck has reached critical mass. And the glacier keeps grinding forward, impervious to the heat of our contempt, pulverizing traditional cultural values, traditional standards of public behavior. One wants not to add even an ounce to its weight, and since no one is compelling me to write about you, that's an option I have no reasonable excuse for failing to exercise. Unreasonably, though, I have to say that, for me, you have always been an irresistible subject. I have written about you, in one short form or another, at one time or another, for

2

many years now, never entirely to my satisfaction. When the invitation to write a book was tendered, I thought perhaps I might finally find a way to write about you that would satisfy me without doing you injustice.

I didn't want to write a biography, as such. I didn't want to write a critical study, as such. I distrust biographies of artists, even ones that are composed after the life has been lived and some historical perspective has been gathered. It seems to me that as that life is recounted, the work – which is the only justification a stranger has for poking through the rubble mortality leaves behind – tends to be obscured, diminished. For the drama of creation is an inner drama, essentially unknowable to the stranger and, in any case, difficult to recreate on the page in comparison to professional feuds, marital unrest, illnesses endured, children embittered by neglect – all the stuff that is, alas, imprinted on the memories of witnesses, as often as not imprinted on the surviving documents.

There is, to me, a slightly better logic in a critical approach which permits into the discussion only that biographical information that demonstrably seems to have influenced the artist's work. We understand that the modern actor (particularly the modern American actor), adherent of this or that variant on Stanislavskian technique, must be bringing something of himself, his memories of emotions past, to the creation of his characters, and this in some sense legitimatizes our rummaging through his personal history in search of his sources. But there are defects in this strategy, too, the most obvious of which is that an actor doesn't make up his lines as he goes along. And, of course, the director may have proposed this pause, that gesture. Or the player may be responding to another actor's rhythms, characterization or sense of the scene. In any event, much of what actors do is more obviously suggested by the evanescent mood of the moment than it is by the accumulated weight of life's history. The possibility is that they would have done this or that scene differently yesterday than they happened to do it today. And, of course, tomorrow is still another day.

There is, as well, something removed and distant, impersonal, about this approach to your case – about any case involving movie stardom. We do not, we cannot, perceive a movie star in pure terms, that is to say solely on the basis of his performances. We take in so much more – journalism, publicity, gossip and (nowadays) political and social pronouncements as we form our affections for and disaffections with people like you. Then we add to that muddle of misinformation, disinformation and partial information our own wild and needy suppositions, our own hunger for exemplary emblems – romantic, heroic, what have you – just to complete the confusion.

It seems to me, then, that we need to experiment a little with form and style if we are to encompass in print, in some instructive fashion, significant star careers. This is not new news. Almost everyone attempting to write seriously about the movies in the last three or four decades has read and taken to heart *The Immediate Experience*, the modest volume which post-humously collected all the pieces that a model observer of popular culture, Robert Warshow, wrote on the subject. As early as 1954 – coincidentally the year *On the Waterfront* was released – he wrote: 'A man watches a movie, and the critic must acknowledge that he is that man.' And he added, 'It must be that I go to the movies for the same reason that the "others" go: because I am attracted to Humphrey Bogart or Shelley Winters or Greta Garbo; because I require the absorbing immediacy of the screen; because in some way I take all that nonsense seriously.'

Warshow did not live to finish the longer book in which he intended to apply this principle to a wide variety of movie-going experiences. And most of the rest of us, though honoring his memory and his admirable effort not to distance himself from all that he took into the theatre with him when he went to the movies, have never taken up the challenge implicit in his simple, resonant observation. We back off, strike poses, get prissy, in general refuse to acknowledge the sub-critical (or should I say the supra-critical?) human impulses that draw us to the movies in the first place – and keep us coming back even though much of the time we suspect we might more profitably be doing something else.

Why this denial? Maybe we're lazy – it's much simpler to borrow the manner of traditional criticism and apply it to the movies than it is to invent a new critical language suitable for them. Maybe we're self-important – it perhaps elevates the discussion of what used to be thought of (and still is in some quarters) a low popular art to employ the high mandarin manner of, say, structuralism in writing about it. The possibility of stupidity is not to be lightly dismissed.

In any case, as I started to think about writing something more about you, as I looked at your movies anew, and read up on your life and times with a researcher's concentration, I began to look for a way both to breach biographical convention and cut through critical decorum, to find some way to narrow the distance that customarily separates observer and subject. The more I thought about the matter, the more it seemed worthwhile to see if Warshow's general observations about the way the movies work on everyone – including people with quite sober aspirations for their musings on the subject – could become the basis for a book that attempted to combine practical biography and practical criticism with an acknowledgement that the writer, like any other member of the audience, is an accomplice in the creation of any public figure and that there are particularly strong links between a movie star and whichever generation encounters him in its most impressionable years: the decade between (roughly) the ages of ten and twenty, when the search for heroes, exemplars or role models is especially intense.

In other words, I frankly admit that I was long ago 'attracted' to you in the same sense that Warshow was 'attracted' to the actors he forthrightly named in that same increasingly distant past. And I have tried to analyze the needs you seemed to speak to, the hold you continue to have on those of us who came of age in the years immediately after the Second World War.

So that there can be no mistake about where I'm coming from, let me try to make explicit some of the forces that have shaped the pages that follow. My approach is fundamentally 'generational'. But in thinking and writing about you I have tried to define the term more narrowly than it is usually defined. Those of us who have taken an almost proprietary interest in you are mostly drawn from a group that entered adolescence around 1945, as the social compact that had shaped our culture during the 1930s, and had been extended, pretty much unthinkingly because of wartime exigencies, began to come apart. And we are, for the most part, drawn from a relatively narrow segment of that generation. We come from that portion of it that is middle class, thus sufficiently leisured and educated to be intellectually and aesthetically aspiring, and thus ultimately, if perhaps unfairly, defining to social history as it is usually written. You know – Our Crowd: the book-buyers, theatre-goers, cineastes. We saw in you, or more properly in your screen character as it was initially defined in the period 1950-55, a period that roughly coincided with that period in life – late adolescence, early adulthood – when we were groping for self-definition, something of ourselves. Not something of what we were, but something of what we aspired to be: rude and sensitive, inarticulate but painfully aware – living oxymorons, if you will. This thought also vaguely nagged: if only we could slip down a few notches in class, we might be freed, as your screen character sometimes was, to mobilize our contempt for Fifties nicities, hypocrisies, acquiesences as you seemed to be doing.

A rum lot we were in the Fifties – by modern standards certainly: the last adolescent generation that did not have a full-scale demographic identity of its own, a popular culture that was exclusively ours' and actively off-putting to everyone older than we were. That culture – more wistfully rebellious than actually so, until it was crudely politicized in the Sixties – coalesced in its first primitive form around you – not that you or we were entirely conscious of what was going on at the time, not that anyone would begin to see what was happening until the first heroes of rock 'n' roll appeared a few years later to erect the first impenetrable sound barrier between the generations.

Indeed, you might say that you fulfilled a need we didn't know we had until you appeared and clarified it for us. It began with something that seems painfully obvious now: what we required was someone who was not Clark Gable or Gary Cooper or Jimmy Stewart; was not someone we had been taught from childhood to love, honor and obey; was not, in short, our parents' movie star. What we needed was our very own star. Who turned out to be you – just enough older (about a decade) to have achieved something we could look up to, but not so much older that you were distanced from us.

Were our requirements in this respect more exigent than those of previous adolescent generations? I think so. A few short-lived curiosities aside (one thinks of Frank Sinatra in his first swoony incarnation), younger generations had pretty much shared their elders' regard for the stars of movies, popular culture in general. But then, as the great wet blanket of prosperity, conformity and *politesse* settled down over middle-class America in the early Fifties, the oncoming generation needed to find someone who appeared not to accept the corporation as a model social institution, was scornful of bourgeois manners and habits of mind, was capable of emblemizing the soul's immutable need to say – well, all right, mumble – 'no' on our behalf.

We were quite capable of complicating this matter still further, of course. At the time, the writer Donald Malcolm suggested that the reason we had become 'the silent generation' was that we were too preoccupied with self-analysis to speak up and out about anything. In any case, 'Alienation', a novel word that yet fell trippingly from our tongues at the time, was a preoccupying topic. *The Lonely Crowd* was anatomized in 1950, and the fear of drifting into its clutches was lively in us. *White Collar* was on our brick and board bookshelves, and we saw how the eponymous object seemed to be choking the life out of earlier generations. *The Man in the Gray Flannel Suit* stalked our nightmares and soon enough *The Organization Man* would join him there, though, of course, even as we read about these cautionary figures, many of us were talking to corporate recruiters about entry-level emulation of them.

Opposed to these characters we had the exemplary work (and as we learned more about him) the exemplary life of Albert Camus. 'One must imagine Sisyphus happy,' he concluded his noble essay against suicide, and so we did. We also imagined ourselves happy following the mythic example he had chosen for his central metaphor – pushing our boulders up the hill, knowing full well the scoffing gods would send us (and our burdens) tumbling back down just as we attained the summit. But yet there was joy – albeit, a muted, Fifties kind of joy – in our 'acceptance' (another word that was big with us) of our meaningless fates. There was even a sort of romanticism – again, of a very Fifties sort – in calmly proceeding with our struggles despite their cosmic inconsequentiality. (I've often wondered, did you read Camus, too? Is that why ritual beatings administered by representatives of the uncomprehending world, but passively accepted by you, were such regular occurrences in the lives of your characters?) The point for now is: not quite knowing what we were doing, but not quite *not* knowing what we were doing either, we were looking around at that moment for someone to embody a rebel hero of Camus's kind for us, and there you were.

We knew you (or thought we knew you) before we ever saw you, since your reputation, gained in the Broadway production of *A Streetcar Named Desire*, preceded you to the screen. We knew, of course, that you were an actor in the full sense of the term, not someone some studio hireling found on a stool at Schwab's and gave lessons in deportment and elocution (though naturally the imbecile Hollywood press immediately suggested that you were in dire need of both). But we gathered something more than that from the buzz surrounding you. We gathered that you were after some new kind of truthfulness in your work, though that was only vaguely defined by you and ignorantly defined by the many commentators on your efforts. Above all, we gathered a sense of your otherness, a sense that you represented a renewed and revised conscience in your profession.

The publicity attendant upon your first forays into Hollywood reinforced this impression. For as the showbiz reporters began probing your private life, delicious hints emerged of what read as Bohemian excess (well, anyway, non-conformity) during your New York days. Since you were among the first of a new breed of workshop-trained actors, we were not yet as familiar with the accompanying lifestyle as we have since become. More importantly, your assaults on Hollywood's hard-won, tenuously held gentility – blue jeans in Bel-Air, insults to Louella Parsons and Hedda Hopper, public crotch-scratching and nose-picking, general gnarliness with the moguls – were also widely reported. It seemed to us that you were, in your way, trying to say for us what we were merely thinking about conventional middle-class values, and since the profiles of you indicated that you were a product of that class – our class – your escape from its constraints and conventions made your behavior seem all the more enthralling. And, in some way we could not yet define, potentially useful to us. Maybe you would help us define *our* otherness.

Your first movies were not quite up to that task. But they did not disappoint us. Far from it. No one had seen anyone quite like Ken, the paraplegic in *The Men*, at the movies before – such heights of rage, such depths of self-pity; we were used to more stoic confrontations with fate on the screen. Nor had we seen anything quite like Stanley Kowalski's rutting masculinity in *A Streetcar Named Desire*. For that matter, the inwardness and insecurity of Emiliano Zapata, a Latino revolutionary, thus a type from whom we had been taught to expect heedlessness and fiery speeches, was also a novelty, albeit a less potent one at the time. (*Julius Caesar* was, of course, quite a different matter, a demonstration that the new American theatrical accent could be compromised, blended more or less unobtrusively, even stirringly, with the traditional English elocutionary manner.)

The generational quarrels stirred by these performances largely revolved around your vocal mannerisms – the great mumble war. Older people, used to the tradition of the well-made actor, were appalled. Younger people were enthralled. Couldn't they – our elders – see what you were trying to do? God! This discussion was mostly irrelevant, of course, a way of evading what was really discomfiting about you. The issue was not your alleged inarticulateness, it was rather the previously unspoken topics you were trying in your way to articulate – psychological matters that had heretofore been subtextual (at best) in American movies. Ken's despair over his fate, his impatience with well-meaning sympathy, his anger over the need to exercise traditional masculine self-control in ghastly circumstances – these had not been components of movie heroism before. And though stars like Gable had always implied ballsiness, they had also covered their tracks with comedy and little boyishness. No one had ever flaunted sheer, cocksure maleness with the brutal arrogance you did in *Streetcar*. Or contrasted it so vividly with weepy vulnerability when that sexuality was thwarted. If we had seen men come to moral and political consciousness in the movies before, we had never seen one come to it as hesitantly as you did in *Zapata*.

From your publicity and your performances, then, an impression of unprecedentness was created, and since, like all adolescent generations, we were convinced of our own unprecedentness, the bond we had begun to forge with you back when you were not much more than a half-scandalous rumor grew stronger with each new movie, each new magazine story about you. For artistic and social compromises elicited nothing but contempt from you. You had 'integrity'. You were not 'selling out'. You were telling the 'truth'. You were doing what we desperately hoped to do, you were achieving success on your own terms.

But it was not until your fifth picture, four years along in your movie career, that the bond between us was fully sealed. It was when you dressed yourself in black leathers and black shades and came vrooming down the archetypal Main Street of an archetypal American small town in *The Wild One*, there to do menacing, entrancing wheelies, sending the dear hearts of its gentle people into cardiac arrest, that gossip and screen image finally came together definitively.

'Hey Johnny, what are you rebelling against?' 'Waddya got?' Oh, Lord, it was glorious. We were thrilled down to our toes curling cowardly in our white bucks. For those words, the sum and substance of our secret thoughts spoken out loud, made it official: you were now our designated outlaw. We didn't really care that this generally inept movie actually ended on an ambiguous note, a conciliatory implication about the generational conflict. We were used to ignoring those lurching, screeching last-minute right turns into the high, safe road. We understood they were required by Cardinal Spellman or J. Edgar Hoover or somebody equally scary, risible and, in the largest sense, irrelevant.

And then, immediately afterwards, in *On the Waterfront* there was Terry Malloy. Young man actually finds halting words for his moral anguish, escapes corrupt, corrupting organization. Inherent sensitivity – the silent generation's strongest suit – takes a terrible beating but wins at least a provisional victory in the end. You, too, of course – the Oscar. That was a yet more marvelous (if, as it turned out, ambiguous) victory – of the new acting manner over the old, of the new movie manner over the old, of course. But it seemed to be something larger than that, as well; it seemed to be a generational triumph. If Marlon Brando could no longer be dismissed as a fad, a passing fancy, then perhaps we, too, could expect to be taken seriously. Or, at the very least, not be forever dismissed as merely, if worrisomely, silent.

I have no way of knowing if you were aware of the effect you had on so many of us. I'm inclined to think that you were simply embarrassed by our adulation, dismissing it as just the kind of silly fandom that had always made movie stardom anathema to serious actors, not different in kind from the giddy fatuity that had been visited on Rudolph Valentino and others of his ilk almost from the beginning of the movies. I'm also inclined to think that you may at the time have been even more concerned to avoid another kind of cultural heroism, as exemplar and tribune of the movement for theatrical reform that had been building since Stanislavski's Moscow Art Theater visited the United States in 1923. The Laboratory Theater, the Group Theater, Piscator's classes at The New School (where you enter the story), the Actor's Studio – so many brave beginnings, so many frustrations before the breakthrough (though it was more of style than of substance) achieved by your acting generation. These zealously committed people had needed a star, someone who could embody their message to the world, far longer than my generation had, and neither Franchot Tone nor John Garfield had quite fulfilled their hopes. They, too, had settled on you. Since they had been your teachers, your directors, your acting colleagues, they could get to you (emotionally as well as on the phone), and I imagine that you perceived them not as dismissable strangers but as the truly clear and present danger to your individuality, your integrity, the development of an uncorrupted acting self.

I believe that your disgust with the importunings and impositions of both groups, the need to escape their clutches, has been the ruling reality of your life, that most of your career can be read as an attempt to run from the responsibilities other people wanted to thrust upon you. I also believe, having made such study as a stranger can of your early life, that this is not a late-starting star trip. For almost every reliable witness to your childhood, your adolescence, your early days as an actor, speaks of an individuality purely (if eccentrically) defined by you, and of the quickness with which you perceived threats to it.

These are matters to which inevitably we must return. The main themes of your life are to be picked out of this tangle. For the moment, though, it is perhaps sufficient to observe that all of us – your distant fans and your closest friends – posed a danger to you that was not different from that posed by the hateful Hollywood moguls. For we all wanted to incorporate into our mental landscapes, the better to project outward on to the great American landscape, not your full human nature, but a usable version of you. To be falsely, or too easily, understood is what has always driven you crazy. It is, I imagine, why you have hidden behind so many accents; it is also I imagine why you have in late years turned yourself into a fat man; it is certainly why you have become the Abominable Snowman of our culture – your tracks everywhere, your flitting shadow frequently reported, your actual presence only rarely authenticated.

Speaking of shadows, I suppose honesty requires me to admit that another sort of shadow, the shadow of irrelevance, is cast on these pages. The world moves on, and a crowd of actors including your neighbor and sometime co-star, Jack Nicholson, Robert De Niro, Dustin Hoffman and

possibly Al Pacino, all of whose careers you made possible, have succeeded you as the actors knowing audiences accord respectful anticipation,
a measure of indulgence in performance and a certain interest in the
enigma of creation as they practice it. Even your recent re-emergence, in *A
Dry White Season*, rewarded by Hollywood's shyly encouraging, sweetly
forgiving Oscar nomination (for a two-scene role), and *The Freshman*, in
which you gathered such welcoming reviews, cannot disguise the fact that
the best of the younger audience doesn't quite know what to make of you,
and the rest of their age group is preoccupied by the likes of Tom Cruise
and Mel Gibson. As the critic Peter Rainer put it in an excellent recent
article lamenting your lack of contemporary relevance, 'For most young
moviegoers, film history doesn't extend back much beyond a decade – at
best.'

Yes, one still sees the poster-size photograph of you in your *Wild One*
black leathers, straddling your hawg, on some dormitory walls. But for
today's middle-class college kids that is less a portrait of a specific and emotionally potent artist as a young man than it is a generalized symbol of their
(by now) *de rigueur* contempt for bourgeois niceties. For many of them, it
carries not even that much psychological weight; it's just this semester's
cheap decorating solution, replacable for a few dollars the next time something catches their eye at the campus nostalgic merchant.

For, to tell you the truth, the kids are more interested in Marilyn Monroe – she reads more easily than you do. In the Fifties you may have
seemed the icon of the era, while she seemed no more than the latest icon
of availability. But times change, and her apparent victimization has made
her into a feminist martyr, symbol of oppressions past, and a cautionary
figure when we contemplate oppressions current and future. Besides, she
left behind all those terrific photographs – so useful when people need to
reach quickly for a vivid symbol of an increasingly vague past.

To tell you what may be a more awful truth, later generations are more
interested in James Dean. Can you imagine? The kid who copied you!
Who used to annoy you by calling up and trying to make friends! Who
(accidentally) got out when the going was good. There is much to be said
for dying young in circumstances melodramatically appropriate to your
public image. There is very little to be said for living long and burying that
image in silence, suet and apparent cynicism.

Of course, if you can get a youngster to watch all of *A Streetcar Named
Desire* or *On the Waterfront* he will respond – they are powerful films and
the power of your performances remains manifest. But the rest of your
movies? Frankly, you have to bring something of a shared past to them. It

requires a serious exercise in historical imagination for a kid today to see the felicities that I perceive in *Sayonara* or *Mutiny on the Bounty* or *One-Eyed Jacks*. And I wonder if I could convey to my daughters, for instance, that sense of triumph we felt when we saw *Last Tango in Paris* or *The Godfather*, that sense that our patience with you, our steadfastness against the scoffers, our 'fandom', through the long season of dismay you endured in the Sixties, had at last been rewarded. In that time, in return for past favors, we indulged *Morituri* on your behalf, sympathized with your victimization by Chaplin on *The Countess from Hong Kong*, eagerly exchanged appreciations of the truths you achieved in the curious context of *Reflections in a Golden Eye*, responded to the improvisational brilliance of your work in *The Missouri Breaks*. But if a viewer has not shared a past, an imaginative life with you it is hard to distinguish most of your pictures from all the other dim footage lurking in the shadows of late night cable. Before you came back in your two recent pictures, a cruel young newspaper writer asked: what do Elvis Presley and Marlon Brando have in common? The answer: many people believe both of them are still alive. Funny at the time, I suppose. How come I didn't laugh?

Because, manifestly, here you are. And here am I. Exasperated yet somehow content, I am stuck with you, just as you are stuck – more exasperated and less content – with that partially false self we unconsciously conspired to create for you some forty years ago. We can't escape our pasts. Pointless to go on trying. Besides, I don't know how to write about Tom or Mel. I lack motivation. They belong to the inner life of another generation.

Look, old friend, old comrade in the generational wars, it comes to this: you are now 66 (67 before this book is published) and – truly unimaginable, this – you, our rebel angel, are eligible for social security. I am not as far behind as I wish I were. You are about to become 'historically significant'; I am about to become historically irrelevant. Before either of those things happens, let me try to take all the 'nonsense' about you 'seriously', make what 'sense' I can of it before we both must surrender our shared history to the thronging, uncomprehending young strangers, submit ourselves and our times, which you, certainly, helped to define, to their heedless and ignorant deconstruction.

You may, if you wish, imagine me happy.

Sincerely,
Richard Schickel

AGE OF INNOCENCE

I f this is a book as much about audiences as it is about an actor, let it begin with Marlon Brando's first fully appreciative audience, an audience of one named Stella Adler.

There had been, of course, small audiences before – parents, teachers, schoolmates. But Adler was the first to see in Brando's rough, unrehearsed act something treasurable. To her, as opposed to virtually everyone who had been exposed to it before, the self-portrait he had worked up by late adolescence seemed utterly unique and, in most important respects, admirable – well worth polishing, finishing, exhibiting.

There would be, obviously, huge audiences later. But Adler was the last to see the actor's potential in its pure form, unsullied by artifice and adulation (or, perhaps more properly, the flight from adulation). And she was the last to have a large and helpfully shaping influence on his gift. After her, that gift would mostly be shaped, for better or worse, solipsistically.

It was not a role, according to her, that she was eager to accept. Not at first, anyway. For Adler's first glance at the young man – eighteen going on nineteen – who turned up in her acting classes at the New School in Greenwich Village in the wartime winter of 1942-43, revealed two aspects of his nature. On the one hand, there was originality and vitality. On the other, there seemed to be something hurt and hidden about him. His air of bravado did not quite succeed in covering a vulnerability that was, to her, equally apparent.

It was possible, she thought, that the self-explorations and revelations demanded by the study of acting could unhinge a spirit rather more delicately balanced than most. Here, perhaps, was someone who was not merely entitled to his privacy, but more needful of its healing balm than most of his contemporaries.

Moreover, Adler could not help but contrast him with the other young people who came to her. They were, most of them, already firmly dedicated to the theatre, willing to let a strong-minded, strong-willed teacher take them over and remold them in the shape of their desires. Brando's presence in her classes seemed to Adler not to represent an act of commitment of that order, but rather an experiment in self-definition.

In sum: 'I thought there was something terribly sensitive, the kind of thing you don't want to touch. This puppy thing – I didn't know if I should.' And so, decently, she hesitated. But not for long.

For Brando was irresistible to her, just as she was irresistible to Brando. It may be too much to suggest that their encounter was fated, but the timing certainly could not have been improved upon. For they met at the moment when their mutual needs were impeccably matched. If Brando was at that time a character in search of a defining author, Adler was an author in search of subjects, that is to say, actors who could embody her theories of performance in major roles. Since these theories had been gestating for close to a decade, there was by this time a certain urgency in her search for instruments by which she could assert herself against her enemies within the theatrical community and, perhaps, impose her beliefs on its future history.

Admittedly, this sounds rather melodramatic. Passion of that kind – even from the never dispassionate Stella Adler – seems improbable to us now, when the American theater is bereft of serious artistic or intellectual dispute (or, so it often seems, general cultural interest), when Broadway is mostly a haven for imports, and even the sometimes promising regional theater movement often resembles opera, dependent on subsidies and a cult following for survival. But in those days Adler was a woman embattled, and many people cared greatly about the outcome of the struggle in which she was engaged, believing that the very future of the theater as a relevant social institution might depend on how the several issues agitating its most committed people were resolved.

It is impossible to say how aware an adolescent newly arrived from the middle west was of how much history was about to be applied to his remodelling. It is equally impossible to say how aware Brando is of it now, so much history of his own peculiar making having crowded his memories. But I don't think we can begin to understand what became of him without recalling what came before him. For he was – quite uniquely so – burdened, and possibly bent, by a weight of dreams that were not of his own devising.

When she met him, Stella Adler was 42 or 43 (at least – her birthdate is not a matter on which she has ever felt a strong compulsion to accuracy), not quite the *grande* and rather terrifying *dame* she would soon become, but with her legend nonetheless on the way to solid establishment. Beneath her flamboyance, however, there was shrewdness, a belief in the theater as a morally and intellectually serious enterprise, and an authentic, if

14

relatively new-formed, passion for teaching.

She was, of course, the daughter of the legendary Yiddish actor, Jacob Adler, and she began her career in his company, then moved on to Broadway. Wooed by the idealistic spirallings of director-theorist-critic Harold Clurman's rhetoric (she would later marry him), she joined The Group Theater at the time of its foundation by Clurman, Lee Strasberg and Cheryl Crawford. She gave what is generally thought to be her greatest performance in The Group's production of Clifford Odets' *Awake and Sing*, but she never took to the communitarian life of the organization. (She is reputed to have said she could live in any communist country if she were its queen.)

That shared life (The Group took to the country in its early summers to live, study and rehearse together) was one leg of the intellectual tripod on which it suspended its large hopes for theatrical reform. Another was its ideological commitment, which was to a (mostly) innocent Stalinism and to new plays that were (mainly) realistic in manner, often about lower middle-class life, generally didactic in intent. The last, but most lasting in influence, of The Group's underpinnings was its commitment to Stanislavskian technique in acting – 'The Method', as Strasberg, the Russian director-theoretician's self-appointed American disciple, started calling it as he began to build *his* legend.

This relatively new, psychologically oriented manner of performance, introduced to the US when the Moscow Art Theater visited in 1923, and propagated thereafter by a great, forgotten man of theater and film, Richard Boleslavski, at his American Laboratory Theater, was an integral part of The Group's reformist efforts. It would give actors a tool enabling them to play a grittier kind of drama than was then prevalent in the commercial theater, and it would help them maintain their air of veracity, when these works made their inevitable swerve toward the unveraciously rhetorical – in other words, when it came time to state an uplifting moral (something The Group often insisted its playwrights supply as they rewrote for production). But the most important thing about The Method was that it was in itself a kind of moral statement. It proposed a codifiable discipline, a teachable tradition, for acting, and a standard toward which performers could work through intensive study. Though no one seems to have put it in precisely these words, Strasberg and his disciples implicitly believed that with Stanislavskian theory as a base (and perhaps with Lee Strasberg as Minister of Theatrical Culture), acting could become a true profession. And if it did, that might well have a profound effect on a theater dominated by the star system and drowning in (as they saw it) commercial trivia.

From the start, however, Adler was dubious about Strasberg's 'Method'. He placed particular emphasis on 'affective memory', that is (to put it simply), insisting that the actor draw on his own psyche for emotions analogous to those of the character he was playing. As Adler would put it later (and often), she felt this led to 'hysteria' on the part of the actor. Moreover, she believed that the plunge into subjectivity could not serve, and might very often subvert, the playwright's text and intentions. Finally, it seemed to her, as it did to others (notably Bobby Lewis, another Group member, and an actor-director who would also become an influential teacher), that the Method was the enemy of styles other than the realistic – not much use in Restoration comedy, for instance, or in Brecht. Or for that matter in Shakespeare.

Adler's opposition to Strasberg, however, did not crystalize until, by chance, she encountered Constantin Stanislavski himself in Paris in 1934, and accused him of ruining her life as an actress with his theories. Her charges puzzled and intrigued the Russian, who informed her that he had substantially modified his views. He no longer held with affective memory, he said (or she said he said), and was now placing his emphasis on observation and imagination rather than self-examination.

This was a revelation to Adler, and she spent six weeks at the master's side, returning home with a diary in which she recorded his revised thoughts. When she confronted Strasberg with it, he was, in her account, outraged. According to her, he insisted that Stanislavski had fallen into error, that he, Strasberg, was now the one true keeper of the one true theoretical flame. Their contention did not break up The Group, which continued to produce plays, though in increasingly straitened economic circumstances, through 1940. But like many of its most gifted actors and playwrights, she began working elsewhere, even doing a couple of movies – the source of all corruption as far as hard-core Group members were concerned – her brief appearance in *Shadow of the Thin Man* powerfully and memorably interrupting its slick banter. She made one last film in 1947, and continued to take occasional parts in the commercial theater while she established herself as a teacher. She did not entirely abandon performance until after she founded her own acting school in 1949.

What Adler was primarily looking for among the young actors who presented themselves to her for instruction were observers, sympathetic students of human behavior – their own and other people's. On an excellent television documentary about her life and work, first broadcast in 1989, she by no means discounted the uses of memory as a fuel for performance. But her definition of the usable past, for actors, was not Freud's – or

Strasberg's. 'The actor has in him the meaning of everything he has ever tasted or touched or eaten. And he is by nature gifted with memory. He can go very far back, and he does go very far back. . . .'

That, in a sense, brings her to Brando, and Brando to her. A puppy he may have been, but he was her kind of puppy, and perhaps one she had not imagined finding at The New School. For its Dramatic Workshop was the creation of Erwin Piscator, disciple of Max Reinhardt, refugee from Hitler's Germany and a formidable *avant-gardist*, with a taste for theatre on an epic scale. Piscator was not a Stanislavskian, and realism was not at the center of his aesthetic. He tended to see actors as extensions of the director's will and the director as the servant of the playwright, interpreting his work. He was, nonetheless, tolerant of Stanislavskians on his faculty (Lee Strasberg also taught there), and Cheryl Crawford would later say that Piscator's workshop formed the most important link between The Group Theater and The Actor's Studio in the seven years between the former's demise and the latter's founding.

Be that as it may, almost immediately after Brando enrolled in her classes Adler began predicting that he would soon be acknowledged as the best young actor in America. A few years later, when that prediction had emphatically come true, she was still saying, 'He's the most keenly aware, the most empathetical human being alive. . . . He just knows. If you have a scar, physical or mental, he goes right to it. He doesn't want to, but he doesn't avoid it. . . . He cannot be cheated or fooled. If you left the room he could be you.'

Of course, young Bud Brando (as everyone called him in those days) could not have had ideas as firm as hers about what he was looking for in those days. But she had enough for both of them, and they matched his best instincts. 'Actors have to observe, and I enjoy that part of it,' Brando was to say some years later, after stardom had seriously interfered with what was perhaps his most precious artistic freedom, the freedom to observe unobserved: 'They have to know how much spit you have in your mouth, and where the weight of your elbows is. I could sit all day in the Optimo Cigar Store on 42nd Street and just watch the people pass by.'

But Brando had more than a canny watchfulness to offer. He had imagination and daring, too. Adler, for example, would recall the 'inner scale' of his performance as a priest in a scene from Strindberg. But somehow a story Elaine Stritch, the actress, recently told catches what one imagines to be his truest self in those days. She was in one of Adler's classes with Brando when the teacher set this exercise: a coop of chickens has just learned that an atomic bomb is about to be set off near them; show

17

us their reactions. Naturally most of the students leaped to their feet and started running about, cackling madly. Brando alone kept still on his perch, miming the laying of an egg. But, of course! What does a chicken know about the destructive potential of nuclear fission? Come hell or high water, she will do what she must do – no more, no less. To imagine lack of imagination – and to dare stillness – may be the highest achievement available to a young actor.

One other quality completes the youthful profile of Marlon Brando: consistent autobiographical refusals. And this, finally, made him the perfect challenge for his teacher. If Adler could make an actor out of someone as reticent, as hidden as this young man was, wouldn't that show Strasberg a thing or two? One searches the anecdotal record of Brando's early years in vain for evidence of subjectivity in his work, or for that matter in conversations with friends, and almost nothing comes to hand. Stunts and pranks and general goofiness we hear about, and a ready sympathy for the pains and problems of others, and girl-chasing, naturally; but of personal history, recalled emotions, virtually nothing. Years later, an interviewer elicited this confession of fear about self-exploration in search of a character's deepest well-springs: 'There comes a time in one's life when you don't want to do it anymore. You know a scene is coming where you'll have to yell or cry or scream and all those things, and it's always bothering you, always eating away at you. . . .'

I don't think Brando ever wanted – or intended – to 'do it', to plunge down into the abyss of himself. I don't think he knew, when he wandered into Adler's class, that that effort was now beginning to be widely regarded as a requisite for serious acting. For that matter, it seems unlikely that he knew, definitely, that he wanted to try to make a living as an actor. Yes, his mother had been an amateur actress of some local repute at one time in her life, and, yes, his sister Jocelyn was pursuing a theatrical career, and, yes, the thing he had liked best about prep school had been acting in plays, but in everyone's reminiscences Bud Brando has the air of someone taking a few courses mainly because he couldn't think of anything better to do with his time.

Adler felt his commitment to acting was 'touch and go', and she would characterize him in those days as a young man basically 'against things', adding that when she first met him there was no place where he 'functioned with continuity and discipline'. Adler would confide to an interviewer that, after he began to find himself as an actor, his mother came to her and said: 'Thank you, you've saved Marlon. He had no direction; now he has direction.'

Which may have been true. For a time. But one also feels that perhaps Mrs Brando and Ms Adler spoke too soon. Looking back now, one feels that his pleasure in the young actor's life and his relatively quick ascent to stardom disguised his continuing, and, as we now know, growing doubts about his choice of profession. Indeed, by the early Fifties friends and relatives were predicting early retirement for Brando, a prediction in which he frequently joined.

It made sense. For it was obvious, even then, that Brando would never gratefully, gracefully settle into his success, which, for practical purposes in post-war America, was starting to mean what it now most assuredly means: more or less accepting other people's definition of you, however little that accords with your own sense of yourself, and living to fulfil the peculiar needs of others, among them − once celebrity is attained − perfect strangers.

That, as it happens, was the basic issue with Brando *before* he was famous. Naturally, no one outside his immediate family much cared what was going to become of him in those early days. But *they* cared a lot. Couldn't help it, being middle class, Middlewestern WASPs, thus born fussers after respectability, which always includes an overwhelming drive to see their children placed firmly in the paths of predictability. Here, I think, I can safely impose my experience on Brando's, on anybody's who is a product of that milieu:

You come home from fourth grade with bad marks in arithmetic and your parents immediately see your college career threatened. And if you don't go to college, how do you expect to get a decent job? And if you can't get a decent job, then what? Somehow, they can look at you standing there in your knickers and high tops, as miserable as anyone else about your report card ('Does not apply himself; Not working to capacity'), and project the loss, by you, of all their hard-won gains. Menial labor, itinerancy, petty crime − who knows what disgraces await the dilatory scholar?

Perhaps that anxiety was more vivid for the Brandos of Omaha, Nebraska and, latterly, of Evanston and Libertyville, Illinois than it was for others. The surface impression they created was an archetype of bourgeois solidity in its time and place: Marlon Sr, a stern, taciturn man in a dark suit, implacably, prosperously purveying useful, glamorless products − cattle feed, chicken feed, limestone − to businessmen reassuringly like himself; his wife, Dorothy, known to all as Dodie, in manner rather like the characters Billie Burke used to play − pretty, high-spirited, distracted, always in a bit of a dither, but warm and sweet and (as people used to say) 'cultured'; three children − Jocelyn, born in 1920, Frances, two and a half years younger, and, finally, Marlon Jr, born April 3, 1924. All the Brando children were intelligent and talented – paternally encouraged to accept discipline, responsibility, maternally encouraged to express themselves in whatever manner suited them.

This was a classic 'nice' family according to the standards of its time and place. Their life seems to have been perpetually elm-shaded. One gathers an impression of comfortable old houses, spacious lawns, lemonade on a summer's afternoon, long, lazy Monopoly games when it rained, family sing-songs in the evenings, with Dodie pounding out 'Red Sails in the Sunset' on the piano. Even during the Depression there appears to have been no hint of economic instability.

But emotional instability? Yes. Of course. This was Sinclair Lewis country, after all, not to mention Sherwood Anderson. One expects to find something not quite right hidden behind the comfortable facade. One would be disappointed not to find it – as if, somehow, the family had failed to live up to the role preordained for over-respectable provincials by the literature of the time.

An irony now arises. Privacy – no, secrecy – was, and is, a major value for people like the Brandos. And, gossipy, neighborly speculations aside, they can usually count on maintaining it. Except in one instance. That it is when their fractious, fretted over, difficult child, that dagger in the heart when he is growing up, becomes a consequential figure in the great world. Think of it: you worry for twenty years that your child will not make something of himself, then he goes and does so, and your life suddenly becomes an open book – many open books, in fact. If the boy had indeed fulfilled your worst expectations you, at least, would have remained anonymous and ultimately untraceable, your secrets buried, finally, in the sleeping dust alongside of you.

One almost feels like apologizing for saying it . . . but . . . well . . . Dodie drank . . . and Marlon Sr was an unyielding moralist who was also, typical of his breed, a hypocrite, since he too drank, albeit more secretively. And womanized as well. Of the two, she is the more sympathetic figure, the more tragic figure. He is both more remote and more dangerous.

Dorothy Pennebaker Brando was the kind of alcoholic who could remain sober – and in her case charming and spirited – for long periods, only to disappear on binges, often to be discovered in degrading and even dangerous situations. In the early years of marriage her problem was apparently controllable, or anyway disguisable, for she had in those days an ideal outlet for her talents and energies. She was one of the founders of the Omaha Community Playhouse, which would ultimately become one of the most solidly established, and artistically striving, amateur theatrical companies in the country. It was she who recruited a handsome young man named Henry Fonda to play juveniles in the company, and over the years she would play leads in everything from O'Neill to *Lilliom* to *Ten Nights in a Barroom*, becoming something of a local celebrity in the process. Everybody said that she might have had a professional career if she had not married and had a family.

Doubtless her drinking was, in part, a response to simple disappointment at ambitions unfulfilled. Doubtless it increased after 1930, when Marlon Sr found a larger business opportunity in Chicago and the family moved to Evanston, a much more straight-laced community (the headquarters of the Women's Christian Temperance Union was there). It offered nothing comparable to the Playhouse to deflect and absorb Dodie's troubled spirit.

For we are dealing with something more than a frustrated actress here. The fact is that Dodie had come to see her marriage as a sham. Eventually, it seems she confronted Marlon Sr with evidence of his philanderings. There are also unverifiable claims that he may have beaten her. It is certain that more than once she absented himself from their home for an extended period – trial separations in fact, if not in name.

And little Bud? What did he make of all this? In Jocelyn's nice description he was, in the Omaha years, 'a blond, fat-bellied little boy, quite serious, very determined'. As the oldest sibling she was often pressed into service as something more than a baby-sitter, almost a surrogate mother, while Dodie devoted herself to the Playhouse. One of her most vivid memories was of a little boy climbing up on to the mantelpiece of the living-room fireplace and repeatedly falling, rolling, leaping off of it (a distance of about five feet) – miming movie death scenes, no doubt.

The middle sibling, Fran – closer in age, and as it happened closer emotionally to her little brother – would remember that he loved to win the card games he played with her, and that he was inventive at making up rules as they went along in order to assure that end. Gamesmanship is, in fact, a feature of everyone's early memories of Bud Brando: word games, and made-up games (who can dance faster, balance a match or stand on one foot longer). The family and Middlewestern friends would also remember Bud and Fran running away from home on a fairly regular basis, almost every Sunday for a time. They didn't get far, and such mischief as they got into on those occasions was minor. But these attempts at escape, more symbolic than real – there were other, more elaborate ones later in adolescence – established a lifetime pattern: dodging away, disappearing into clouds of his own creation.

Another salient characteristic also manifested itself early. It began with Bud's concern for the animal kingdom. The household population of pets, always extensive, was constantly added to as he brought home lost and injured creatures to care for. When the family moved from Evanston to a farm in Libertyville, Bud was the only one who could milk a rather mean-spirited cow. People would later remember that the creature would even let him ride on her back when she was put out to pasture. But there was more to this interest than simple sentiment. There was complex sentiment as well. Animals seemed straightforward, trustworthy, unduplicitous in a way that human beings seemed incapable of being – at least within Bud's limited experience of them.

Similar feelings were extended to people who presented themselves as emotionally lost or unusually put-upon. It appears that, wherever the Brandos lived, Bud was always at the center of the neighborhood gang, and even then attempted to use his star power to extend protection to the unfortunate. Fran would recall a little girl with a habit, in games, of getting lost in her own thoughts, coming close to a trance-like state. Bud always chose her to be on his side.

His friendship with funny little Wally Cox, not at all a typical boy's boy, which began in Evanston when they were about ten, had the same sweet protective air about it. And it continued beyond the grave. 'It wasn't an unlikely friendship,' Brando told a reporter in 1976, three years after Cox died, 'because Wally didn't resemble in the remotest his Mr Peepers character.' He had, rather, 'the mentality of an axe murderer'. Brando claimed he had kept his friend's ashes in his house and talked to him all the time. 'I can't tell you how I miss and love that man.'

He was entirely capable of extending his elaborate kindness to strangers as well. A significant moment in family mythology has Bud coming upon a woman who had swooned on the street and insisting she accompany him home, where she was made comfortable and a doctor was called. Fran would also recall, on more than one occasion, her younger brother's first visit to her in New York when she was studying at the Art Students' League. 'Bud was terribly shocked by the things he saw – just walking down Broadway, all the unfortunate people you see.' She would remember him pressing five dollars on a shoeshine man and hurrying away before change could be offered.

In a way, all this is something of a relief. It implies that Brando's subsequent and more famous devotion to such causes as civil rights and the plight of the American Indian was not merely a star trip, that it was the logical extension of something deeply rooted in his nature. We must bear it

in mind when we come to Oscar night, 1973, and the strange case of Sasheen Littlefeather.

We must bear something else in mind as well. Bud Brando was the child
of alcoholics. And one of the things recent research into the psychology of
such children teaches us is that they do whatever they can to deflect attention away from the source of their shame. If, therefore, one can find people
even more troubled, more in need of sympathetic attention than the errant
father and/or mother, and direct concern toward them, it serves the youngster's hidden agenda.

Jocelyn: 'He was drawn to people shyer than he, more in trouble with
their families, who were not able to cope with life as well. I don't like to use
the word "underdog", but anyone he felt was insecure he wanted to help.
Perhaps he was drawn to them . . . because they reflected something in
himself . . . He was defending them, but I also think he was identifying
with something in them.'

Yes. Unquestionably. Though by local middle-class standards it is hard
to see how anyone could be in more trouble – this side of outright juvenile
delinquency – than Marlon Jr habitually was with Marlon Sr. All the more
reason to continue fulfilling the most basic requirement of a successful
Middlewestern boyhood: attending to one's popularity with one's peers.
This, of course, has its practical benefits. It gives one a way of escaping tensions at home. But another element begins to creep into the portrait of Bud
Brando as he headed toward adolescence – reserve, watchfulness, 'shyness'. A friend of the family took to calling him 'The Judge' – the owlish
observer of the world's imperfections.

Shyness! Such a perfect Middlewesternism, that word, as its greatest
modern exigete, Garrison Keillor, has taught us. Little kindnesses of the
kind we have been discussing are an almost perfect expression of a shy
soul's feelings, because they can be modestly shrugged off. ('Oh it's
nothing. Forget it.') Shyness is also a way of muffling the effects of sudden
and quite unpredictable emotional earthquakes of the kind that periodically shook the Brando household – a mother's sudden loss to alcohol, a
father's sudden rage. It is a way of preserving an illusion of untouchability.

But shyness, that vague whisper of a word, defies full, accurate definition, for it also covers a multitude of anti-social mysteries, among them in-
expressable rage and mild schizophrenic tendencies. Speaking here as a
'shy' person, I can say that it is the imperfect articulation of powerfully
conflicting yet inchoate emotions which one cannot bring oneself to put
into words and which one often covers with careful respect and politeness,
especially to one's elders and to authority figures. (In later years, when

Brando's reputation for wildness preceded him everywhere, he was always disarming strangers with attentive mannerliness.) Above all, one wants to avoid direct confrontations. One hides much outrage behind a vague smile, murmurs of false assent and dim denials. ('What's wrong?' 'Nothing – just a little headache.') Finally, one reserves the right not to return phone calls, an art at which Marlon Brando would become one of the world's masters.

The conflict in which he was caught was utterly basic. It was a conflict between loyalty owed on the one hand to his mother – sweet, indulgent, ineffectual and increasingly pitiable – and on the other to his father – strict, unyielding, uncomprehending.

Jocelyn would later put it in a well-turned paragraph: 'Father thought when we were growing up we should have responsibilities, and mother thought we were still growing up and should be let alone. In many ways he [Bud] got along better with mother because the pressures she put on him were of a different kind. Pressures of living, getting along with people, understanding life. . . . She was much more patient during those years than father. Father was not very articulate, and wasn't able to give of himself too well, and his attitudes were much stricter. With him, performance was the thing, not the intention. The opposite with mother. She was a very encouraging person. She had plenty of foibles herself and acknowledged them, so was more tolerant.'

There speaks, in carefully measured words, a daughter dutiful to her family, to the discreet traditions of her time and place, but also to the truth. Foibles! Well, all right, foibles. Let us permit the mild word. But as Bud Brando grew older he was obviously responding to something more potent than 'foibles' in the family drama. We speak now, I think, of endless and terrible parental tensions, and of the corrosive damage being done to Dodie by them. At a certain point her illness (though of course the idea that alcoholism was an illness, rather than a moral failing, was not widespread at the time) became obvious to perfect strangers, possibly even a subject of suburban scandal. It was impossible, needless to say, for the son to intervene between his parents, or to express himself openly on the central issue of his family's life.

So . . . withdrawal. Recalcitrance. Indifference. Drumming. (Yes, drumming, a wonderful way to shut the world out while at the same time driving it crazy, as I, myself a sometime drummer, can attest.) Jocelyn would expand somewhat on her characterization of Marlon Sr and Bud's relationship with him. An 'intense, scared, inarticulate man,' she would call him. 'He thought it best to push Bud. . . . Life hung on an arithmetic problem. Father wanted a lot from him and for him in a practical sense.

"You're not passing here, you're fooling around there." Bud was many times not so practical.'

Bud was many times beside himself. Though, as I've said, it is almost impossible to find among the memories of those who knew him as a young man recollections of him speaking about his past, there is one, that is particularly vivid. Offered by a young actor who aspired beside Brando in summer stock, it is a paraphrase of Bud's description of his father: 'A tall, looming figure who stares down hard at him, but never touches him or makes contact with him in any way.'

Eventually, in mid-adolescence, Bud did find his tongue. Witnesses have testified to overheard battles, conducted at the top of their voices by the two Marlons. There is no record of conventional juvenile delinquency – smashed cars, petty crime, girls 'in trouble'. There is, however, an insistence on serious attention being paid to the quiet young man. Here, again, his parents' problem with drink cannot be ignored. It is fairly typical of children of alcoholics to deflect attention to themselves in order that it not be focused too intently on errant parents. This is something to bear in mind when considering Marlon Brando's seemingly curious behavior half a century later, when his son was charged with murder, notably his sudden loquaciousness with the press after decades of avoiding it. He was drawing attention to himself, away from his son, just as, long ago, he had attempted to draw it away from his parents.

Back then, Military school was, of course, deemed the answer to the kind of problems he presented. 'That'll knock some sense into you, young man.' Goodbye, Sinclair Lewis. Hello, J. D. Salinger.

Military school! There was a time when that threat hovered over the head of almost every middle-class adolescent male in America. Parents would contemplate its salutary effects in voices just loud enough to be overheard by their sulking sons. We would affect indifference, cynicism. But we would sometimes be very good for a day or two, until the current storm blew over. The obvious trouble in Brando's case was that his father was himself the product of – yes – a military school. Dear old Shattuck, in Fairbault, Minnesota. Up at 5.45. Inspection. Callisthenics in the cold Minnesota mornings. Drills. Hikes. Compulsory sports. Study Hall after dinner. Lights out at 9.30. And, at the time, a certain urgency about the whole miserable business. For this was 1942-3. 'Don't you know there's a war on, Buddy?'

Still, true to the Brando heritage of politesse, Bud was at least for a while an obliging student. He went out for football and did well until sometime in his second season a knee injury put him in the hospital (it required an operation, but it probably saved him from the draft). He made the 'Crack Squad', which was a precision drill team in which the school (and his father, who had been a member of it in his day) took inordinate pride. He did well in dramatics – at least three shows, one of which his mother saw. 'That boy can act,' she reported at home.

In other words, Bud Brando did rather well, all things considered. Oh, there were reports of more than usual class-cutting. And there was the matter of the flaming Vitalis. The hair tonic was a colorless oil-based liquid. You could write a dirty word with it on a wall and it would remain invisible – until you touched a match to it and the obscenity came to fiery life. Bud caused another minor (but perhaps more biographically instructive) scandal at his first communion, when he held the wafer on his tongue and, on returning to his pew, took it out and examined it. The school saw it as irreverence. Jocelyn saw it as Bud being Bud. 'He just wanted to see what this stuff was that was so important – see it, feel it and taste it.' (Remember Adler on acting. Brando was hers before he met or heard of her.)

None of these constituted expulsion offenses, especially considering how nicely Bud Brando seemed to be fitting in at Shattuck. But in the fall of his second year, after the football injury, things started to deteriorate. He worked his wound for all it was worth, exaggerating a limp and continuing to drag about long after his knee had healed. Malingering was suspected, and disgust was registered by school officials. Concentration had never been one of Bud's strengths, of course. But the more distant observer has to suspect something else was at work here, something that would recur subsequently in this career. Bud Brando had proved a point: he could be his father's son if he wanted to. But now he had played this role, had pleased his audience, had got out of it whatever good there was to be had from it. Now he was perhaps bored. Why go on repeating himself? He has never learned to accept the basic folk wisdom about the wages of success: 'You don't get to do better, you just get to do more.'

Be that as it may, it seems he was not asked to leave Shattuck because of any spectacular infraction of the rules; fizzling out, he was pushed out. 'Beat, tired, discouraged, and upset' was Jocelyn's description of him after his dismissal. There was patriarchal disgust at home, naturally, and matriarchal patience. New York, where both his sisters were then living, was mentioned – and perhaps the possibility of studying acting. Or not. The record is shadowy. Jocelyn would remember simply that Bud was 'shaky' and didn't know what to do with life when he finally decamped for Fran's apartment, cluttered with her work and her art student's paraphernalia, on West 10th Street in Greenwich Village.

AGE OF CONSENT

I t was a good time to be in New York. As it had been for something like a half-century, the city was, to quote an early metropolitan observer, 'teeming with life, humming with trade, muttering with the thunder of passage' – especially the latter in these war years. It thronged with servicemen on leave, horny, wondering, feverish, many of them, at their impending confrontation with premature mortality. It thronged, too, with refugees from Hitler's Europe – artists, musicians, men of letters, performers of all kinds – and they lent a new edge of sophistication to the city's cultural life, an edge which cut away much of its remaining provincialism.

Nine English-language newspapers were then published daily in Manhattan. Magazines thrived – a dozen that are no more, another dozen that have since lost the youthful vigor they then enjoyed. Network radio was also an animating, glamorizing force, and a means of employment for actors. And though, then as now, then as before, everyone lamented Broadway's decline, it still mounted upward of eighty productions every season. These industries fueled a legendary night-life, of course, but also helped feed an intoxicating mixture of gossip and ideas.

There was a playfulness in New York life at this time that is perhaps the most regrettable of all its losses in recent decades. Above all, this congeries of forces fueled the hopes of a bright, ambitious, upwardly striving population of young adults, drawn from all over the United States in hopes of finding an escape into fame. Or an escape into anonymity – either one, as long as the stage on which their personal dramas were played out pulsed with wayward life.

John Cheever would remember New York at this moment as a place 'still filled with river light' but also one where 'almost everybody wore a hat'. In other words, it retained, as it would for another decade or two, before the urban rot took hold, both spaciousness and graciousness. Think of it: a young artist and a young actor could afford an apartment with a walk-in kitchen and a small terrace from which they could look down on Patchen Place – perhaps catch a glimpse of e. e. cummings stepping out of his little house there.

That was the way of it in New York then. It was not all high rise and bottom line. The city was more a creator of innovation than a consumer of imports. Young men and women beginning careers in the arts or some less grand form of communication could feel that they were in some real sense sharing the world of people who had made, were still making, the tradition they would inherit, perhaps expand upon. In the Forties, for example, George Balanchine's New York City Ballet was beginning to establish itself as a great new creative power in dance, while all around Greenwich Village painters were beginning to form the school that would soon be known the world over as Abstract Impressionism. Uptown, on West 52nd Street, jazz was being renovated by the likes of Dizzy Gillespie and Charlie Parker, and on Broadway, at virtually the same moment Marlon Brando was walking into Stella Adler's class for the first time, *Oklahoma!*, which would revitalize the American musical, was about to open. These were powerful assertions that an indigenous American culture was coming of age, and the force this culture would exert in the post-war world – a force that would match and (to some) help justify America's political dominance of that world – was unimaginable. It was not quite as unimaginable, though, as the fact that by the time the decade turned this same Marlon Brando would exemplify the new, and equally potent, American style of theatrical self-presentation to the world audience.

I speak with some feeling about this New York, maybe more than Marlon Brando would. For while he was living in it, I was dreaming of it, and feeding those dreams with Winchell's column and *Time*'s back of the book, the *New Yorker* and the Sunday *New York Times* – all that teases a young provincial mind and then bends it toward the need to share in some version of urbanity. We were both lucky, I think, that in the Forties, when Brando was there, and the Fifties, when I finally attained the metropolis, the reality of New York still more or less matched our fantasies.

Brando's life in these early days in New York is something of a blur. It is not clear, indeed, how he made a living until he began to get his first acting jobs. We do know that he found work running an elevator at Best's department store, but that it only lasted a week or so. Calling out floors and naming the merchandise ('second floor – ladies' lingerie') to a carful of strangers is no job for a shy person. What we also know is that taking on a new identity, something one can hide one's true self under or behind, is a sovereign cure for shyness.

'Young actor' – that's a good alias under which to travel. And, at the time, a new one. For it was only with the beginning of organizations like Piscator's workshop that aspiring performers began to form a community, a recognizable identity as a group. This, indeed, may have been the most important thing that these new, and by no means stable, institutions gave them: a feeling that they were apprentices to an honorable profession, absorbing a body of lore and legend they could rely on for strength, to help build a self that could stand up to the buffetings of what is, God knows, one of the most difficult and psychologically dangerous occupations on earth.

It has been claimed that Brando may actually have been the first to make blue jeans a standard element in this crowd's dress code, though there is no proof on that point. But we do know that their life consisted of living in lofts, eating in cafeterias, second-acting shows (that is, sneaking into an empty seat at the intermission), nursing a cup of expresso for hours in one of the Italian cafes on Bleecker or MacDougall Street, while an impassioned discussion of a new production or a new acting phenomenon, or just a good performance in yesterday's class, roiled on through the evening. How harshly bad 'work' was condemned; what a sense of awe good 'work' engendered. But what a relief – to be eighteen and in New York, to be judged on what you did, not who you were, to be free of parental anxiety and disapproval, to be broody and gorgeous among people to whom both qualities were a source of attraction rather than a cause for alarm, to be part of a new family that loved easily and forgave readily.

Fran put it mildly: 'They were very intense about their school. They were terribly absorbed in their dancing and their movement and their make-up' [all subjects taught at the Piscator workshop]. The group, she recalled, was 'very closely-knit. . . . At last there were lots of people he could talk to.' Adler, predictably, put it less mildly: 'Young actors as a group are just screwballs. They have nothing to do with ideas. They are a separate group, apart from all. And they cannot be with anyone else – they are not happy.' Commenting almost a decade later she observed: 'Marlon only has to do with them.'

Ultimately, as she implied, that may have been limiting. But for the moment it was a blessing. And it was accompanied by quite startling success. By the fall of 1943 Bud Brando was working in the little scenes that another Dramatic Workshop teacher, John Gassner, used to illustrate his lectures on theatrical history. By January 1944 he was cast in Piscator's production of Gerhardt Hauptman's dream play, *Hannele's Way to Heaven*. It was a dual role: that of the eponymous heroine's beloved schoolteacher and that of a dark angel who haunts the long slumber into which she sinks after a suicide attempt. Such was the power of Piscator's reputation that critics from the major papers often reviewed these plays, and Brando got his first good notices in this, and in *Twelfth Night*, which was staged the same week. Though it was *Hannele* that his friends would remember more powerfully, it was *Twelfth Night* that most interested the first agent to sign him, Maynard Morris, of the Leland Hayward office.

Immediately thereafter, there was some Molière and an appearance as – yes – a giraffe in a children's play written by Stanley Kauffmann, latterly better known as a film and drama critic. The following summer Piscator included Brando in the company, drawn from the Dramatic Workshop student body, which did a fairly serious summer of stock in Sayville, Long Island. The season opened with the *Twelfth Night* of the previous winter. But Piscator had turned rehearsals over to associates while he finished up some work in New York, and deplored the chaos he found when he joined his troupe just prior to the first night. Dodie, who had come out to see it, liked it just as little, and for the same reason. She also came on to his best friend, Carlo Fiore – or so he alleges in the book he wrote about these early years. How one hopes he misunderstood, or exaggerated. In any case, there were two or three more shows, and then another expulsion.

The company had been having the usual swell time associated with summer stock: all-night sessions drinking and talking, plenty of goofing off, plenty of romances. Brando had perhaps the best time of all, for he and Fiore had the best bunk – in the hayloft of a disused barn on the theater grounds, away from the house where most of the company lived, and with a glorious ocean view. It was, obviously, a great place to entertain young ladies. Piscator was not amused. Too much of that sort of thing had been going on throughout the company, in his stern view. And he was especially watchful of Bud Brando. For the director was a theater saint, all dedication and self-denial in pursuit of high ideals; in a business rife with corruptive influences, his type is not unfamiliar, and not without value, either.

Piscator had noted Brando's frequent absences from class all spring, and he suspected a lack of proper sobriety about theater art. Sure enough, snooping around one afternoon he found Bud Brando in what was by all accounts quite innocent congress with one of the girls in the company when he might have been . . . what? Studying lines. Studying Boleslawski's *Six Lessons*. Studying his navel, if nothing else. Both miscreants were asked to leave, though Brando was in this instance somewhat in the condition of a typical Hitchcock hero: on the specific charge blameless, but of a general lack of moral-aesthetic seriousness (at least by Piscator's standards) guilty as charged.

Many of Brando's elders looked upon him in this way at this time. And if they looked to him like potential father figures, in either the forbidding or the distant manner, then he was likely to react rebelliously. For example:

An audition for Alfred Lunt; the usual worklight dimly illuminating the stage; the house, also as usual, dark. From it, the bored, disembodied voice of the great man. 'Say something, just anything.' Panic. Anger. Both piled on top of the normal tensions and anxieties of a reading. One had not been taught to 'work' this way. Quite the opposite. One had specifically been told this was no way to work. Most actors, even today, would swallow those feelings and announce that they had worked up a little something from Shakespeare or Chekhov, whoever, whatever, Not Marlon Brando. 'Hickory-dickory dock,' he declaimed 'The mouse ran up the clock.' Whether or not he got to the end of the nursery rhyme before stalking out is not entirely clear.

Around the same time he had had his first screen test, for Twentieth Century-Fox. As these things go, it was quite simple: they perched Brando on a stool and asked him to turn this way and that, so they could see how he photographed from various angles. At some point the man conducting the test engaged his discomfited victim in conversation. 'What do you want to be?' the director asked. Disgusted reply: 'A yo-yo player.' Or, in the improved version of the story, he pulls out a yo-yo and starts playing with it.

No matter which is correct. The point of both stories is that he did what every actor has always wanted to do: raise a protest against the degrading, demeaning process of auditioning, the whole dreadful business by which (if you're lucky) you are granted five minutes to state your essence, show your skills, strut your stuff. The occasion is meaningless for the grandees lurking in the theater, behind the camera. They've got it made and have buried their memories of what it's like not to have it made. But it is everything to the actor. He is often confronting a question of immediate survival – next month's rent, last month's unpaid phone bill – and he is always confronting career pressure: keeping it moving, keeping himself visible, viable.

Jocelyn, a fine actress who never attained such security as stardom has to offer, knew exactly what her brother was feeling and what he was trying to say to his auditioners. 'Someone out there in the dark, whom you can't see, will judge you. Your life begins or ends at this moment. . . . I mean, to be interviewed by someone you can't even see, in a place where you're drowning. . . . Bud simply felt the whole ridiculousness and awesomeness of it . . . the whole futility of the thing. And then they say, "Oh, that weird boy."'

But not for long. Or, if, perhaps, the likes of the Lunts – perfect exemplars of the mannerly and well-spoken tradition that the Stanislavskian crowd was bent on replacing – continued to think in those terms, most people were soon admitting that this kid Brando had something. For he

31

was scarcely back from Sayville when he got his first Broadway show: *I Remember Mama*. Of all things.

Produced by Rodgers and Hammerstein, it was an adptation by the smooth, commercially-knowing John van Druten of *Mama's Bank Account*, Kathryn Forbes's memoir of growing up poor, but with excellent values, in a family of Norwegian immigrants in turn-of-the-century San Francisco. They were, of course, warm, loving, mildly fractious, sweetly eccentric – in short, appealing and utterly untaxing folks with whom to spend an evening. They were also the kind of people that wartime popular culture loved celebrating: they, and their right to be exemplary were what we were fighting for. Moreover, this family had obvious commercial potential, for they and the vehicle in which they were presented were not far in spirit from the Day family of the comfortably nostalgic *Life With Father*, then about half-way toward setting the record it still holds as the longest running non-musical play in Broadway history.

It is obvious from this description why Brando hesitated when he was offered the role of Nils, the family's youngest son, in a cast headed by Mady Christians and Oscar Homolka, both popular character leads of the time. For *Mama* was just the kind of thing Brando and his peers viewed scornfully, if not with revolutionary outrage – bourgeois theatre of the most blatant sort.

But Adler read the script and urged him to take it. She knew as well as anyone what it was, but she was no Strasbergian purist. She saw that Nils aged a few years over the course of the play, which is always a nice, noticeable trick for an actor to achieve. More importantly, she observed that the role consisted very largely of watchful silences. In other words, the casting was perfect.

When *Mama* opened, the critics were dismissive ('pleasantly undisturbing'), but in a way that signalled to the middle class that they would have a very nice time at The Music Box theater. Though it did not challenge the success of *Life With Father*, the play would run almost two years and became an inescapable presence in American popular culture – as a George Stevens movie (starring Irene Dunne), as the basis for an early television series, and, as late as 1979, the source of a musical scored by one of the original producers, Richard Rodgers. It was only at that late date, despite Liv Ullman's presence in the lead, that the piece finally attained total irrelevance to the audience.

In 1944, the reviewers were so preoccupied with van Druten (whose recent record included *The Voice of the Turtle*, another great wartime success) and the bullet-proof Christians and Homolka that they didn't pay much attention to Marlon Brando. But truly knowledgeable theater-goers, the professionals, did. 'I went to see *I Remember Mama*,' Bobby Lewis would recall a few years later, 'and I noticed this kid on stage. I checked with my program and it said "Marlon Brando". I turned to a friend of mine sitting beside me and said: "This is probably a mistake. This Marlon Brando is probably sick and somebody else is in the part." You know, like they have to put a stage-hand in the role . . . in an emergency. I mean everybody else on the stage was acting or not acting, but this boy was a note of reality. He was so real. He really lived in that house there.'

Edith Van Cleve, the MCA agent whose client Brando would shortly become, had a similar revelation. 'Everybody was watching Oscar Homolka, Mady Christians, Joan Tetzel [who played the narrator-*ingénue* and would soon marry Homolka] and so on. And afterwards everyone was saying, "Wasn't Homolka wonderful?" And I'd say, "Yes, but wasn't the boy good?" "Wasn't Christians wonderful?" "Yes, but wasn't the boy good?" And finally someone said, "What boy? Oh, the one in knee pants who grew up." The way he listened. He stood on that stage for twenty minutes without a line, and when he did speak it was if he had been speaking all the time. You didn't jerk your head around because of a new voice. How extraordinarily he played the scene. He made it seem like he had a long part.'

Van Cleve, who specialized in the movies, sent for Brando, who told her he had representation and wasn't interested in movies in any case. She replied that he wasn't ready for them anyway, but that she'd be glad to turn down offers on his behalf. And that was that for something like six months. Then in the midst of a blizzard, when no work was being done, no phone calls were being made, Brando appeared out of the storm at her office and announced he had fulfilled all obligations to Maynard Morris (who would subsequently join MCA) and was ready to sign.

The problem now was getting Brando to leave *Mama*. The pay was steady, the work light. Adler, in particular, felt obliged to pry him loose from the play she had talked him into, for it was beginning to feed his natural laziness, she felt. She said he ought to think about doing a *Peer Gynt*, which was a great casting idea. But nothing came of it. What did come of the withdrawal from *Mama* was almost a year without theatrical employment. But, again, Adler to the rescue – or so she would recall.

In 1945-46 her husband, Harold Clurman, had formed a producing partnership with Elia Kazan and their first presentation was to be Maxwell Anderson's *Truckline Cafe*, with Clurman directing. She recommended her student for a role as a psychopathically troubled war veteran, and

33

despite doubts, they hired Brando. It was, for all concerned, a moment more significant than it seemed at the time. For *Truckline Cafe* would turn out to be a true theatrical rarity: a consequential flop, a play of no great merit that would, nevertheless have several unintended effects on the course of future history.

Setting aside Tennessee Williams's *The Glass Menagerie*, which had opened just before the end of the war, and which was, in any case, a less blatant – if ultimately more effective – assault on the status quo, *Truckline* can be seen (perhaps was in part seen by its creators) as the first post-war challenge to Broadway's pre-war mentality. For it represented a coming together of two important strands in the recent history of the American theater. Clurman's involvement in the production obviously signals the influence of The Group Theater on everyone's calculations. So does the presence of Kazan, who had been an actor and general factotum in the company. (Hence his nickname, 'Gadge', short for Gadget, which symbolized his all-purpose usefulness in the old days.) The two would become perhaps the most significant figures in shaping American theatrical history in the post-war era. Between them they would direct a majority of the most important plays of the era, introducing significant new American voices to the theater and, in the case of Clurman (whose manner, paradoxically, was that of a passionate *boulevardier*), many of the more interesting European modernists. Kazan's work as a movie director would, of course, be as important as his Broadway career, and Clurman would soon take up duties as a drama critic (for *The Nation*) of uncommon knowledgeability and influence – especially on theater people.

Given their backgrounds and convictions, it is significant that at this moment they chose to do a play by Maxwell Anderson. With Robert E. Sherwood and Sidney Kingsley, he had been for almost two decades one of the most highly regarded of Broadway's serious playwrights. Anderson was drawn alternately to high-flown historical pageantry (*Elizabeth the Queen, Mary of Scotland*) and contemporary socio-political issues (*High Tor, Key Largo*) but, whatever his subject-matter, fatally attracted to blank verse, and his work has not worn well. Still, at the time he was taken very seriously as a 'playwright of ideas', not least by himself. In any case, it was no small thing for this establishment writer to link his fortunes with Group alumni, and there was high interest in what they would bring forth.

As it happens, *Truckline Cafe* found Anderson going among the low-lifes, a group by chance gathered one evening at a roadside diner perched on the Californian coastline. From the start, and typically, Kazan felt the writer needed to do more work on his text. From the start, and also typically, Clurman was more interested in subtext: the unspoken material he had, with his shrewd critical sense, winnowed out of the script and, as well, hoped to winnow out of his actors.

Brando's role – a supporting one – was that of Sage McRae, a psychopathic war veteran returning home and discovering, in the course of the drama, that his wife, played by Ann Shepherd, has been unfaithful. Sage murders her and swims out to sea to dispose of her body, but then returns to the stage, dripping wet, (stage-hands doused the actor with cold water just before this entrance), teeth chattering and, almost beatifically, awaits the arrival of the police and eventual doom.

Brando dieted down to almost wraithlike proportions, the better to suggest his character's tormented nature. But rehearsals were troubled. Karl Malden, whose career would for some time be intertwined with Brando's, was in the cast and remembered him as 'a terribly shy, sensitive boy', who had trouble projecting. To say the least. Anderson couldn't hear his precious lines, and Clurman fretted anxiously over a performance that refused to take shape. People did not yet know that this was one of those actors whose rehearsals are terrible to behold – groping, erratic, crazy-making for directors and fellow performers. Clurman guessed correctly that he was unable to voice his deepest emotions because 'it hurt too much.' Unfortunately, despite his many excellent qualities, Clurman was a talker, delightful to listen to in private life, but tedious as a rehearsal speechifier – especially to someone like Brando. The actor did not respond at all well to the hours of pseudo-analytic dialogue in which the director engaged him.

Malden, watching, was wiser. 'I guess actors are formless,' he would say later. 'Nine-tenths of the people who become actors are that way.' The point was, he suggested, that his young colleague needed to lose himself, and his shyness, in a role – and that loss happened not when he was thinking about the part, and talking about it in rehearsal, but when he was doing it under performance pressure. Or, as Malden put it to a reporter, 'Once on stage, he became a character so much he wasn't Marlon any more.'

Too bad Arthur Penn wasn't around to consult with Clurman about Brando. Years later, having directed him in two pictures, he would say, 'He doesn't put on a great scene on how acting is acted. He just gets up and does it. He's like a natural hitter in baseball. He doesn't take 25 swings . . . he just steps up there and hits it out of the park.'

I suspect we come close, here, to one of the prime reasons Brando abandoned the stage. A play in the making is a cave of the winds, everyone talking actor-talk about motives and emotional recall and what-have-you – trying to get into the very stuff our subject became an actor to avoid getting

35

into. Movies are different: the production schedule sets the pace: get up and do the scene – bang – then move on to the next set-up and the next. There's no time for self-examination, and no demand for it. The actor can indulge in it if he wants, but in his trailer, in his hotel room, in his own time. On set or location he's just supposed to hit his mark and say his lines. In other words, and despite all the contemptuous words he has lavished on the medium, Brando's psychological priorities suit the exigencies of the movies better than they do those of the stage.

Yet a performance – and by all accounts an astonishing one – did at last emerge in *Truckline Cafe*. Pauline Kael, the movie critic to be, happened to catch Brando in it. Arriving late for a performance, she settled into a second row seat 'and saw what I thought was an actor having a seizure on-stage. Embarrassed for him, I lowered my eyes, and it wasn't until the young man who'd brought me grabbed my arm and said, "Watch this guy!" that I realized he was *acting*.' The reviewers in their variously dim ways agreed for the most part. But everybody hated the play. It would close after a week's run.

But not before the producers who could not bear to see their work buried in the mass, unmarked grave reserved for short-lived Broadway failures, make a fight for it. Clurman and Kazan took out an ad in the *Times*, attacking the critics. 'There is a black-out of all taste, except the taste of these men,' they wrote, urging the public to come and see the play and make up its own mind. '*Truckline Cafe* has faults,' they conceded, 'but it is the kind of play that, in our opinion, every theater lover should see. That is why we did it . . .' Anderson, 'a great, shy bear of a man, rich in humility and conscience,' as John Mason Brown, the drama critic, described him, chimed in with a far more intemperate, and quite out-of-character attack on the critics. 'A sort of Jukes family of journalism,' he called them in a Sunday newspaper letter. 'It is an insult to our theater that there should be so many incompetents and irresponsibles among them.'

These assaults, more than the play itself, constituted a gauntlet flung down. Saving the gentlemanly and open-minded Brooks Atkinson of the *Times*, no sub-group of a generally benighted profession more deserved chastening. Ever since Alexander Woollcott had set the preciously personal tone of New York drama criticism earlier in the century, the subject-matter of the reviewers had been often as not themselves – that is, their subjective states as they watched a production – rather than the work itself. Not that they ever betrayed sensibilities worth examining, or dug into them with powerful tools. Rather, they took pride in announcing their sleepiness or restlessness at the theater, or the point at which they walked out. Needless to say, they were most often bored at plays that courted some sort of artistic or intellectual danger, offered some kind of challenge to the audience. Indeed, their loyalty was never to the theater as an expressive form, but to the narrow and timorous sensibility of the middle-class audience which the reviewers always ended confidently, usually quite directly, advising to go or not to go to a given play, as if, somehow, their opinions were perfectly representative of everyone else's. If their approach was reprehensible, their writing was as a rule unreadable, and one must regard the attack on their smugness by Kazan, Clurman and Anderson as belated and mild in comparison to the offenses they had committed in the name of criticism.

This particular show was beyond saving, but these unprecedented diatribes against a breed that – Walter Kerr excepted – has not notably improved over the years, did send a message: that the non-commercial (indeed, anti-commercial) radical fringe of Thirties theater was starting to move on the center, and that it would find there surprising allies like Anderson. Add to this its importance in Brando's personal history, and *Truckline Cafe* was rescued from the dustbin of history. Though unread and unplayed today, it clings to life at the bottom of the page, a teasing footnote in modern American theatrical annals.

It performed two other significant functions as well. It brought Brando to the attention of Kazan, and that had, as we all know, a major effect on both careers, as well as on the larger history of American theater and film. More immediately, according to Kazan, it precipitated renewed thoughts about creating some kind of theatrical institution that would perform some of the functions which The Group had once performed. For one thing, he would remember saying to Clurman, 'We needed our kind of actors to play the leading roles in our productions.' Besides Brando, he had liked Malden and some of the others in *Truckline*, but many roles he had thought 'inadequately performed'. He also harbored hopes of restoring some of the communal spirit of The Group at its best. Clurman agreed, and said he'd mention it to Stella. No thanks, Kazan thought, having had his difficulties with her in the past. So he took the idea to Bobby Lewis, and in the course of an afternoon's walk in Central Park, The Actor's Studio was born – for good, ill or some combination of the two. (If Lee Strasberg was mentioned at all in that conversation it was as someone who might teach a course or two in the history of the theater, according to Kazan.)

No matter to Marlon Brando, all these plans. He had a job. Guthrie McClintic, Katharine Cornell's husband's manager and director, had seen him in *Truckline*, and conceived the odd, daring notion that he was right to play Marchbanks, the palely loitering poet, opposite Cornell in a revival of *Candida*, with Sir Cedric Hardwicke cast as her pastor husband. And so our young rebel was again thrust back into the well-spoken mainstream, with one of theater's designated Great Ladies (the others were Helen Hayes and Lynn Fontanne), who, as it happened, counted Shaw's play one of her great triumphs of a decade ago.

Curiously, nothing bad came of this involvement. Actors in the company would recall Brando being extremely reserved and polite to his elders, though Cornell's theatrical manner and McClintic's directorial style – he was a curious blend of the prissy and the volatile – were clearly antithetical to him. On opening night, it is said, Brando either went up in his lines or indulged in shameless upstaging, or both. But the show opened to respecatable, if not wildly enthusiastic, notices. Some reviewers even liked Brando in it, thinking he caught the skittish inwardness, the tormented shyness, of unformed youth. Others thought he somewhat flattened out the character. The play had a short Broadway run and moved on to Chicago for a few weeks (Cornell remained a great draw on the road), where Brando's performance is reported to have deteriorated, possibly as a result of proximity to his parents on their home ground.

In the fall of 1946, more work, more theatrical legends: Ben Hecht, Luther Adler, Paul Muni. The former, co-author of *The Front Page* and *Twentieth Century*, one of Hollywood's most brilliantly facile screenwriters (and a renowned script doctor), had abandoned his lightsome ways for a passionate commitment to Zionism. In aid of a cause that would eventually cost him his movie career – he supported the Irgun terrorists and denounced the British protectorate in the Holy Land, leading to a boycott of his work in Britain – Hecht wrote *A Flag is Born*. It was a sort of propaganda pageant masquerading as a play, with music by Kurt Weill. Luther Adler, Stella's brother, and a man of immense ego, was engaged to direct it. Muni, who had also begun his career in the Yiddish theatre, and was held in general awe as an actor, agreed to star.

There was no question about Brando's participation when he was asked. These were certainly more his kind of people than Cornell and her crowd had been. And surely there was a timeliness, and a controversialism, to the subject-matter that was absent from yet another Shaw revival. Indeed, the establishment of a Jewish state, welcoming the homeless survivors of the holocaust, was a cause that naturally enlisted Brando's sympathies. This would be the first time, but hardly the last, that he insisted upon placing the demands of his conscience ahead of professional calculation. But it must be admitted that the role, that of a heroic young freedom fighter who has the play's concluding inspirational harangue, after the Muni character has sacrificed his life, was not without its obvious appeals.

Finally, the opportunity to work with Muni was irresistible. That seems a little odd now, for Muni's reputation is no longer what it was. He had been the original *Counsellor at Law* on Broadway, and *Scarface* in the movies, and had worked marvellously in another touchstone film of the 1930s, *I Was a Fugitive from a Chain Gang*. But he had gained his greatest fame in a succession of movie biographies of great historical figures, hiding behind heavy accents and make-ups. He had great technique, but he had a way of 'humanizing' these figures that was somewhat in the vein of George Arliss. They twinkled more than was absolutely necessary. Still, he had found a way to hide in plain sight while the 'real' Paul Muni – if there was one – eluded detection. And that intrigued Brando.

Not that rehearsals went smoothly. Muni had trouble getting hold of his part (much fuss over the shape of his beard) and his lines – particularly a lengthy didactic speech. Adler, and occasionally Muni, entered the usual complaints about Brando's rehearsal habits, which were again slow and diffident to the point of inaudibility. Finally, in performance, there was an incident that passed into showbiz lore and legend. When Muni finally expired on stage Brando was supposed to drape him in the flag of Israel and then launch into the ringing peroration that brought down the house. Muni, though, was not entirely content that his face be hidden from view, and on this occasion he tugged the flag down, bit by careful bit, while his young colleague was in the middle of his speech, until the famous face was once again revealed. Titters, of course, ensued.

Yet the reviews, especially of Brando, were good; *A Flag is Born* achieved a respectable run (127 performances); and of all the actors Brando worked with he has remained most voluble in his admiration for Muni. Thirty years later he would tell a reporter: 'Night after night that man gave me goosebumps. Most plays you go mad with the boredom of repetition. But Muni was electrifying, the best I've ever seen. . . .' I think we may be talking role model here, a demonstration of a way to make a living as an actor without indulging in prodigies of self-exposure. All that make-up, all those accents later on. Muniesque.

Of course, not every encounter with a legend works out so well. Consider Tallulah Bankhead and *The Eagle Has Two Heads*, which was certainly one of Jean Cocteau's lesser fancies. A dour Graustarkian fable, in which a queen's mourning for a mate done in fifteen years earlier is interrupted (somewhat belatedly) by the intrusion in the bedchamber of a revolutionary. He has come for murder, but he stays for love. At the end, both queen and commoner die for their sins – or maybe just to provide the play-wright with a big finish. One of the work's appeals to Bankhead was that death scene, which required a spectacular fall down a long flight of stairs. Another was a first-act monologue, said by some historians to be the longest soliloquy in theatrical history; it took her 30 minutes to get through it at the beginning of an endless pre-Broadway tour in Wilmington, 22 minutes in Boston, 17 when the play finally reached New York – still a mouthful of words.

By that time Marlon Brando was long gone. The question is why he was invited to come along in the first place. Edith Van Cleve and John C. Wilson, Bankhead's tame, socialite director, thought he was her kind of hunk. But first impressions should have told all concerned that he was not ideally cast in this situation, if only because of Bankhead's notorious alcohol problem. Brando has always been forthright in his disapproval of drink, for good and obvious reasons. (One of Maureen Stapleton's major memories of him in student days was of him calling her and a room-mate 'drunken hags', because they had had a nip or two one night before going out with him.)

Still, a job was a job, and an interview was arranged. Bankhead had a home in Westchester, not far from Bobby Lewis's weekend retreat. It was arranged that Brando and a date should have luncheon with Lewis before going on to meet Bankhead. A wrong train was taken, a carelessly discarded cigarette started a minor fire among the dry leaves on Lewis's lawn, and the young actor was perhaps not in the best of humors when he finally encountered the star. She, predictably, was well along in drink when he arrived, and when she offered him something he asked, 'Are you an alcoholic?' 'No, Darling,' she replied, 'just a heavy drinker.' She also had certain sexual expectations of young men associated with her in theatrical enterprises (Kazan, who directed her in her last great success, *The Skin of Our Teeth*, could have told young Marlon a story or two in that regard), and she was soon trying to grope Brando through his jeans. It would not be her last pass.

For, strangely enough, she engaged him. It was a truly monumental – or even risible – mistake. As everyone discovered in Wilmington. Up to now, the gap between the new generation of actors and the previous ones had been papered over. Ultimately, mutual respect had been formed between Brando and Clurman, Brando and Muni. But Tallulah was not just a star. She was a star turn. And she was surrounded by people who catered to her iron whims, even found in them moral imperatives. Words like 'discipline' and 'respect' were often on their lips. Lewis put the matter well. 'Tallulah

. . . clung to the old tradition of certain stage stars, namely that when they are holding forth in a scene, everyone for miles around should be immobilized. They count every move or reaction from the other actors as distractions. Marlon, on stage, is the kind of actor who has a continuous life going for him, a life which results in scenes rather than star arias surrounded by accompanying robots. Tallulah even placed spies out in the audience to report to her if Marlon was acting behind her back in sections where she couldn't keep her eye on him.'

Compare this account with that of Richard Maney, a self-styled Broadway 'character', who was Bankhead's press agent and drinking companion for a quarter of a century. He was a master of quotable epithets and of a prose style, as Brendan Gill once remarked, 'so ornate that pigeons could have nested in it' – sort of an Alexander Woollcott on the cheap. He contained within his bulky frame virtually everything that was wrong with the old Broadway: toadying star worship, a love of superficial glamour and, above all, hatred of anything that suggested the new and untried. As Maney would tell it in his autobiography, Brando passed rehearsals in his customary state, described as 'trancelike', arrived surly in Wilmington, and then proceeded to upstage Bankhead's treasured first-act 'aria'. 'He squirmed. He picked his nose. He adjusted his fly. He leered at the audience. He cased the furniture. He fixed his gaze on an off-stage property man instead of on his opponent.' Maybe it was pure wickedness. On the other hand, it may well have been acting. Brando's character was supposed to be a loutish peasant, after all.

The death scene was, in Maney's account, even worse. 'On cue, he plugged the Queen and watched her pitch headlong down the stairway. Then, in defiance of Cocteau, Wilson, and Equity's Board of Governors, he refused to die. Instead he staggered about the stage, seeking a likely spot for his final throe.' Bankhead sneaked a wary peek from her elegantly prone position as the audience broke into giggles. 'Why wouldn't this misbegotten clown cash in his chips,' Maney has her wondering. 'Marlon had been mooning about for a full minute on the apron when he suddenly collapsed as if spiked by an invisible ray. The curtain came down with the audience in hysterics.'

Brando was not fired on the spot, but in Boston he achieved that highly desirable end. And, though his only real rival among his generation of actors, Montgomery Clift, was interviewed for the part, he was in fact replaced by that great actor, Helmut Dantine. The temptation, of course, is to see all this symbolically – the old Broadway versus the new, or, if you prefer, the new mannerism versus the old. I'm going to yield to that temptation. Old-fashioned star acting on the stage, as opposed to the movies, where it was quite different and infinitely more refined, had by this time become a bore: ageing ladies and gentlemen receiving heedlessly respectable New York notices, then trotting their tired turns around to wow us provincials.

It was always the same with them: a swirl of rich costumes; graceful gestures, such as one never saw in life, infinitely prolonged; delicate diction that seemed to turn everything they touched into a Freddy Lonsdale comedy. Maybe Brando was cruel to Tallulah – it is definitely not nice to make fun of older people. Maybe it was just acting up, sheer youthful devilry. Maybe something deeper was at work as he played opposite an alcoholic woman who was roughly his mother's age. But with the critics supinely indulgent of the names they had built up in the past, and the public glamorized by press agentry, let's see Brando's behavior on this occasion as what it surely was in some measure – a small gesture of disgust with the status quo (which, excepting *Truckline Cafe* and certain aspects of *A Flag is Born*, had ruled his professional life up to now), a sign that maybe times were beginning to change.

Perhaps faster than he might have guessed. For by the time *Eagle* (which people had taken to calling 'The Turkey with Two Heads') finally crash-landed on Broadway for a run of 29 performances in March 1947, Kazan's production of Arthur Miller's *All My Sons* had opened. Its success, combined with the earlier trimph of *The Glass Menagerie*, suggested that the Broadway theater might finally be entering upon its long predicted new era.

There is, of course, a certain irony in the linkage of Miller and Tennessee Williams as the leading figures of this period in the American theater, for it is hard to think of two more antithetical sensibilities. Except for this: at their early best both of them wished to explore the torments of that most basic of institutions, the family. Miller was, self-consciously, a playwright of ideas, Williams, equally self-consciously, a poet of the theater. But *Menagerie* explored the relationship between a mother and a daughter, *All My Sons* that between a father and a son, and both of them did so in near-tragic terms.

In any event, the success of *All My Sons* emboldened Williams to get in touch with Kazan to direct his next play, even though, as he said, 'Gadge likes a thesis and I haven't made up my mind what the thesis of this play is.' *A Streetcar Named Desire* was to be produced by a newcomer, Irene Mayer Selznick, daughter of Louis B. Mayer, estranged wife of David O. Selznick: in Broadway's mind, a picture person, to be looked at somewhat askance; in her own mind a novice, needing to tread cautiously.

Her first choice as director was Joshua Logan, who was then, arguably, the theater's most reputable director, though not perhaps an ideal choice for a Williams work. Her first choice for the role of Stanley Kowalski was John Garfield – another dubious idea. He was a good actor, but he was a slight man, who though he had played tough city types, had tended to play them in a rather romantic and boyish vein. There was nothing of Stanley's animalism – or menace – about him. And, at 33, he was perhaps a shade too old for the role.

In any case, a stage wait ensued. Kazan went off to Hollywood to direct *Gentlemen's Agreement* (in which Garfield co-starred), continuing to campaign subtly for the assignment to *Streetcar*, as did Williams, who came to the coast to work on script revisions with the director. There, also, they found their Blanche du Bois, or perhaps, as Kazan came to suspect, had her subtly thrust upon them. Hume Cronyn, knowing Williams was in town, and also knowing the one-act play that was the sketch for *Streetcar*, staged it an at LA actors' workshop with his wife, Jessica Tandy, in the leading role. Williams and Kazan came – and were conquered.

When he wrapped his picture, Kazan returned to New York, and at last was officially awarded the play by Mrs Selznick. He also professed himself content with the casting of Garfield. Kazan, in addition to his several other virtues, was a shrewd man of the theater, and thus not averse to a little star insurance, especially if it was in the form of an old Group Theater colleague who apparently shared his theatrical values.

The problem was that 'Julie' Garfield (as he was known to his old pals) was now more movie star than theater idealist. He would only commit to a four-month run in the play, and he wanted first refusal of his role if a film was made of *Streetcar*. He was also casting longing eyes at another play, Jan de Hartog's *Skipper Next to God*, which contained a part more comfortably within his range, and which he did, in fact, do – though with no great success.

The *Streetcar* people began looking elsewhere, and Kazan, recalling Brando from *Truckline*, and perhaps receiving a helpful hint from Bobby Lewis, began looking for Brando. Not an easy task, for this was a period when he had no fixed address, because, it is said, he was attempting to avoid the several young women who were simultaneously pursuing him. Be that as it may, it is Kazan's recollection that he gave Brando twenty dollars for his fare and sent him to Cape Cod to read for Williams, himself a wanderer, who had briefly settled there. Kazan thinks Brando spent the money on food and then hitched his way to the cape. Or maybe he just decided to proceed at his own pace. In any event, he was three days late, arriving when the house was in chaos – electricity out, the toilet overflowing, Williams in a tizzy. Brando fixed the fuses and the plumbing, then transfixed Williams with his reading. The part was his – for ever, as it has turned out, since every actor who has attempted it since has had to compete against everyone else's memory of Marlon Brando in, if not the play, then the movie adaptation.

The rehearsals were in some ways like all his rehearsals, in some ways not. Mrs Selznick, for example, couldn't hear Brando in the back of the house. And Ms Tandy found him erratic. 'If he felt bored or tired, he acted bored or tired. If he felt gay it would go gay. I remember Karl Malden [playing Mitch, Blanche's would-be boyfriend] smashing his fist against the wall because it was so frustrating.' In short, 'I can say I enjoyed acting with him sometimes and other times, God knows, I could have wrung his little neck.' Not that she thought there was anything malicious in this behavior. She always felt Brando was trying to make things easier for the rest of the cast, but that he went about it 'the hard way', by which she meant, among other things, that he did not take direction quickly. Kazan would give him an idea, but she would not see it emerge in performance until weeks had gone by, and Brando had processed it and made it his own in some fashion mysterious to her.

In some ways, however, the rehearsals were different from any that preceded them in this brief theatrical career. Brando seemed to get hold of the basics of the part sooner and more firmly than he had any earlier one. There was some natural affinity with this character that he had not found before. Looking back on Brando in *Streetcar* in the spring of 1990, Kazan would say: 'He is exactly the thing I like in actors. There's a hell of a lot of turmoil there. There's ambivalence there. He's uncertain of himself and he's passionate, both at the same time.' But there was in Kazan's view yet more to the mixture of motives with which Brando invested the part, something the director would describe as 'ambivalence . . . between a soft, yearning, girlish side to him and a dissatisfaction that can be dangerous.' This was perhaps more than Williams consciously knew was inherent in the role as he wrote it, but he delightedly recognized it when Brando summoned it forth. In Kazan's words, the writer developed a 'crush' on the actor, which was not sexual, but was full of gratitude for the subtextual ironies and the driving force he was bringing to the play. Williams proved to be enormously supportive at times when Kazan began worrying that Brando might be unhinging the delicate balance of the play. Brando was so strong, and Tandy was so tentative in the beginning, that the sympathy was flowing toward Stanley Kowalski instead of toward Blanche Du Bois, which was not Williams's intention – at least as Kazan saw it. The author, however, remained serene. He kept saying that his play wasn't so finely poised that its moral weight could shift, depending on casting and perform- ance. In some sense, of course, the point was academic. For as Kazan would later ask: 'What would I say to Brando? Be less good.'

And good he was, in a way that was different from the ways he had been good before. Later, the actor would attribute his success to hard work of a conscious kind. 'I made a study of guys like Stanley Kowalski. You know, guys who work hard and have lots of flesh, having nothing supple about them. They never open their fists, really. . . . They grip a cup of coffee like an animal would wrap a paw around it. They're heavily muscled in body and manner of speech. You see, Stanley Kowalski wasn't interested in how he said anything. He didn't give a damn how he said it. His purpose was to convey his idea. He had no awareness of himself at all. . . .'

Well, yes. All that was certainly there if we may judge a stage perform ance by its film record, made some three years later. But something more was operating, and it too was something that the role drew out of the actor's essential nature. 'He challenges not only the woman,' Kazan would later say, 'he challenges the whole system of politeness and good nature and good ethics and everything else. . . . He did that in life. He never knew where the hell he was going to sleep, you didn't know who he was with, you didn't know who he was running away from or who he was angry about. You never knew. Every day there was a drama that he brought on the set with him.'

All of that appealed to Kazan, the tough, charming, very smart im- migrant lad who had scuffled and scrapped to the top of his profession. And he recalls that he didn't have to do much to encourage this other migrant, a migrant not from foreign climes, but from cautious respectabil- ity, to rip away at genteel convention in whatever ways his spirit moved him. In his director's notes for the play, Kazan referred to Stanley as a 'hoodlum aristocrat', and his task, he remembers, was doing nothing to dis- courage him from acting out all the impulses contained in that nice phrase. 'I liked him so much,' Kazan would say over four decades later, smiling affectionately. 'I still do.'

One is obliged to report that Brando has for years denied the possibility that he found anything in his own nature that was analagous to Stanley's. 'Why, he's the antithesis of me . . . a man without any sensitivity, without any kind of morality except his own mewling, whimpering insistence on his own way,' he would tell an interviewer. There was fear as well as loathing

45

in the performance, he would say. 'Kowalski was always right, and never afraid. He never wondered, he never doubted. . . . And he had the kind of brutal aggressiveness I hate. I'm afraid of it. I detest the character.'

Intellectually, that's doubtless true. But as Kazan has recently asked: 'What is a person to detest but his own faults? – I wish I weren't like that.' There is, of course, something else he may detest: the forces in his past that shaped – bent – that self. The most obvious element in this character- ization, the stuff that was to become the basic source of Brando imitations for years to come, was the almost satanic satirical spirit he loosed on the fine literary-romantic pretensions of his visiting sister-in-law. His rooting sexuality had already knocked that nonsense out of Stella, and now, quite literally cocksure of himself, Stanley was glad to perform the same service for Blanche – resorting, of course, to rape after his verbal assaults had failed. Before that, however, his manic anger at Blanche's genteel airs, his paranoid suspicions of her past and of her future intentions, his sheer dis- gust at her lack of reality – none of which, by the way, is entirely misplaced – becomes, in effect, an assault on the manners and morals of an entire class.

We cannot help thinking of the Brandos, with their guilty secrets and their striving for respectability, as being at least cousins to Blanche, cousins, indeed, to almost all of us who came out of the same anxious pro- vincial milieu. Let us take the thought a step further. Let us imagine that Brando also found in *A Streetcar Named Desire* a symbolic representation of the basic family drama that was crucial in forming him. Was there not much of Dodie in Blanche – the drinking, the sexual teasing, the lost hopes that somehow must be kept alive in fantasy? And was there not something of his father in Stanley – the impatience with the impractical, the endless demands for a stern, realistic accounting of 'poetic' behavior, the threat, perhaps, of physical violence to enforce his version of reality on others?

Finally, was there not something of Brando's present self in his Stanley? In his notes, Kazan stressed Stanley's hedonism, his need to preoccupy himself with immediate physical pleasures in order to avoid confronting his deeper dissatisfactions, the deeper hopelessness and cynicism. There was certainly nothing elegant about his sensualism, and there was nothing ele- gant about Brando's as he pursued his young actor's life. But they were similar in their quick and greedy grabs for the sweetness of the moment, their need to avoid thinking of the past or the future. As he thought about Stanley, Kazan also began to see him as a man ferociously defending what we have since learned to call a 'lifestyle', believing it a fortress that, if vio- lated, would lead to his downfall. In the course of the play, as Kazan read it, he moves from rough, amiable acceptance of Blanche to outright hostility as he begins to see that her airs and pretensions threaten the defensework he has constructed. Brando, I believe, perceived the ambitions of the American Stanislavskians – soon to be, as we shall see, focused on him – as an analogous threat to his fortress lifestyle.

Thus were great riches brought to bear – semi-consciously, unconsciously – on this performance. But if, in it, Marlon Brando could not avoid himself or his past, it is also true that the elevated language of the piece, its setting, with its odor of the exotic, the melodramatic imperatives of its powerful structure, lent it just the right metaphorical distance for him, and helped to relieve the psychological pressures of its themes and subtexts. There is nearly always an element of luck in stardom, and *Streetcar* was this actor's luck – the right play at the right moment in his life, something he could handle, and live with, and yet also use to draw out of himself what needed now to come forth.

Who knew, who could even guess at the time, all the factors that had gone into the making of this production, this performance? What everyone could see was that something extraordinary was taking place on this stage. Even out of town, in New Haven and in Boston, *Streetcar* was a hit. Kim Hunter, that perfect Stella, would say later that 'we had to work hard against overconfidence,' that the company's chief anxiety was 'that we couldn't live up to the reputation the play had before it opened.' But they could, and did. Even the daily reviewers could not mistake the play's originality and power – and Brando's. It must have been – let's put it mildly – terribly fulfilling, a justification of all that he had been, and, more important, all that he had refused to be, across the first decades of his life.

But it was also, in its way, a threat. Which was implicit in this opening night telegram: RIDE OUT BOY AND SEND IT SOLID. FROM THE GREASY POLACK YOU WILL SOMEDAY ARRIVE AT THE GLOOMY DANE. FOR YOU HAVE SOMETHING THAT MAKES THE THEATRE A WORLD OF GREAT POSSIBILITIES. EVER GRATEFULLY, TENNESSEE WILLIAMS.

Oh, God. No place to hide now. Responsibilities – to himself, to other people's hopes for him, for the reformation of the entire theatrical enterprise – were implicit in this success. It was incumbent upon him to find new ways of evading them.

THREE

AGE OF REASON

'We who saw him in his first, shocking days believed in him not only as an actor, but also as an artistic, spiritual, and specifically American leader.' Thus William Redfield, sometime colleague and close friend, looking back in sorrow, anger (and smugness) at Marlon Brando's career in his *Letters from an Actor* in 1967. That 'we' is not hyperbolic: Redfield accurately summarized what many of his theatrical generation expected of Brando. And the actor, with his preternatural sensitivity to other people's unspoken agendas, was not unaware of these entirely unrealistic yearnings.

They were a cruel burden to place on anyone, but most especially on a young man who would not turn 25 until after he had disembarked from *Streetcar*, a young man who had not, and never would, show the slightest inclination to lead anything, particularly a 'spiritual' revolution. His response was, or should have been, quite predictable.

In the theater he role-modelled the responsible, dedicated acting professional. He did not miss performances, he worked hard and inventively to keep his work fresh, stayed on in his role longer than some people perhaps imagined he might. He also kept up with his acting classes. This kind of leadership – leadership by example – was within his range in those days. In the rest of his life he clung desperately hard to that young actor's way of life that he had embraced on his arrival in New York and that had proved so congenial, so liberating, ever since. Again, one feels, he was setting an example. No one was going to catch him striking star poses, living big, talking big, throwing his weight around.

To his professionalism there is much testimony. For example, here is his co-star, Kim Hunter, as recorded by Lillian and Helen Ross in their invaluable book, *The Player*. 'It is a tremendous experience to play in relationship with him; he yanks you into his own sense of reality. For example . . . the way Marlon played the scene where Stanley goes through Blanche's trunk. Stanley had found out a little bit about her at that point in the play, and is starting to question her, and he begins to go through the things in her trunk, while Stella tries to protect her sister's belongings. Marlon never, never did that scene the same way twice during the entire run. He had a different sort of attitude toward each of the belongings every night; sometimes he would lead me into quite a fight with him, and other times I'd be seeing him as a silly little boy. I got worn out after many months in the play, but I never got bored. . . .'

As he sought out Blanche's mystery, night after night, Brando, as we've seen, seems to have been seeking out the answers to some of the mysteries in his own life. It's the most reasonable explanation for his ferocious and lengthy engagement with the role. The fact that, aside from a larky summer stock tour in *Arms and the Man* in 1953, he never returned to the stage supports this view. Perhaps he did not look very hard, but clearly he never found another role that he felt could absorb (or divert) him sufficiently to balance the boredom (and terrors) of a long run.

That motivation probably extended to some of his other activities. The high school drop-out was, as he has remained, a devoted autodidact. Karl Malden shared a dressing room with him and he remembered Brando immersing himself in heavy tomes about anthropolgy and psychology, rarely bothering with fiction less weighty than Dostoevsky.

This sobriety extended to what we might risk calling his world view. It was essentially an extension of his childhood and adolescent sympathy for the tormented and the damned. Stella Adler recalled going with him to see a film about bull fighting and casually remarking afterward that she was more sympathetic to the man than the beast in their encounter. He did not speak to her for a year thereafter she claimed, perhaps exaggerating somewhat. Brando himself would recall a yet more thought provoking encounter with filmed images that dates from this period. It was footage taken when the Nazi concentration camps were liberated by American troops. 'It was,' he said some thirty years later, 'the greatest trauma of my life. The film poured sulphuric acid on my hopes for the future of the human race. I was – and still am – shattered by the experience.'

For the moment at least, neither success nor despair interfered with his obligations to Stanislavski, though he left Stella Adler's tutelage – amicably, since she later called the break 'completely mature' and he has remained a supporter of her work – to join the Actors Studio, which opened just two months before *Streetcar* did. There he was for a while a conscientious, and occasionally brilliant, student. Bobby Lewis dined out for years on his story of Brando's work in a scene from *Reunion in Vienna*. In an early version of the tale we find Lewis insisting on the actor doing something far out of his natural range, something, say, from Alfred Lunt's repertory: 'Where you have to be elegant, speak beautifully, play the prince with a monocle. "Anything but put your feet on the table – and by the way

49

take them off the table right now." I badgered him and badgered him, told him he could do it and had to do that kind of thing, even if he played Kowalskis all his life.' In a telling aside to his interviewer, Lewis observed: 'You know, Marlon and all those kids think if they speak well and move well they are compromising their manliness, that if they sweat and grunt they're manly.'

Brando and his scene partner, an actress named Joan Chandler, worked dutifully on their roles, but procrastinated over performing in front of the class. Finally Lewis told them either to bring in their scene or to quit class. They rented appropriate period costumes, and Brando not only wore a monocle, but added a sword and a tiny mustache to his get-up. They also brought in a phonograph to play on off-stage waltz. The results were not the comic fiasco many had expected. He and Chandler were, in fact, electrifying. The class burst into applause at the end of their turn. 'Well,' Lewis remembered, 'it was then that we knew Marlon was bigger than Kowalski. We knew he could do anything.'

We must not, of course, discount another explanation for his dedication to *Streetcar* and the perfection of his craft. We must suppose that even Marlon Brando was not, in those days, immune to the infinitely pleasurable possibilities opened up for him by the greatest personal triumph enjoyed by any actor in Broadway's immediate post-war era. We must imagine that the sheer fun of being the hottest ticket in town sustained him as much as his nightly exertions at the Ethel Barrymore Theater.

For public life doesn't get much better than it was for Brando in this first year of his fame. His achievement was handsomely recognized, by a knowledgeable, small and therefore unthreatening public, and the word on him was slowly but comfortably spreading beyond the relatively narrow confines of Broadway. He was making what seemed to him good money ($550 a week), and there seems to be no question that his new prominence (and Stanley's stud-ish image) did him no harm in his romantic adventurings. Though he would later claim that after running for a couple of months in *Streetcar*, 'one night – dimly, dimly – I began to hear this roar,' he was not yet an international or even a full-scale national celebrity. He was still able to live as he chose and, more importantly, to move about as he chose, that is to say, freely and anonymously.

He remained devoted to his mother and his sisters. Dodie, on one of her absences from home, moved in with her son for a time, sharing vicariously in his sucess. And when his sisters had children he was often a doting baby-sitter for their offspring. He even achieved a curious rapprochement with his father. Because he was always broke (mainly because he was a soft touch for out-of-work colleagues) he began turning his weekly pay-checks over to Marlon Sr and living off an allowance the old man doled out. This was in one way astonishing, since his essential relationship with his father was unimproved, but in another way it was not. Adolescents are used to living on allowances, and what Brando was clinging to, despite his grown-up success, was an adolescent, or, at best, post-adolescent, lifestyle.

About the only thing he was not eager to sample in those days were the life, luxuries and nervous respectability of the upwardly mobile. On $150, which is what Dad permitted him, Brando lived not as a star, not even as a working actor, but as one still aspiring. His dress remained a scandal, he lived in walk-ups in slovenly chaos, and his eating habits were strictly take-out. The sometime snare drummer had at some point switched to the bongos and he was often content to stay home thumping away at them or watching TV, especially if he could find a Laurel and Hardy re-run, or, indeed, anything by the comedians of the silent or early sound eras, who apparently remain favorites of his to this day.

He was rarely alone, however. Rumors of homosexual behavior were rife during his early fame, but there is every evidence that they were started by his sometime roommate in this period, wicked Wally Cox. There is also some evidence that Brando rather enjoyed these rumors. In any case, he remained devoted to Cox, no matter what gossip Wally started behind his back, possibly with Brando's complicity. There is, of course, a theory that womanizing to the extent that Brando practiced it then and later betokens suppressed homosexual tendencies, but theory is just theory, and the patchy but somehow persuasive historical record runs counter to it.

According to eye-witnesses his romantic life mostly involved young actresses, and that it was by all accounts rich and varied, and sometimes involved sweet serenades with the recorder he had taken to playing. It was also conducted in a communal context, for he continued to cling to the company of young actors, who generally tend to travel in packs. His door was nearly always open, and people constantly floated in and out, for he still loved to be the center of a group, just as he had in adolescence. He often scared his pals with his penchant for perilous, showy stunts involving open windows on high floors, and he continued to recruit them for games in which he could star. Jocelyn would remember a game of essences, in which a participant was supposed to give metaphorical descriptions of another player while the rest tried to guess who it was. 'He's an old, fragile, beautifully embroidered Chinese ceremonial robe with a couple of 3-in-1 oil spots on it,' was one of Brando's contributions. She immediately recognised Wally Cox, but kept asking questions in order to let her brother continue his descriptive flights.

There was an element of manipulation – apparently benign manipulation – in his command of this crowd. He told Truman Capote that he made friends very warily, circling around and around a potential candidate for intimacy, touching ('ah, so gently') then pulling back, then coming nearer again. In his infamous *New Yorker* profile of Brando, Capote quoted him thus: 'They don't know what's happening. Before they realize it, they're all entangled, involved. I have them. And suddenly, sometimes, I'm all *they* have. A lot of them, you see, are people who don't fit anywhere; they're not accepted, they've been hurt, crippled one way or another. But I want to help them, and they can focus on me.' At this point Brando used the curious phrase that gave Capote the title for his article. 'I'm the duke. Sort of the duke in my domain.'

In other words he had a star's retinue even before he was a star in the full sense of the word, though there is no evidence that in his ducal doings he exercised the kind of sadistic control of his train that is not uncommon among the hugely celebrated. Yet there can be no doubt, either, that his needs were in certain respects as powerful as those to whom he extended his protection. Capote also quoted an anonymous 'past tenant on the ducal preserve' who observed that Brando never talked to more than one person at a time as he moved through his court. Each person was singled out for a full dose of charm. 'Makes you feel that you're under his protection and that your troubles and moods concern him deeply.' He added: 'You have to believe it; more than anyone I've known, he radiates *sincerity*.'

Capote's informant wondered what the point of all this was, what was in it for Brando? Then he shrewdly answered his own question. It was affection Brando was after. 'Affection that lends him authority over you. I sometimes think Marlon is like an orphan who later on in life tries to compensate by becoming the kindly head of a huge orphanage. But even outside this institution he wants everybody to love him.' Put the point more directly: Brando was trying to spare others the loneliness and disaffection he had himself known as a boy, while at the same time gathering to him, however belatedly, some semblance of the love his variously preoccupied parents had so often been too distracted or too unyielding to provide.

Not that Brando's young manhood was entirely devoted to compensatory behavior. Many of his pleasures were simply and perhaps predictably *jejeune*. He had, for example, a period of some 20 minutes in the middle of *Streetcar* when he was offstage, and these he usually passed in the alley outside the theatre, hanging out with other idle members of the cast and crew, chatting up passersby (particularly, of course, young women). He was also something of a physical culturist in those days – as the old torn T-shirt stills attest – and he organized boxing matches among members of the company in the theatre basement. In fact, he owes his nobly broken nose to Jack Palance, his understudy in *Streetcar*, who landed a solid punch in the course of one of these encounters.

His one indulgence was a motorcycle – every boy's dream straddle. He was a familiar sight vrooming around the theatre district aboard it. Jessica Tandy, who, as we have seen, did not completely share Kim Hunter's delight with his on-stage unpredictability was once appalled to discover that his kindly offer of a lift home entailed hopping on the back of his bike. The responsible adults in his life, people like Irene Selznick and Edith Van Cleve, worried about accidents, since Brando had poor eyesight and refused to wear glasses. Younger colleagues were generally less pernickity, and he was arrested on one occasion for piling too many of them on the machine with him. He thought it might be a useful experience to spend a night in jail and may possibly have been disappointed when Selznick sent her dignified theatrical lawyer, Arnold Weissberger, around to post bail.

Looking back at all this from a time in which the excesses available to the suddenly celebrated include obscenely conspicuous consumption, life-threatening addictions, every kind of uncloseted sexual behavior and all manner of weird moral-political assertiveness, one cannot supress a certain amount of amusement at the titillation, even scandalization, that was stirred up by this innocently Bohemian life, these trivial poses of rebellion. Indeed, Brando's desire to cling to what he knew and trusted, even though he surely saw that his success foredoomed the effort, can be read as a sign of integrity. 'Why so fast?' Edith Van Cleve would remember him saying. 'Everything's so immediate. So *big*.' Freedom of the kind he was enjoying, and the lack of obligations it entails, are not, and probably should not be, easily surrendered. For the sense of how stifling the active pursuit of a career is going to be, of how pleasant it is to delay entering that chute, is impossible to avoid.

But other reactions are permissible. There may be no imperative to glide about in limousines or to lease a penthouse, but there is some small imperative for a man of 25 to start growing up, to accept the inevitability of adulthood, however reluctantly. Sooner or later one has to begin testing how to live with some semblance of integrity in that complex condition. That's particularly true in cases like Brando's. For his fear and loathing of 'phoniness' (to borrow a term that another great young cultural hero, Salinger's Holden Caulfield, would soon make famous) were, in ways

Brando surely did not perceive, limiting. Acting, almost by definition, involves an embrace of phoniness. For at its highest and most testing level it involves imagining oneself as characters far more profoundly alien – 'unnatural', even – to a contemporary male than Stanley Kowalski. Orestes and Hamlet, Uncle Vanya and Rosmersholm all require the modern actor to strike strange and taxing poses, require him to run the risk of 'phoniness'. Indeed, in modern America, with its narrow theatrical culture, its lack of historical sensibility and its resistance to unfamiliar stylizations, simply confessing an ambition to attempt these roles is itself generally read as 'phony'. Or, at the least, 'pretentious'.

But if we perceive on Brando's behalf an obligation, owed primarily to himself, to try to transcend this attitude, we must also admit that at the time the American theater lacked the large numbers of institutions, performers and other theatrical professionals, which were needed to help him break free of such cultural constraints. The wiser heads among the older heads who were close to Brando in those days (Adler, Bobby Lewis, Kazan) all seconded this point. Adler, for example, pointed out that Gérard Phillipe, in France, and Olivier, in England, had endless opportunities to challenge themselves and to grow by playing classics that remained part of a living tradition, thanks to their national theaters, and, indeed, to a commercial theater that still found it economically viable to mount new productions of these sustaining works.

Kazan would also observe, a few years later, 'It's not a natural thing for a man to be an actor now, as it was, say, in the nineteenth century.' Without the plays, playwrights and directors to provide truly meaningful work, he said, 'there is something trivial about it.' He thought Brando's great predecessor, John Barrymore, had fallen into 'self-mockery', and Brando's potentially great contemporary, Richard Burton, into the idle pursuit of money in 'foolish' enterprises, precisely because there was so little grown-up work to do.

Unfortunately, the Stanislavsky tradition, at least as it was developing in New York at the time, with its stress on self-exploration and its emphasis on a rather limited and realistic repertory of plays, was of small help to Brando in dealing with this issue. It tended to keep his attention focused inward, and it did not often propose theatrical ventures taking up themes that might catch his attention or stir his imagination. To put the point simply, the school of acting which had unquestionably helped him 'find himself' (to the degree he may be said to have done so), and to which he owed at least some part of his success, was no longer helpful in that regard.

None of which is, *per se*, an argument for going into the movies, though they certainly must have had an escapist appeal that Brando dared not speak aloud – especially if Billy Redfield and his ilk were in the room. In any case, the first offers from Hollywood began arriving immediately after *Streetcar* opened, and as he was expected to do, Brando received them scornfully, that is, with a mixture of contempt and fear. The reasons for the former attitude are less obvious now than they were then, when the superiority of the stage over film as a venue for serious writing and performance was unquestioned by everyone. As for the fear, that was based not merely on the temptations to greater wealth and fame the movies offered a performer, not merely on the untempering ease of the work most actors were called upon to perform in them, but also on what theater people saw as the sad fates of promising colleagues they had seen off to the west coast only to observe their spirits weaken, their talents soften, after a few years under the Los Angeles sun. The Group Theater alone could cite the decline of such sometime stalwarts as Clifford Odets, Franchot Tone and John Garfield (to whom, ironically, Brando owed so much). They were cautionary figures to young actors of Brando's generation.

On the other hand, perceptive people were beginning to observe the first hairline cracks in the monolith that was the old studio system. Having achieved the height of its economic power during the war years, and having enjoyed the greatest single year in its history in 1946 (when ninety million movie tickets were sold), Hollywood's prosperity began to weaken visibly in the late Forties. In peacetime, even before television became the overwhelming medium, other diversions were drawing customers away from the movies; pre-war stars and the pre-war generic formulae were losing their hold on the mass audience; and the ageing moguls who had managed the studios with conspicuous success for over two decades no longer seemed adaptable and energetic enough to cope with these changes. Moreover, in 1948, the studios signed a consent decree in a long-pending antitrust action which obliged them, over the next few years, to sell off their economically stabilizing theater chains. This was a devastating blow to the industry's confidence. And its cowardly official response to the notorious House Un-American Activities Committee investigations into alleged Hollywood Communism, which began in 1947, had an equally unsettling effect on its sense of community.

The situation in Hollywood was suddenly analagous to that of Broadway. Both were institutions confronting a shrinkage in their audiences, therefore a shrinkage in power, and both appeared open to reform, possibly radical reform, as a result. Since the idealism of The Group Theater tradition had never been confined merely to a theory of acting, or to

5 5

socially committed drama, some among its adherents certainly sensed the possibility that the long-awaited moment for full-scale revolution might be at hand.

Ultimately history would betray that hope. Adjustment, not revolution, would preoccupy Hollywood in subsequent decades. And Marlon Brando would be a particular victim of the large, false promises of freedom it offered, a particular victim of that curious blend of indulgence and oppressiveness with which it treats people whose talent simultaneously tempts and terrifies it. Still, it was obviously becoming possible for actors like him to avoid some of the traps in which their predecessors had been caught. It was not necessary any more to live in Los Angeles in order to work in the movies, and it was not necessary (soon it would be impossible) to contract oneself to a single studio for a seven-year term. You could live where you wanted, in whatever manner suited you. You could accept and reject projects freely, return to the stage whenever you liked, do or say what you pleased without a studio hierarchy monitoring your every move. It was now also possible, at least in theory, to work full time in movies that aspired to make serious social, political, moral and cultural statements.

It was not that Hollywood had failed to make such pictures before, despite all the loose critical talk about its routinely appealing to the infamous fourteen-year-old mind. It was not that all of the movies it was now beginning to make on 'adult' themes were actually preferable, by any standards, to, say, a Preston Sturges comedy or, for that matter, *Double Indemnity*. What was happening was a relatively slight mood shift, but one which the press and the middle-brow public picked up on eagerly, and possibly made too much of; a modest trend that, as it worked itself out in the mid and late Fifties, did not fulfill its promises in ways that could sustain a career like the one Brando wanted to pursue, or, for that matter, fully engage the most sophisticated segment of the audience.

That's a matter we will perforce return to. For the moment it is enough to note that whether we are discussing *The Lost Weekend* or *The Best Years of Our Lives*, *Crossfire* or *Gentleman's Agreement*, *The Snake Pit* or *Pinky*, the movies were beginning to take up, in an appropriately sober (sometimes too sober) manner, issues that, not incorrectly, serious people believed needed to be addressed by a mass art. That, taken together with the economic evidence suggesting the motion picture industry had to make new kinds of arrangements with creative people and find new ways of appealing to its audience, was encouraging to the new theatrical generation. Maybe, just maybe, it would be possible to work in the movies without 'selling out'.

Not that Brando leaped at the chance. A screen test he made in this period still exists. It is for a project called *Rebel Without a Cause* (not to be confused with the James Dean film of a few years later), and in it he plays, rather warily, a young criminal urging his girlfriend to join him in fleeing the law. His 'soft, girlish' side is very much in evidence here, and so is a desire to show that he can enunciate as clearly as the next guy. But the work is extremely tentative, not at all that of a young actor determined to take Hollywood (or anything else) by storm. An interview, included on the same reel, finds him in a dark, neat suit and tie, and in a nervously affable mood, also quite unprepossessing.

In fact, and perhaps predictably, Brando's first serious flirtation with the movies was not directed toward Hollywood. It was free-spirited, ambitious and, in its particulars, quite marvelously hare-brained. The French director, Claude Autant-Lara, who specialized in historical drama and adaptations of classic fiction, was contemplating a production of Stendhal's *The Red and the Black*, and he invited Brando to visit locations in France. Hoping to lure him into the lead, the director offered the actor expenses and a small salary for three weeks to familiarize himself with the people and places of the planned production. Autant-Lara was the kind of formalist the New Wave would soon invent itself to oppose, and Brando soon drifted out of his orbit. He booked into a raffish Left Bank hotel and fell into the company of a down-and-out actors' co-operative. Maynard Morris, his sometime agent, happened to be visiting Paris at the time, and was startled one night to hear his name called out from a group of what he took to be street people. It was Brando, of course, addressing him.

Nothing immediately came of Autant-Lara's ambitious project, which was delayed until 1954, when the director finally filmed Stendhal's novel in a three-hour version starring Gérard Phillipe. But before returning home, Brando also visited Italy, in search of the sources of Neo-Realist cinema, and he would later insist to interviewers that the only moment of perfect happiness he had ever known occurred on this trip. Visiting Sicily, he lay down in a field of flowers, stripped off his shirt and, lulled by the Mediterranean sun, fell asleep, and into a paradisical dream.

Doubtless, he exaggerated, and certainly he, like everyone else, understood full well that perfect happiness was never to be vouchsafed by the movies. Even so, the project in which he at last agreed to make his film debut carried a solid promise and, when all was said and done, a decent measure of fulfilment. For *The Men* represented a reasonably good early example of the new Hollywood independence, the new Hollywood 'seriousness'. Set largely in the paraplegic ward of a veterans' hospital, it

57

soberly took up a sobering subject: the attempt by grievously wounded soldiers of the late war to reintegrate with society and, perhaps more importantly, to reintegrate their permanently damaged bodies with minds and spirits whose wounds, the film tried to show, need not be permanent.

This, obviously, was a story to appeal to a heart ever sensitive to the outcast and the downcast, and it was also a project in which a serious young actor could easily justify taking part; there was nothing flashy or trashy about it. It was the kind of enterprise of which even earnest William Redfield would have trouble disapproving. And it was also an enterprise that would, for a few months, get him out of town, away from the overheated concerns of such people.

It is impossible to say which of these thoughts, placatory or escapist, was foremost in the mind of our reluctant cultural hero. But it must have been with a sense of relief at ending his own, and everyone's, anxiety about his next move, that he committed to *The Men* on the basis of an outline – and the offer of a $40,000 salary, which seemed huge to him in those innocent, relatively non-inflationary times. Indeed, Brando joked about it. 'I don't have the character to turn down such big money,' he said.

As he left for Hollywood he reassured an anxious theatre community that his relocation was only temporary: 'I may do a picture now and again, but mostly I intend to work on the stage.' And he told a friend: 'If I ever invite you to the MGM commissary, you're to cut me dead.' As if to make certain he would avoid all temptation, his entire wardrobe for the trip consisted of white T-shirts and blue jeans, plus one suit with holes in the knees and a rip in the seat of the pants. His accommodation was the couch in an aunt's living-room in Eagle Rock, distinctly unfashionable suburbia. Even the trim young agent, Jay Kantor, assigned to this difficult case by MCA, turned out to be, beneath the dark suit the agency insisted all its representatives wore, a soulmate – a shrewd and protective friend who, even after he became a production executive, remained a trusted adviser. To put it simply, Brando had gone to Hollywood, but he did not 'go Hollywood'.

The atmosphere surrounding the production to which he reported was austere by traditional industry standards. The producer was Stanley Kramer, a sometime film editor and post-production supervisor who, after Signal Corps service in the war, formed a company committed to low-budget films about serious matters. His earlier releases, *The Champion* – about the spiritual corruption of a boxer – and *Home of the Brave* – about racial prejudice in the army – were very much in Hollywood's new spirit and had achieved quite respectful critical attention and reasonable box office returns. *The Men* was written, after much first-hand research in a

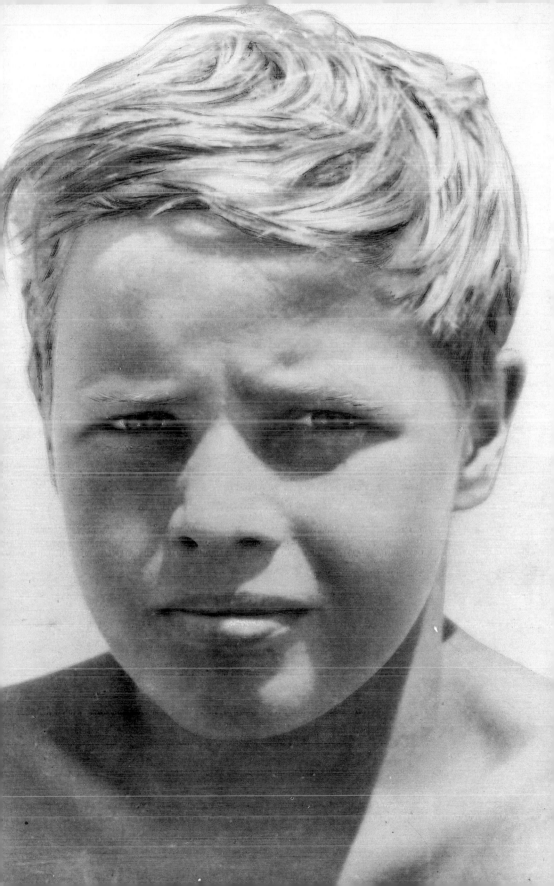

Aged 2, wrapped up for winter.   Aged 4, in his own backyard.

PREVIOUS PAGE Marlon at 10: a good-looking boy.

Aged 7, enjoying the beach.   Aged 8, preparing for westerns!

LEFT Aged 8, playing Indians.
RIGHT Looking tough at the same age.

Brando with Jocelyn and his mother.

LEFT Studying hard at 13.

RIGHT Marlon at 14 with his sisters.

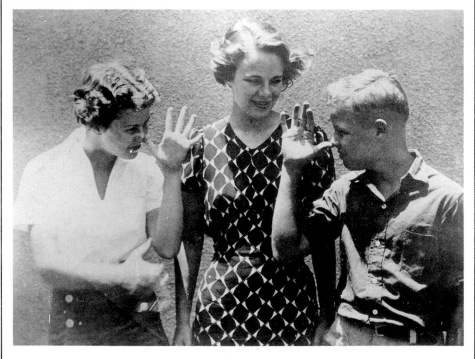

Frances, Jocelyn and Marlon.

LEFT Marlon at military academy, age 16.

RIGHT Brando at 17 just before he went to New York.

In uniform, but Brando never enlisted.

ABOVE As Nels in *I Remember Mama*.

BELOW Marlon with Ann Shepherd in *Truckline Cafe*, 1946.

OPPOSITE *I Remember Mama*, 1944. Brando's first stage appearance.

Truckline Cafe closed after only thirteen performances.

OPPOSITE Brando poses against a literary backdrop.

Brando plays a WWII veteran who murders his unfaithful wife in *Truckline Cafe*.

The Broadway production of *A Streetcar Named Desire* ran for eighteen months to great acclaim.

Brando's first film *The Men* was released in 1950.

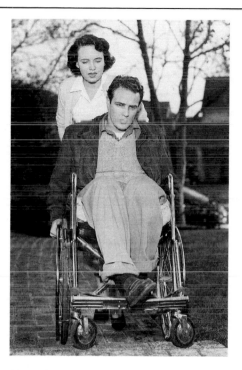

Brando, an embittered paraplegic war veteran with fiancée, Teresa Wright, determined to make him face up to life in *The Men*.

Studio publicity for *A Streetcar Named Desire*.

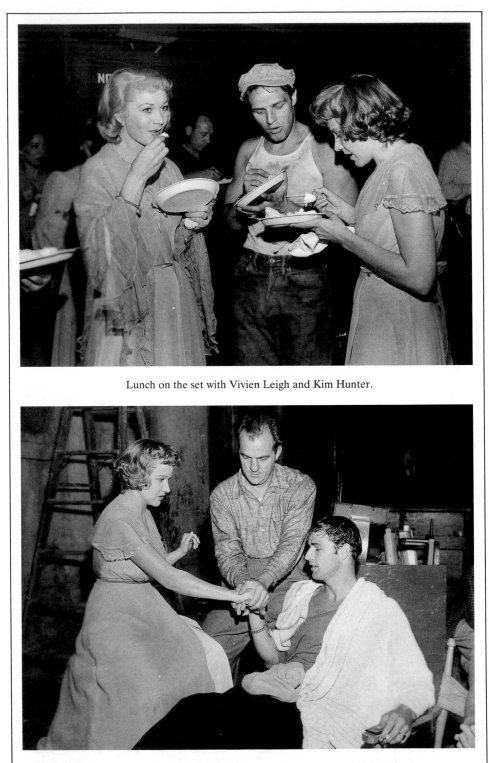

Lunch on the set with Vivien Leigh and Kim Hunter.

With Kim Hunter and Karl Malden on the set of *A Streetcar Named Desire*.

Brando had to wet up
for the sweat and fight scenes.

A shower was rigged up
on set for the purpose.

As Stanley Kowalski in *Streetcar*.

With Anthony Quinn in *Viva Zapata*!

OVERLEAF On the set of *Julius Caesar* amongst a host of javelins.

Jean Peters teaches Zapata (Brando) to read.

hospital, by the literate and liberal-minded Carl Foreman, and it was directed, mainly on location in a VA hospital, by the self-effacing Fred Zinnemann, a humanist who was also one of the most meticulous film craftsmen to emerge in the Fifties. The cast mixed professional actors with actual paraplegics, whose brave and often touching presence lent the movie a high degree of realism. In all obvious respects, then, this was a more than usually conscientious film, intelligently made, socially useful in its plea for the humanity of the handicapped, and frequently inspiring in its portrayal of their small triumphs over their condition. In short, *The Men* satisfied most of the standards Hollywood's critics had been advocating for its works.

Brando joined in the spirit of the production. He prepared carefully for his role, spending some weeks living on the paraplegic ward of the Van Nuys veterans' hospital, where much of the film was shot, learning to manipulate a wheelchair and, more importantly, learning what it felt like to be unable to move about unaided. On set there was some initial concern over his throw-away rehearsal style, some tension between him and the other professional actors in the company (Jack Webb and Everett Sloane in particular). And one has the feeling that the austere Zinnemann, though respecting Brando's gift, never warmed to him personally. He was drawn to the more mannerly mannerisms of Montgomery Clift, whom he had just directed in *The Search* and whom he would soon fight to include in *From Here to Eternity*. Clift's preparation for a role was less visibly messy than Brando's, thus more appealing to the fastidious and carefully controlling director. Still, when the camera turned, Brando was there, with all his power mobilized and focused, and his work won over even those doubters who never took to him personally.

Our first ever glimpse of Brando on the screen presents him, in fact, as a middle-class figure, a young infantry lieutenant, named Ken Wilocek, leading his platoon into a European village that appears to have been deserted by the Germans. His uniform is Hollywood-neat and the angles on him are conventionally heroic, very much those of the standard Second World War combat film. The idea, of course, is to set up a contrast between our recent fantasies of war and the realities of its aftermath, with which the rest of the film is concerned. Equally important is the contrast which is set up between Ken's confident vigor and the near-helpless condition in which he will spend the rest of the movie. The sequence ends on a broadly ironic note, for it is as Ken turns to gesture his soldiers forward that he is shot by an unseen sniper.

Blackness. And then a voice – Brando's: 'That's funny, that's very funny. I was afraid I was going to die. Now I'm afraid I'm going to live. . . .' The accent is Stanley Kowalski's, only a trifle diluted. But it is also entirely appropriate. For Ken is also a 'Polack', also of working-class origins. There, however, the resemblance between the two characters ends. For Ken is an orphan, whose lack of family ties may have had a liberating effect on him, permitting him to try to work his way up through society, unencumbered by awkward reminders of his beginnings. Before the war he attended college (possibly on an athletic scholarship), and it is also possible that his army commission originally seemed to represent another lucky break for him, something he could trade on in a post-war civilian career. Finally, it is obvious that his extremely respectable girlfriend, Ellen (Teresa Wright), represented, for him, a step upward as well.

In other words, a class tragedy provides a subtext for physical tragedy. The sniper's bullet has put Ken back where he started, among polite society's outcasts. Only now there is no way to escape: no learned behavior that can cover the humiliation of being handicapped, no acquired charm or grace to divert people's attention from it. His only defenses seem to be anger, cynicism, withdrawal.

The movie is, in fact, entirely about getting Ken to overcome these attitudes, to achieve what so many 1950s movie heroes had to achieve: psychological 'adjustment' – no matter what the situation. Early in the film Ken is moved out of his private hospital room on to a ward, where socialization begins with ragging and ribbing by fellow paraplegics. ('He doesn't want to be a paraplegic.' 'That's funny, I thought everyone wanted to be a paraplegic.') Soon Ellen is visiting, applying the poultice of sweet patience to his problems. He keeps sending her away – and not politely either. ('Can't you understand English, you stupid idiot.') She does not take the hint. Teresa Wright never took the hint. Patient suffering was her speciality, and one always hoped in vain that she would show a little spunk. Her simpering performance is one of the minor things wrong with *The Men*.

At one point in the film someone tells Ken, 'Before you can change the world, you have to accept the world as it is,' which is one way of stating not only this film's theme, but what would turn out to be another great theme of popular culture in the 1950s, which was the insistence that everyone moderate their rebellious or excessively self-assertive ways for the good of the community – and of themselves, of course. After a few setbacks – the death of one of the most popular men on the ward, a humiliating wedding night (paraplegics, we learn, cannot handle alcohol), a drunken driving charge – Ken Wilocek does indeed achieve this peculiar state of grace. At the end of the film, as he faces an obstacle he cannot navigate in his wheelchair, Ellen asks simply, 'Do you want me to help you up the step?' and he replies, even more simply, 'Please.'

Here we begin to confront the movie's major flaw, which is caution. *The Men* does not aspire to rise above a safe middle range of emotions, and is perhaps even more anxious not to sink below that range. Or, to put it another way, there is no wildness about it: very little of the black humor that we might logically expect to find in young men whom chance has singled out for a dreadful punishment; and, even worse, not much of the still blacker despair with which one also imagines them grappling. The ideal to which everyone is encouraged is pep, good cheer, normality in the face of abnormality. It seems, indeed, that once a man reacquires his get-up-and-go, despite the fact that his basic problem is that he cannot get up and go anywhere unaided, he is, so far as the institution is concerned, cured, ready for a return to 'normal' (i.e. middle-class) society.

Vocally, Brando does his best to play that line. It has not generally been remarked that his famous mumble becomes less and less pronounced as the film proceeds. Far from being carelessly mannered, his verbal style in *The Men* is carefully calculated. In the beginning, when he is in despairing withdrawal, he is quite inarticulate; but as he re-enters the world he begins to enunciate much more clearly; by the end of the film his tone is firm, even 'normal'. What Brando is doing is called acting, and it is acting of an order one still sees only rarely in the movies, in that it conveys something about the spiritual state of his character in quite a delicate way, risking the kind of jocular, uninformed criticism that was visited upon his work at the time.

But in other respects Brando's performance keeps subverting the smooth, straight-ahead progress to which the narrative aspires. One just does not quite believe that Ken Wilocek, as Brando plays him, all rage and self-pity, could be reached, and turned around, as quickly, and by such simple therapeutic devices, as the film employs – the hearty camaraderie of his buddies, the patient love of his sweetheart, a little psycho-babble.

It is Brando's preparation that is largely responsible for the way he unbalances the film. One of the most famous Brando anecdotes dates from this period. As the story is told, he joined some of his new friends in a wheelchair excursion to a nearby bar, where they were approached by a drunken woman who urged upon them the healing powers of evangelical religion. God, she insisted, could often cure what medicine considered hopeless conditions. Brando encouraged her, before pretending, finally, an on-the-spot conversion. At which point he struggled to his feet, faking a miraculous restoration of his ability to walk. He then (and here various accounts diverge) tap-danced through the bar, or leaped capering on to one of its tables – something hilariously dramatic, anyway – much to the delight of his actually crippled companions.

His lifelong sympathy for the afflicted surely animated this work. But so did something else, a subtext which he did not speak of publicly at the time. Sexual impotence is, obviously, a concomitant of lower body paralysis; so is incontinence. The movie speaks only briefly of the former (Jack Webb's character informs Wright, 'It's not in the nature of a normal woman to love one of us'), and not at all of the latter. But Brando spoke, off the record, about both. He referred to the stag movies the paraplegics rented, ran and desperately hooted at, for example. And he spoke still more frankly about their inability to control their bowels, their inability in some instances to smell it when they did lose control of themselves, their inquiring of one another about whether an accident had occurred. For someone of Brando's nature – despite his outward carelessness, he was compulsively tidy about his person, the kind of man who changes underwear and bedding constantly – there was genuine horror here. And it is that emotion, obviously, that he is trying to convey, without being able to speak openly of it, particularly in his exchanges with Teresa Wright. It is that emotion, finally, that unhinges the film's essential prissiness.

Given the gentilities enforced by the Production Code, not to mention the standards of 'good taste' which society in general still imposed on the movies, one perhaps should not criticize *The Men* for avoiding important topics. It is better to focus on what Brando accomplished despite such limitations. For across the years the movie retains its largest interest as Brando's screen debut. In retrospect, considered in relation to what had preceded it, and what has followed it, Brando's work is utterly original: a redefinition, an expansion, of the issues a star performance might embrace. For anything comparable one needs to refer back to quite a different piece of work, that of James Cagney in *The Public Enemy* (which was not a debut), to see a movie actor exploring, and implying, the unwritten deeps and darks of a screen character, extending the boundaries of the acceptable a perceptible degree.

Of such achievements, Brando did not speak. It was known at the time that he was unhappy with the film's ending, apparently made more hopeful than it was in the original script. But in a later interview he was content to call *The Men* 'worth doing' for the attention it brought to an ignored minority. (It is perhaps worth suggesting that increasing public sensitivity to the needs of the handicapped probably begins with the movie.) It remains one of the rare films Brando has not subsequently decried for failing to live up to what it initially seemed to promise either to its subject-matter or to him as an actor. *The Men* did not make Brando a movie star in the same sense that *Streetcar* made him Broadway star. We came, we saw, we were interested. But there was nothing in the film or his role that was intrinsically sensational, nothing to blow anyone away. It was a liberal-minded movie that did not entirely stifle the actor's radical spirit, but did manage to contain it. We reserved judgement.

But not for long. For Brando almost immediately went into the movie version of *Streetcar*. William Redfield spoke for all theater snobs when he insisted that if you had not seen Brando's original stage performance you had seen only the shadow of his greatness. 'Forget it,' sneered this founding member of The Actor's Studio, and self-appointed keeper of the flame. Who knows? Maybe he was right. But eventually no one will know, because all who were present at the creation will be gone, and only the film record will exist to remind us of this turning-point in theatrical history. And it is not discreditable – to put it mildly. It is wonderful – to put it quite precisely.

For just as there had been nothing like this performance on the stage before, there had been nothing like it on the screen, either – no comparable blend of menace and black comedy and near-parodistical maleness. 'In the state of Louisiana we have the Napoleonic code, according to which. . . .' 'Wadya you two think you are, a pair of queens?' And, of course, the 'colored lights', which only Stanley could get going for his sexually enthralled Stella. And that says nothing of the giddy airs and graces affected by Blanche, who comes to her tragedy along a similarly wayward and ambiguous line.

It is hard to believe that any nuance of Tennessee Williams's writing was lost in the extraordinarily faithful screen adaptation. Indeed, the sweaty intimacy of the hot, over-crowded French Quarter apartment may have been heightened by the intimacy with which the camera viewed it, though Kazan thought audiences experienced a greater sense of entrapment with these tormented souls in live performance. He also conceded, however, that in one of the play's crucial moments, when Stanley forces a naked light bulb close to Blanche's face, to reveal its lines, her psychological nakedness (and her terror) was powerfully enhanced by the close-up camera. One believes, as well, that it must have revealed nuances in Brando's performance that were lost on the stage.

This debate is, however, pointless – we innocents were charged up by the screen *Streetcar* in the same way that the stage version had electrified 'sophisticated' Broadway. We had no sense of the theatrical and cultural history that was made and unmade by this work, this performance of

Brando's. Yet we instinctively sensed that this was an event to which our generation owed an allegiance, something that helped define youthful us in opposition to decrepit them.

At first glance we were, of course, reading the most obvious element in the performance, the 'dangerous' side of it, in Kazan's formulation. The perception of its 'girlish' side did not come until subsequent viewings. Even now, when I return to this film, I find myself laughing delightedly at Stanley's rip-and-snort anti-bourgeois message, his inarticulate articulation of my own – *our* own – unspoken impatience – it may actually have been fury – with the conventions that hedged us round. Here, in this movie, is where my generation's bonds with this actor were formed.

But, for all its importance, there is, curiously, little anecdotal material about the filming of *Streetcar*. Jessica Tandy was the only performer not asked to repeat her stage performance, for independent producer (and former agent) Charles Feldman yielded to studio pressure for a more widely known name, and everyone settled on Vivien Leigh (who had played the role in London) for box office insurance. Kazan expressed regrets about hurting Tandy's feelings (and career), but she had not really expected to get the part a second time, for she understood that she was virtually unknown to movie audiences. Moreover, Kazan, not particularly wanting to re-do the piece (he had permitted Harold Clurman to stage the road company production of the original play), thought maybe a newcomer in the company would stir his imagination – especially after the failure of his original plan to 'open up' the play with a good deal of location shooting, which he had seen as another way of quickening his interest. When the first-draft screenplay was completed, he saw that it diluted the work's original power.

In the end, a multi-story set that successfully replicated, in movie terms, Jo Mielziner's famous Broadway setting, was built on a Warner Bros. sound stage. It proved felicitous in ways that may not have been predicted; the look of the film has a nice dislocating quality. Not quite a photographed stage play, it is not quite a film, in the usual sense of the term, either. It seems to occupy its own imaginative territory.

Vivien Leigh also proved a felicitous choice. She gave Kazan a few problems during the first week or two of production, when she refused to abandon what he regarded as bad habits she had acquired doing Blanche on stage, but he soon settled her down. 'She had,' he later wrote, 'a small talent, but the greatest determination to excel of any actress I've known. She'd have crawled over broken glass if she thought it would help her performance.' And that, in effect, she did. Kazan correctly judged her

64

'excellent' in the scenes that counted, possibly more fragile and vulnerable than Tandy, whose natural spirit is of quite a different order, although Kazan insists that, on the whole, his first Blanche was his best Blanche.

Leigh, it would seem, was also rather a better sport than one might imagine. At their first meeting, it is said, Brando trotted out his two best tricks for his new Blanche; his curious skill at surrealistic verbal cartooning, and his less surprising talent for mimicry. He asked why Leigh used a heavy perfume, and got a predictable response: 'Because I like to smell nice – don't you?' No, said Brando, deadpanning, he didn't even take baths. 'I just throw a gob of spit in the air and run under it.' She laughed, and, it is also said, was an appreciative audience for Brando's send-up of her husband, Laurence Olivier's, Agincourt speech from *Henry V*.

On the whole, then, production proceeded smoothly, though Brando twice suffered minor injuries – once in the bowling alley sequence, when he couldn't extricate his thumb from a ball as he let it fly; a bit more seriously when he suffered a dislocated shoulder in the fight scene, where his poker partners have to wrestle the drunken Stanley into a cold shower.

The more significant troubles that afflicted the film took place either away from the set or after shooting was completed. It was while working on it that Kazan got the first hint of the political problems that would soon engulf him and permanently mar his reputation (which should be much higher than it is) among cineastes. For it was while he was in Hollywood that the radical right, led by Cecil B. De Mille, made an assault on the Directors Guild, seeking to recall its president, Joseph L. Mankiewicz, and impose a loyalty oath on its members. Kazan, a sometime Communist, was one of their chief targets, and he ducked a confrontation (at a famous Guild meeting, at which De Mille and his cohorts were turned back). But he also understood that there would soon come a time when he would be unable to avoid a confrontation with his political past (and former political allies), could not avoid a painful public break with the Stalinists and, eventually, the opprobrium they furiously orchestrated against him and the others who testified about their past political affiliations (and affiliates).

Before his reputation was damaged, however, his picture itself was, in his view, damaged. He and the studio had maneuvered the *Streetcar* script past the Breen office, enforcers of the industry's increasingly odious self-censorship code. Explicit references to the homosexual lover and the nymphomania that were part of Blanche's past were excised (though clear implications of both remained), and the rape scene – which Breen had wanted elminated – was staged less brutally than it had been on Broadway. Now that the picture was finished, however, the final cut ran afoul of the enforcer's enforcers, the Catholic Legion of Decency. The motion picture code, written by a Catholic priest and largely administered by Catholic laymen, had been drafted mainly to avoid open conflict with the Legion, to shape scripts and edit finished films in such a way that they would avoid its 'C' (or condemned) rating, which effectively triggered a Catholic boycott. But the shrewd Martin Quigley, publisher of exhibitor trade journals, friend of Cardinal Spellman among other princes of the church and, in fact, the man who had invented the code almost two decades earlier, was proposing just such a rating.

He probably felt he had no choice. As an adaptation of a famous and much-honored play, one that anyone could see represented an expansion of all previous definitions of what was acceptable subject-matter on stage and screen by a new generation of artists, *Streetcar* was a more than usually visible enterprise, one on which the Catholic moralists were obliged to take a stand. Moreover, as a lapsed Catholic, Tennessee Williams was, for them, an irresistible target (there was a similar assault in Kazan's production of Williams's far less dangerous *Baby Doll* a few years later). There are, in fact, middle-aged women who today look back with astonishment at demands that they pray for the wandering soul of Thomas Lanier Williams when they were Catholic schoolgirls.

Equally significant was the temper of the times. Both the Code administration and the Legion were beginning to feel what would ultimately become an irresistible pressure for change. Foreign films, full of material forbidden to American movie-makers, were proving to have a large appeal to the most loyal members of the shrinking movie audience – adolescents and the older, more educated crowd who were beginning to accept the notion that film was an art. Moreover, within the American industry itself there was a growing sense that the presentation of more openly erotic material and the use of more realistic language were a requisite for survival. On the high road, movie people argued for this loosening of outdated standards in the name of artistic freedom; on the low they could see it was a way of differentiating their products from those of their great new competitor, television. This discontent also encouraged the Catholics to take a stand here and now, on this eagerly anticipated work.

So, with Feldman and the studio in collusion, an editor was set to work behind Kazan's back, trimming the picture to Legion specifications. These were men for whom accommodating censors was a normal aspect of business. Particular attention was paid to the relationship of Stanley and Stella, for it was their unquenchable sexual heat, not the mistreatment of Blanche, that to churchmen seemed a particular threat to public morality.

Defending his work, Kazan confronted first Feldman and Warner Brothers, then Quigley himself, but with no success. Finally, he wrote a letter to the New York *Times*, exposing the issue.

All of this was to no avail: the picture was cut. But the censorship was unavailing as well: the complicated (and ambiguous) things Williams wanted to say about the ways we confront and evade our sexuality, and about the costs of both strategies, are built into every line and situation of the play. They are not excisable by conventional means. The vividness of his characters and the force of his clean language could not be blurred or blunted by the censors' usual tools either. In other words, we got it. And we have carried it with us ever since. Stanley Kowalski and Blanche Dubois are modern archetypes. And, from the moment this movie went into general release, so was Marlon Brando.

That moment, however, was more than usually delayed by the lengthy process of reaching accommodation with the censors. Something like a year passed between the completion of principal photography and the film's premiere. Ultimately, of course, *Streetcar* would become a major critical and commercial success, culminating in no fewer than twelve Academy Award nominations, including one for Brando, though Hollywood, teaching the bumptious boy a lesson, withheld his Oscar (and Kazan's) while awarding the prize to all of the film's other major players (Vivien Leigh, Kim Hunter and Karl Malden). But in the meantime Brando was granted one last year of freedom from full-scale movie stardom; one more year in which he could continue to employ the strategies he had more or less successfully employed to evade the responsibilities that had been thrust on him when he attained theatrical stardom; one more year in which he would be allowed to avoid the more pervasive and complex demands of a much greater celebrity.

FOUR

GOLDEN AGE

L ooking back on 1950 with such perspective as four decades may afford, we can see that as the new decade began Marlon Brando was, all un-knowing, already embarked on one of those rare, brief cycles of good fortune that few actors ever enjoy – a period when everything they do turns out to be the right thing to have done. (For precedents one might, perhaps, look to James Stewart, circa 1938-40, from *You Can't Take It With You* to *The Philadelphia Story*, and Bogart, 1941-47, from *High Sierra* to *The Trea-sure of the Sierra Madre* – and perhaps one or two others.) It is not that every film the actor makes during such a passage is a box office success or achieves legendary status. But with at least a couple of each – and no not-able disasters in between – he establishes a clear-cut (and, yes, marketable) image of himself as a known quantity, an image that he and the public can rely on, and which will help him through the bad patches that may follow. To put the point simply: one of these success cycles can set an actor apart for ever in people's minds from the George Brents and the Dana Andrews of the profession.

This process began for Brando with *The Men*, released in July 1950: *Streetcar*, when it finally emerged from its trial by censorship in the fall of 1951, would hugely enhance it. Thereafter, *Viva Zapata*, *Julius Caesar*, *The Wild One* and, in 1955, the culminating *On the Waterfront* would, each in its way, confirm his uniqueness and his archetypicality – those seemingly contradictory qualities which are the basis of a great and authentic star-dom. For all of these were films that combined serious intent with con-scientious craftsmanship; all were films for the press and public to conjure with, however they fared critically and at the box office; and all were films that burned at least a few powerful images permanently into the mind.

In 1950, whatever satisfactions (or dissatisfactions) he felt about his work in his first two films, Brando could sensibly – one might even say prudently, considering his lack of immediate prospects – retreat to New York after completing *Streetcar* and pick up his old life, as if nothing had changed (or was about to change). He did rent a somewhat more spacious apartment than before (though it was still a cold water flat) in a building across from

Carnegie Hall, taking in two new room-mates. One was Wally Cox. The other was Russell. Russell the raccoon, that is. The creature has become a legend within the Brando legend – a messy, nasty little guy who appears to have been the only animal utterly insusceptible to Brando's famous way with them. He bit. He scratched. He clawed. Indiscriminately. Unpredictably. Eventually, he drove Cox out of the apartment. Finally, even Brando gave up on him. But for a couple of years the actor and the animal were inseparable. Brando even brought Russell along when he went west to shoot his next movie.

That, however, was a winter and a spring away. For the moment he filled his days and nights in his accustomed fashion: large groups of friends gathered to goof off with him; a number of young actresses appeared and disappeared in his life; The Actor's Studio continued to claim his largest professional interest. There he studied direction as well as acting. He staged the first act of *Hedda Gabler* (resetting it in a crumbling Southern mansion – perhaps in tribute to Williams's influence), and he appeared in one well-recalled acting exercise as the aged Professor Sebryakov in *Uncle Vanya*, wearing pince-nez and stooped under the weight of years and the many scholarly volumes he carried for his entrance. What people remembered from the performance was what, increasingly, one would remember from his later, more public works – a breath-taking behavioral moment. Trying to juggle his books and get at a pad and pencil, Brando's professor would drop first one volume, then another in an inventive, comic and finally quite touching display of the character's absent-minded unworldliness.

While Brando idled, however, his mentor, Elia Kazan was, characteristically, hard at work on what would turn out to be the least well-remembered, but in some respects the most interesting of Brando's early films, the one that would eventually be known as *Viva Zapata*. In Kazan's account, he had first thought of making a film about Emiliano Zapata, the Mexican revolutionary, as early as 1944. Photographs of the Mexican Revolution of 1910-15 stimulated his eye. Zapata's peasant background stirred his imagination – he drew an analogy between the unyielding harshness of his native Morelos province and the equally bleak landscapes of Anatolia from which his own Greek family had emigrated in roughly the same period. Finally, he found a political metaphor in Zapata's life which awakened his controversial instincts. In Kazan's reading of his life (a reading that is disputed by some historians), Zapata voluntarily renounced power after the revolution succeeded. He retreated instead to his home ground, oversaw land reform there (the need for which had drawn him to revolution initially), and was assassinated by the troops loyal to the very government he had helped put in place. Kazan, whose youthful flirtations with communism had long since turned to liberal anti-communism, saw a parallel between Zapata's fate and that of the idealists who had supported the Russian Revolution and had then been betrayed by Stalin in its after-math.

The idea of doing a movie about Zapata was not a new one. It had been proposed as early as 1938, by one Edgcomb Pinchon, a romantic revo-lutionary who had been co-author of the book on which MGM had based Hollywood's last major film about the Mexican Revolution, *Viva Villa*. Shelved during the war, the Zapata project was revived in 1947, by pro-ducer Jack Cummings, one of Louis B. Mayer's nephews and man with a particular fondness for Mexico. Thanks to the intervention of the Mexican film unions, he obtained promises of $1.5 million in production assistance from the Mexican government. He began envisioning Ricardo Montalban in the lead and engaged the Stalinist writer, Lester Cole, to draft the screenplay.

Needless to say, Cole's interpretation of Zapata's life was nothing like the one Kazan was toying with at the same time. With its 'clear, un-equivocal revolutionary content', Cole regarded his seventy-page treat-ment as the basis for a movie that was potentially 'the climax of my writing career. . . .' At MGM? With Montalban? Marxist fantasies have a way of making ordinary Hollywood dreaming look paltry.

Alas for Cole, the project did not move far beyond this preliminary stage, for just as he was setting to work on his first draft screenplay he was summoned before the 1947 House Un-American Activities Committee hearings on Communism in the movie industry. He became, of course, one of the Hollywood Ten. MGM almost immediately dismissed him and joined with the other studios in blacklisting him and his cohorts. In this cli-mate – distinctly down market for revolutionists – MGM decided not to proceed with the Zapata story, no matter what its authorship.

By this time Kazan had discovered that John Steinbeck shared his en-thusiasm for (and attitudes toward) the Zapata legend; indeed, the novelist had been approached by a Mexican company to write a script based on it in 1945. Kazan prevailed on him to attempt a screenplay on speculation, with the understanding that he, a hot property in Hollywood at the time, would help sell it. When it was done, in 1950, he brought Steinbeck and his first draft to Darryl F. Zanuck, chief of production at Twentieth Century-Fox. By this time, Fox, perhaps because Kazan had been expressing interest in Zapata for so long, possibly for other reasons, had acquired MGM's Zapata material for $60,000.

Which is not to say that Zanuck was thinking along the same lines as Cummings and Cole or, for that matter, Kazan and Steinbeck. *The Beloved Rogue* was one working title for this project at Fox and Zanuck had conceived the notion that Tyrone Power would be right for the lead; after all, a few years before, Power had successfully played a somewhat different sort of Mexican revolutionary in *The Mark of Zorro*. That battle Zanuck lost too. But he never entirely abandoned the idea that the picture was essentially a western – poor homesteaders versus rich ranchers.

On the basis of his first draft script, Zanuck gave Steinbeck a $20,000 advance, with a promise of $75,000 more if a revised scenario went into production, and Kazan and the writer headed for Mexico to scout locations and the possibilities of Mexican co-operation in the film. Like Cole and Cummings before them, they met with Mexican film union leaders. Unlike their predecessors, however, they received no promise of assistance on their project. Quite the opposite: they were turned away. Communists had a dominant influence in these unions. They may not have retained residual loyalty to their comrade Cole's project, but Mexican Communism had long since appropriated Zapata (whose historical relationship to Marxism of any kind is dubious) for their revolutionary mythology. They were not going to let a pair of anti-Stalinist leftists, whose work would not treat the party line kindly, exploit a treasured symbol.

Clearly, the Zapata project was acquiring subtexts long before it had a generally agreed upon text. For the Cole-Cummings attempt at this story represented the final effort in the long struggle by the Stalinist left to insert what it liked to call 'progressive' values in the movies, while the Steinbeck-Kazan version, as it finally evolved through several drafts, marks the first (but also the last) attempt by the anti-Communist left to respond to their sectarian enemies by showing, albeit metaphorically, how Stalinism inevitably corrupts the revolutionary process. In other words, though no one connected with either project saw it as such, the effort to recount on screen the story of a man who had probably never seen a motion picture and whose life, in any case, is so enigmatic that its few known facts are open to almost any interpretation, comes to seem in retrospect a symbolic turning-point in the socio-political history of American movies.

There is, of course, an irony in this – no good Hollywood story is complete without an irony. It is this: neither at MGM nor at Fox did any executive care much about the political games their hirelings were playing. Except for the war years, when their Popular Front rhetoric suited everyone's needs, Hollywood's Stalinists had always been forced to speak in metaphors, and their bosses knew that almost without any conscious effort on their part those could be muddled and blunted by the very process of picture-making as they practiced it – rewriting, reshooting, re-editing. Their interest, ever and always, was in simple, straightforward story-telling, and that imperative ultimately steam-rollered all digressions from the true narrative path, whether they were political or poetic.

But it was another habit of the moguls' minds that saved Kazan's project. That was their dislike of having their wills thwarted by outsiders. When it became clear that there was no hope of assistance from Mexican sources for *Zapata*, Kazan feared that Zanuck would cancel the film. It was a risky venture economically, and some subvention from below the border would have alleviated those risks somewhat. Moreover, Mexico and the rest of Central and South America were obviously an important market for this picture. Without the endorsement implied by official sanction of the production, those markets might well be adversely affected (as they were, in fact, when it was released). But Zanuck was not going to be intimidated by far-away figures with strange-sounding names. The Texas side of the border (and the Fox ranch north of Los Angeles) could easily double for Mexico, he suggested. By this time, Kazan was convinced that the House Un-American Activities Committee would soon summon him to testify on his leftist past, and told Zanuck that he feared public exploration of his political past might taint the picture. Zanuck then called in a pair of high-ranking Fox executives, and asked them if people on the lot perceived this enterprise as 'Communistic'. Assured that no one did – which squared with Zanuck's reading of the script – Zanuck indicated that he was not going to tolerate meddling from Washington in his plans either. If there was any meddling to be done, it was Darryl Francis Zanuck who would do it.

And he did. As soon as he had given Kazan the go-ahead, he began complaining about the director's ideas for casting. Brando and Julie Harris, Kazan's first choice for the role of Josefa, Zapata's bride, were made to film a test in New York. The production chief complained that he couldn't understand either of them. Zanuck also thought that, at $100,000, Brando was overpriced, since he did not believe that *Streetcar* would turn out to be the sensation it would soon become. Once again the spectre of Tyrone Power was raised. Or, as an alternative, Zanuck proposed Anthony Quinn (who eventually worked in the picture – and won a supporting actor Oscar – as Emiliano Zapata's brother, Eufemio).

In order to obtain Zanuck's consent to Brando, Kazan had to give up on Harris and accept contract player Jean Peters in her stead. Even so, once the picture began shooting the head of production kept up a steady chorus of complaint: Kazan was falling behind schedule; he didn't like Brando's mustache; he still couldn't understand him. And so on.

One can see what was discomfiting him. This was a Latin revolutionary the like of which Hollywood had not seen before. To begin with, Brando took seriously the issues of make-up and accent. The former went much further than the matter of his mustache. His coloring was extremely dark, he had the make-up man flare his nostrils and impart a slant to his eyes. Some thought he looked more Oriental than Indian, but, in fact, he quite closely approximated to the image of the revolutionist as it had been stylized in their portraits and murals by Diego Riviera and the other Mexican radical painters. Brando worked equally hard on his accent; it was not just a matter of erratically stretching heez ees in the accustomed fashion of Gringos aping the Latin speech pattern. His vocal manner was much richer and subtler than that. To put the point simply, he was not giving an impression, he was attempting a characterization, approaching this role in much the same spirit he had approached in class the problem of acting figures who were equally foreign to him – a Viennese nobleman or a Russian scholar, for instance. For the first time on screen, but scarcely the last, he was entering Paul Muni country.

But these were superficials. It is the spirit of his performance, disturbing to others besides Zanuck at the time, yet for the same reason mysteriously compelling, that imparts much (but not quite all) of the movie's continuing claim on us. He was not a conventional revolutionary firebrand – there is no reckless *machismo*, no beloved roguishness here. Rather, this is a performance in which a pair of more interesting forces are in conflict. On the one hand, Zapata is shown to be a man harboring personal as well as idealistic ambitions (this was the source of one objection Marxist reviewers raised to the finished film); his attraction to Josefa is to some degree based on her middle-class status and the opportunity she offers for him to rise above his station. Meanwhile there is a suggestion that he may have some Spanish blood and that the need to claim the privileges of that caste may be driving him, too. On the other hand, Brando's Zapata is full of the peasant's watchful wariness and the illiterate's sense that words can be used to spin an entrapping web. (One of the film's more touching scenes is the wedding night of Emiliano and Josefa, where he asks her to teach him to read, since he fears the educated leaders of the revolution he is joining: 'My horse and my rifle won't help me.')

Brando got some help on the part from Anthony Quinn. Their relationship was edgy, but Quinn is, after all, half-Mexican, and he had almost as a birthright certain attitudes that Brando needed to absorb, which he did simply by hanging out with his fellow player. And Kazan, justifiably, took some credit for at least one aspect of his star's work. 'I spoke a few words of help: "A peasant does not reveal what he thinks. Things happen to him and he shows no reaction. He knows if he shows certain reactions he'll be marked 'bad' and may be killed." And so on.'

But, as the director also observed, no one entirely directs Brando: 'You release his instinct and give it a shove in the right direction.' He would, in those days, get the idea before it was fully enunciated, turn away, think about it and then take it further than the director imagined he might, perhaps further than the actor himself could predict he might go, since, as Kazan put it, 'His gifts go beyond his knowledge.'

But not, as it happened, beyond the instinctive, first-glance appreciation of his younger audience. For psychologically Brando's Zapata was something of an adolescent, that is to say, an innocent, not quite knowing what to make of the world he had inherited, unsure about the extent of his ability to assert himself in it, yet also restless, needing to test the limits of his wit and strength.

This anti-revolutionary revolutionist was also a very Fifties kind of a figure – although, this early in the decade, we were perhaps less aware of that than we would be later, after we had seen many a good man in the movies, and in popular fictions of all sorts, turn his back on large enterprises, the better to tend his own garden. But it may be that Brando's Zapata was the first to articulate that message, in the process, implying the exhaustion of the old left's energies as well as its metaphors. Daniel Bell, the sociologist, would not actually proclaim 'the end of ideology', in the book of that title, until 1960, but in the preceding years those of us who were naturally of a liberal persuasion felt increasingly bereft of ideological comfort, too wise to accept the old rallying cries of the left, but not acute (or passionate) enough to make up new ones: In short, we remained silent, as in 'silent generation'.

Kazan and Steinbeck were surely not so prescient that they saw, as of 1951, when they were in production, that the behavior of their principal character was going to prove generationally predictive, that young people would soon learn to distrust great ideas, great causes and, above all, 'great' men. But they did understand that conscience seeks belief, requires it as a bulwark against selfishness and anarchy. So they gave Zapata this speech to his followers: 'You're always looking for leaders, strong men without faults. There aren't any. They change. They desert. They die. There are no leaders but yourselves. A strong people is the only lasting strength.'

It works dramatically, in the context of the movie. And as a generalization it is impeccable. One might even translate it into the politics of the moment without too much discomfort. If the Cold War was the only available political metaphor, it made sense to leave it to someone else – for example, those 'tough-minded' liberals who somehow ended up on the CIA's payroll in this period, and made their way to The New Right subsequently. But, looking back, it is clear that the example of industriousness and personal morality that the rest of us – 'a strong people', if you will – were determined to set did not transform society any more successfully than the ideologues had.

So in retrospect, as a postive statement of a practical political alternative to the ideas, left and right, which had preoccupied its creators' generation, *Viva Zapata* fails. What does not fail, what in fact seems most interesting about the movie as one re-encounters it now, is its quite specific and quite sophisticated criticism of the Stalinist mentality. Indeed, I would suggest that nothing offered in popular entertainment in that era of no-nothing anti-Communism, compares with it. I don't think most of us (my generation) noticed it, so focused were we on Zapata's struggles with his conscience. In any case, most of us were not then politically shrewd enough to know what to make of the character known as Fernando and played – very well – by Joseph Wiseman. But he does carry much of what Kazan and Steinbeck most urgently wanted to say politically.

He appears out of nowhere, wearing a Gringo suit, carrying a typewriter and looking for some native unrest to turn into a full-scale revolution. Given his way with words and his love of war, he seems for a while to be a Trotsky-like figure. But no, as the story develops, he takes on a more Stalinesque outline – while Zapata, of course, becomes something like this revolution's Trotsky. Like his model, Stalin, Fernando is not quite at the center of the revolution's ruling councils. Rather, from its fringe he constantly whispers an evil realism in the ears of its principal leaders. It is he who proposes the assassination of the liberal leader of the provisional post-revolutionary government, Francisco Madero (read Kerensky), whose execution is one of the film's masterful sequences. And after Zapata exiles himself from leadership it is Fernando who understands that, like Trotsky, a man of Zapata's popularity (and military skills) cannot be tolerated as a potential rallying-point for 'counter-revolution'. He is present when Zapata (who, it is hinted, is aware of what awaits him, and may welcome death as the ultimate release from the temptations of temporal power, the ultimate means of asserting spiritual power) is lured into his final, fatal ambush – another magnificent directorial set piece. Without this wily antagonist, Zapata's martyrdom would not be nearly so effective. We need Fernando's worship of power to ennoble Zapata's rejection of power.

And the film's conclusion, with Zapata's body being dumped with a resonant thump on the well in the center of his town square, while peasant
women in black watch impassively, and its coda, in which his beloved white
stallion is seen galloping free in the hills, symbol of a spirit free at last of
the world's constraints and importunities, is, indeed, tragically and
romantically potent. That horse, so corny and yet so effective, was, by the
way, Zanuck's contribution: he remembered the device from some earlier
film in which he needed to take the sting out of a hero's death, leave the
audience with something uplifting to dwell upon as they left the theater, so
he imposed it on *Zapata*.

Much good it did him. The picture was reviewed reasonably well, largely
because of the reputations of its writer, director and star for serious work
and, like Quinn, Brando was nominated for an Oscar, though he did not
win. It also opened well, largely because of the commitment we – the
younger audience – had made to Brando. But it had weak legs and it dis-
appeared from the theaters quite quickly, even though it remained a staple
in the revival houses throughout the decade.

For all its metaphorical relevance, the picture seemed distant to most
people, and not romantically colorful enough to make up for that defect.
Kazan and Brando were ambivalent about it as well in the final analysis.
The former remembers describing it at the time to Arthur Miller as
'another "almost"'. Kazan believed that he had not yet mastered the
movie medium, that he was still more a director of actors than of the
camera and of action, though, in fact, the worst one might say about his
work on *Zapata* was that the influence of John Ford, whom Kazan greatly
admired, was still visible in it. But he was not, at the time, a reliable witness to his own work, for soon after the picture was cut he had his first
direct encounter with the House Un-American Activities Committee investigators; and he would spend the winter and spring of 1952 agonizing
over whether or not to name the other members of The Group Theater's
Communist cell of two decades earlier. This, ultimately, he would do, for
what he believed were good and sufficient reasons, some of which he had
placed on the screen in this film.

As for Brando, he has always maintained a certain reserve about *Viva
Zapata*. The longest statement from him about it that I've been able to find
is: 'Zapata was a hard characterization, which I don't think I fulfilled. It
was a good workout.' Brando was not then, and has never been, a political
sophisticate, and it is possible that he was unaware of the film's specifically
anti-Stalinist subtext until it was pointed out. At which point, it also seems
likely, he might have been dismayed to discover he had been used to

mouth a seemingly establishment viewpoint.

In other words, as part of the most troubled passage of Kazan's life the film was in some measure tainted both for him and for the actor, who at this time in his life regarded the director as a mentor. We have the testimony of Brando's next director, Joseph L. Mankiewicz, that when it came out in the early summer of 1952 that Kazan had voluntarily given the committee a list of his sometime Communist associates Brando was stricken by the news. Mankiewicz, who was also a friend of Kazan's, recalls the actor coming to him on the set virtually in tears over Kazan's action, unable to believe that a man he loved and trusted could have done something of which he so deeply disapproved. Mankiewicz, with a picture to finish, and with a more sophisticated knowledge of the sectarian wars of the left, remembers telling Brando not to judge his mentor too quickly or glibly; and reminding him that whatever one felt about Kazan's political activities it should have no bearing on one's judgement of him as an artist.

The film on which Brando and Mankiewicz were working was *Julius Caesar*. And it was very much the product of the 'new' Hollywood. Its producer, John Houseman, was a famous man about the theater and movies. He had been Orson Welles's partner in the Mercury Theatre, and his name had since been associated with a number of literate, distinguished film and theatrical projects – of which the most recent had been the Louis Calhern *King Lear* on Broadway. When Dore Schary, the sometime screenwriter and producer noted for his serious, socially conscientious – or should one say well-meaning – work, replaced Louis B. Mayer as head of production at MGM, he almost immediately recruited Houseman and charged him with making 'prestige' projects.

Caesar was on Schary's agenda when he hired Houseman. It was, in fact, a project that had interested several movie people, among them David O. Selznick, who had registered the title with the Motion Picture Producers Association, which forced Schary to wait until that claim expired before proceeding. It was probably Welles's famous modern-dress *Julius Caesar*, at the Mercury before the war, that stirred this interest, since it demonstrated that the play, which of course offers obvious opportunities for cinematic spectacle, could be read as anti-totalitarian in intent, even if Shakespeare had no notion of what a modern dictatorship looked like. In any case, by the time Selznick's title registration ran out in 1952, Schary, oppressed by management duties, had to abandon his hopes of producing the film personally. But he also saw the possibility of reusing the sets and costumes the studio had created for quite another sort of Romanesque spectacle, *Quo Vadis?*, for this new enterprise, thus drastically lowering the cost of a *Julius Caesar*, and so he turned it over to Houseman. Mankiewicz, who two years in succession had won both writer and director Oscars for *A Letter to Three Wives* and *All About Eve* (an unprecedented and still unduplicated achievement), was not only a logical choice to direct (he had proved beyond doubt that he could handle extensive dialogue in a graceful, lively fashion), but one sure to impress observers who had read Schary's ascension at conservative Metro as an omen that times were changing in Hollywood.

True to his Mercury heritage, Houseman wanted to use as many American actors as possible in the production, and, remembering how well Brando had handled the big climactic speech in *A Flag is Born*, was inspired to suggest him for Marc Antony, much to the initial dismay of Schary, Hollywood gossips and, perhaps at first, Mankiewicz as well. He was in London, signing John Gielgud for Cassius and thinking seriously of testing the young Paul Scofield as Antony, when Houseman cabled him the idea. Actually, of course, Houseman's idea was an excellent one. For Antony is, after all, a man trying to sort out his loyalties, decide what a good man must do in a confused situation. It is, ideally, a young man's part, and very right for this particular young man. Nevertheless, all agreed that Brando would have to prove his ability to handle Shakespearian verse, and he agreed to make a recording of his major speeches.

Brando wanted the role, and was eager to prove, as he later put it, that he was not 'Big Chief Slobbermouth'. According to Mankiewicz, he bought many recordings of the great English Shakespearians and studied them closely before making his own record. This he played for the director at his New York apartment. Whether or not Russell was present for this meeting is not known, but Mankiewicz's opinion of Brando's effort is. 'You sound like June Allyson,' he told the actor. Apparently Brando re-did the record, for both Houseman and Schary were impressed by whatever was forwarded to them, and Brando was quickly signed for the film.

He was never more caring in his approach to work. Everyone was impressed by the seriousness with which he addressed his role and the deference he accorded his fellow players. He took a particular shine to Calhern, whose weary and nervous Caesar is one of the film's ornaments, and Gielgud would recall him as 'charming to me . . . I liked him enormously.' In a recent television interview he offered an affectionate portrait of Brando on the set: 'He was very self-conscious, nervous. He used to come on the set looking perfectly wonderful in this sort of tomato-colored toga and straight fringe [bangs] with a cigarette in one corner of his mouth. Then he'd take it out and put it behind his ear to show he wasn't being posh. He was awfully afraid of being sent up silly in his costume.'

Houseman remembered Gielgud, the modern theater's reigning master of Shakespearian melody, as enormously helpful to the entire cast with questions of speech. He was also an all-purpose morale builder for a disparate group drawn from all over the acting world – movie stars, Hollywood character people, London and New York stage players. Gielgud himself was anxious not to seem to be pulling rank ('They all thought I was coming to Hollywood to teach them how to play Shakespeare, so I kept a very low profile'). He was careful not to volunteer advice, but to wait until he was asked for it. Which, indeed, Brando did when they were about to do one of their two scenes together. 'I went to his caravan,' Gielgud recalled, 'and went through the scene and showed him where the phrasing and the color and so on should be different, and the next day he came down and played it using everything I'd given him.'

Gielgud would later wish Brando had asked for some help with his great scene, the funeral oration over Caesar's body in the forum. Though he has since revised upward his opinion of Brando's work, he thought at the time 'he was just imitating Oliver [always something of a sore point with his great rival] . . . he did some great shouts and things.' Houseman, on the other hand, was grateful for the unflagging energy Brando brought to a sequence that required him to do bits and pieces of a very taxing speech over and over again so that it was covered from every angle a editor might want and so that the crowd reaction shots, vital for its success as a movie scene, could be made.

Perhaps because of Houseman's something-for-everyone casting (besides those already named, James Mason, then at the height of his broody-romantic phase, contributed a very well-judged Brutus, and Deborah Kerr and Greer Garson played small, wifely roles, while most of the character parts were filled by familiar players), perhaps because everything about the movie was crafted with such obvious conscientiousness, perhaps because it really was better than such ludicrous Hollywood assaults on the Bard as the Norma Shearer-Leslie Howard *Romeo and Juliet*, the film received very supportive reviews. Since reviewer response was crucial to its commercial success, it also did well at the box office. Many critics indeed read the film exactly as they were supposed to, as a sign of the movies' new 'maturity'. Those of us who didn't know any better than to believe in their prescriptions (and proscriptions) naturally agreed with them. And, of course, we were proud that our own generational champion held his own with all those well-spoken veterans in a classical piece – no mumbles, and, at the end of the day, another Academy Award nomination.

One is now a little less sure of one's first response both to the film and to Brando's performance. Mankiewicz is a man who idealizes the theater and, despite his success in film, confesses that he wishes he had been a playwright instead (Restoration drama is his particular passion). He could not quite bring himself to a full cinematization of his *Julius Caesar*. Much of his staging has something of the theatrical about it, and though that is sometimes effective, sometimes it is not. We often see his sets as sets, that is, as stylizations of reality rather than as reality itself – and as rather underpopulated sets, at that. The staging of Caesar's assassination requires, on film, an intimacy and a horror that Mankiewicz backs away from, and the crowd massed for Antony's funeral is not well handled either. The camera is rather passive and distant and, as a result, the rabble's volatility never seems as dangerous as it should. Much work was done on the dubbing stage to give them, at least, a louder, more menacing voice, but it still rings hollow – often literally so. The Battle of Philippi, too, is thin and perfunctory. Budgetary restrictions surely hampered the director, but it must also be admitted that this kind of movie-making was not in those days Mankiewicz's strength. He is much more comfortable and effective in the more tightly wound scenes of the conspirators plotting and at his very best with Mason's Brutus on his sleepless, guilt-ridden night before Philippi.

As for Brando, this is the most problematical of his early performances. His own modest evaluation was that he 'gained ground as an actor – not so much in end performance'. It is not an inaccurate summation as far as it goes. All the evidence is that he probably put more *conscious* effort into this performance than he did into anything he has ever done, before or since. But thinking back on his earnest study of his great predecessors – and knowing his uncanny skills as a mimic – one can't help but think Gielgud's first reaction to it was correct. Whether or not he was, in fact, doing his well-practised Olivier imitation, this surely is an actor imitating other actors acting, never quite getting inside this character by means of his own devising. He has all the right moves, and many of the right tones, but he never seems to inhabit the role fully.

Over the years it has become a cliché to regret that Brando did not attempt more of the classical roles. And it may be that, had he overcome his natural laziness and his understandable fear of these parts, he might have become, technically, a more reliable actor, possibly even a 'great' actor in the conventional (or should one simply say the English?) mode. But it may also be that his only brush with Shakespeare showed him the limits of his gift. Or the limit of his patience.

'If you care about it, it's no good,' he once said to John Huston, meaning

ing, as the director correctly interpreted, 'You've got to get into a role to the point that you're no longer acting.' His way in consisted primarily of a withdrawal into himself, a withdrawal so deep that only a director like Kazan, capable of honing his ideas into a few very sharply pointed sentences, could penetrate it, and then only momentarily. 'Acting is such a tenuous thing,' Brando once said. 'A fragile shy thing that a sensitive director can help lure out of you. Now, in movie acting, the important, the *sensitive* moment comes around the third take . . . by then you just need a whisper from the director to crystallize it for you. Gadge can usually do it.'

Similarly, Brando tended to isolate himself from his fellow actors, from the entire rehearsal process as he searched his instincts, and his remembered observations of behavior, for the material he needed. (Around this time Stella Adler spoke of his fear of 'real' theater people – stage actors, that is.) This is not the way a serious modern actor serves a classic text. A much more consciously intellectual, and communal, process is involved in that work. The aim, ultimately, is a compromise between the actor's personality and the demands of the text. To borrow Arthur Penn's metaphor, you don't just step up to the plate and take your cuts at Shakespeare or Sophocles or Chekhov. To put it another way, Brando's instincts spoke up in defense of themselves, of their sovereignty in the acting process as he practiced it. Or so it seems.

Not that any of us cared, or noticed, at the time. We felt, as he perhaps felt, that a test had been honorably passed. In a gentlemanly context a well-spoken, gentlemanly performance had been given – and deserved at least a gentleman's 'C' (maybe even a 'B') as a grade. Fine. Time to move on.

There was no lack of paths open to him. In this period Brando was offered a number of interesting – in one or two cases, potentially elegant – projects. What he chose to do was *The Wild One*. Not exactly elegant. But topical, and, as Brando saw it, capable of being a force for enlightenment. Besides, he'd get the chance to ride his Hawg on screen. For the film was based on a magazine account of a weekend when a motorcycle gang effectively siezed possession of little Hollister, California, terrorizing its citizens. Most important, the picture (which was produced by Stanley Kramer) had – and continues to have – this to recommend it: it was the first major movie to confront the seismic rift that opened between the generations in the 1950s.

Before this decade, twentieth-century American adolescents and post-adolescents had always seemed a little – well – different. they had ridden about in jalopies with funny slogans painted on them, talked in curious –

sometimes briefly indecipherable – slang, danced to new and different jazz drummers. But everybody always said, tolerantly, 'they'll grow out of it,' which, of course, they generally did. They had never looked like aliens to their parents, or to the authorities. Now, seemingly overnight, they were aliens – irredeemably so, manacingly so.

'Juvenile delinquency.' Suddenly the phrase was on everyone's lips. There were senate hearings and best-sellers on the subject, and the newspapers were full of tales about gangs rumbling, usually with one another (as they do, eventually, in *The Wild One*) but, of course, dangerous to nice people who happened to get caught in the middle (as they are in this picture). The conventional explanations were: divorce and/or two-earner families, which led to neglect of the kids; affluence, which either put enough money in young people's pockets to permit them freer range than they had known before, or made those who didn't have it envious enough to try getting it through criminal means; the discovery by American capitalism that youth was 'a market', just a short step or two away from being a separate 'culture'. (Drugs were not yet a major factor in defining this market, and as of the year *The Wild One* was released, neither was music, as its mouldy fig score proves.)

In those days the official line was that America was in the process of eradicating all the old class distinctions, that everyone was, or soon would be, middle class. Therefore, this thought was unspeakable: that much juvenile delinquency, and most of its more violent manifestations, were motivated by class (and racial) envy and involved kids for whom traditional education was irrelevant, most of the work they could imagine being allowed to do, enervating, hopeless.

Apparently the movie's original script made this point quite firmly, and stressed, as well, the notion that the rootlessness and alienation of motorcycle gangs were not subject to amelioration by conventional means – psychiatry, social work, tinkering with school curricula, that sort of thing. The original intent, so Brando thought, was to show citizens of the occupied community responding to their threatening invaders, unprogrammatically and non-violently. He thought they would be seen coming one by one to an emotional understanding of these troubled toughs.

No way the Breen office was buying that line. To begin with, the film's original script seemed to imply that there was something institutionally wrong when a society was producing youths of this kind, and social criticism of that sort did not go down well with Breen and the other Catholic conservatives on his staff – not in an era when the likes of Joseph R. McCarthy were drawing their most vociferous support from their more reactionary co-religionists. It smacked of covert leftie propaganda, just the sort of thing Congressional committees were currently determined to root out. Moreover, the conventional wisdom of the Cold War, now in full cry, was that real men answered force with force, not by turning the other cheek. If one looked at this story of heartland Americans confronting an invasion by alien forces one could see that, in its original form, its bleeding heart was in quite the wrong place.

Rewrites were in order – and ordered up. The result is that confusion of motives still visible today. *The Wild One*'s opening sequence, in which Johnnie (Brando), in sunglasses, cyclist's cap and leathers, is astride his machine, leading his gang down the road to town, is wonderfully charged with menace. So is the vrooming, stunting establishment of their beach-head on Main Street, and their slouching, sneering take-over of the town café which is (a) owned by the town's cowardly constable and (b) managed by Kathie (Mary Murphy), his daughter and the love interest – dramaturgi-cally very convenient. In these passages Brando is, yes, hell's angel – beautiful, insolent, seductive: Joe Breen's, all of Middle America's, worst nightmare suddenly made manifest.

The café is the setting for that famous exchange that was to become a Fifties emblem, this response to Kathie's question about the gang's motives: 'Hey, Johnnie, what are you rebelling against?' 'Waddya got.' It is also the setting for Johnnie's almost equally famous attempt to explain to the girl that, no, they are not exactly looking for a picnic spot, nor a place to go fishing on their weekly outings: 'Man you're too square. I have to straighten you out. You don't go to any one special place . . . you just go to . . . the idea is to whale, to make some jive. Do you know what I'm talking about?'

Well, no, not exactly. Evidently Brando, unhappy with the rewritten script, improvised this and much of his other dialogue. But she – and we – got the general, thrilling idea. The trouble is that the movie doesn't de-velop it. On closer acquaintance the Black Rebels turn into mild ones. Their sins are all against decorum, not against the Ten Commandments. They drink beer on the streets, swagger a bit under its influence, talk too loudly, but they don't do dope, swing chains or carry switch-blades. And they are without the kind of hair-trigger unpredictability they need to maintain their menace. Moreover, Laslo Benedek's direction quickly settles into a kind of cool formalism, stand-offish and objective. It does not – shall we say? – whale.

Nor does the narrative have the kind of erratic pulse, constantly surpris-ing and alarming, that would keep us edgy. It heads smoothly, conventionally toward quite predictable confrontations. The arrival of a rival gang, an off-shoot of the Black Rebels, predicts imminent violence, which gets serious when its leader, Chino (Lee Marvin), is jailed and his gang goes on a rampage. As we know he will, Johnnie rescues Kathie from their depradations, then is himself mistaken as a possible rapist, and is savagely beaten by town vigilantes. This was the first of the many ritual beatings characters played by Brando would absorb in his films, punishment for being an outsider *and* sensitive – a hip messiah in the pop mythology of the time. After that, he tries to leave town, but one of the citizens throws a tire iron at him, he loses control of his bike and accidentally kills an old man. After which a lynch mob gathers. He is rescued by the arrival of the country sheriff, strong and sensible – authority with its best face on. In his calming presence Kathie testifies that Johnnie was not a menace but her savior, and another citizen testifies that it was a townie, not a biker, who threw that tire iron. In other words, everyone shares more or less equally in guilt for this unfortunate incident. Johnnie is ordered to leave and never return, which he does – still inarticulate, still unable to put words to his feelings about what has happened.

This tale is, then, mostly a series of accidents and misapprehensions. About all it proves is that mutual mistrust – especially when there are a few bad apples in the barrel – is a sad, possibly preventable thing. It takes neither the radical view that middle-class America could use a good shaking up from Johnnie and his kind, nor the reactionary one that they are animals in need of the whip and the cage. Either one would have been preferable to the ameliorative inconclusiveness of the movie that finally emerged on the screen.

For, like so many films, so many other artifacts of Fifties popular culture, *The Wild One* wanted to patch things up. And patch things over. It looked, finally, to a firm but essentially benign – yes, Eisenhowerish – authority to accomplish those tasks. What was essential to its mission was the assumption that there was nothing profoundly wrong with a kid like Johnnie, or the society that produced him – nothing that couldn't be fixed by an honest airing of finite grievances, and the even-handed application of commonsensical justice to them. By taking this tack, the film tamed the craziness of the historical incident on which it was based – the shocking, and at the time, unprecedented intrusion of violent anarchy on settled ordinariness. In other words, the very qualities which had made the incident something of a journalistic sensation and which had drawn the moviemakers to the topic in the first place were softened, explained away.

In one of his subsequent comments on the picture, Brando got it right and got it wrong. He was right in his overall assessment of the film: 'We started out to do something worthwhile, to explain the psychology of the hipster. But somewhere along the way we went off the track . . . instead of finding out why young people tend to bunch into groups that seek expression in violence, all that we did was show the violence.' But out of some modesty or perversity, he also got one aspect of the film wrong. Discussing his own character with another journalist, he said: 'This was a man so possessed with inner struggle and strife that he was almost beyond the realm of articulating his feelings and almost not caring any more. I wanted to show that underneath all those things you could find a yearning, a desire to feel love – but so twisted and wrenched by disappointment that it no longer had the face of love. I wanted to show that gentleness and tolerance is the only way to dissipate the forces of social destruction. Well, it didn't come off at all. . . .'

But, of course, it did. Or, anyway, his intentions did. For, in effect, he was following his own agenda in *The Wild One*, acting in the film he wanted to make, subverting as best he could the compromised movie everyone else was doing. All right, he was playing to us, to the self-romanticizing self-absorption that was beginning to redefine adolescence. And he was not critical of it, or even ironic about it. But, undeniably, he was on to something here, something that was new and problematical in the psychopathology of everyday American life. And equally undeniably in this film, so compromised and devious in its larger aspects, he shrugged off all metaphorical disguises and made, at last, a direct connection with his primary audience, his young fellow yearners after love and understanding.

This message, quite obviously, came through to others as well. For all the twistings and turnings that had been imposed on the producers of *The Wild One*, for all the compromises they voluntarily made, Johnnie's dangerousness – the only true menace in the movie – remained obvious. And he neither apologized for it nor explained it. He leaves the picture as inarticulately as he entered it. Here and there around the US, municipal moralists were outraged that he and his gang were not seen to be more firmly punished, and some fears were expressed that the film might prove to be an incitement to riot among its adolescent viewers. In Britain, indeed, censors banned the film outright for something like a decade and a half. They were responding not to a picture, but to a presence – and a performance – that was all suggestion and insinuation, and therefore, infuriatingly, no more censorable, finally, than the text of *Streetcar* had been.

Thus was the last link forged in the bond between Brando and those of us who were and would remain his most devoted audience. For *The Wild*

One accomplished what none of his previous pictures had: it took a screen character (or an image, if you prefer) that had first been glimpsed crippled, and then had been presented to us in variously exotic, distancing settings – the Vieux Carré, Mexico, ancient Rome – and thrust it, in full health and vigor, into completely familiar territory, where he confronted what were for us completely recognizable (if melodramatically heightened) issues. Judged by conventional critical standards, *The Wild One* may be the least of his early movies. But in terms of Brando's career, it is probably the most important of them. All he needed now to confirm his status as the greatest star of his generation was a role that was well within both his range and the range of his developing audiences sympathetic expectations in a film that was incontravertably well-made and thematically compelling; something everyone could take seriously, had to see. In short, what he needed was *On the Waterfront.*

He almost didn't get it. *We* almost didn't get it. For the history of that film's development was vexed, if not, as it must have sometimes seemed, hexed. It begins, perhaps, with another script about longshoremen, called *The Hook*, which Elia Kazan and Arthur Miller developed in the late Forties, but never sold. In part this was because (ironically, as matters would develop) it seemed insufficiently anti-Communist in outlook to people like Roy Brewer, the red-baiting head of the International Alliance of Theatrical and Stage Employees, whose opinion on such matters was being sought – or perhaps foisted upon – studio executives when a property seemed to be politically 'controversial'. Miller and Kazan dropped the project, and then, after Kazan testified about his past associations in the Communist Party, they dropped their friendship as well.

In 1952, unapologetic – actually defiant – about the correctness of what he had done, Kazan sought out a man he had never met, Budd Schulberg, the novelist, who had also identified former comrades to the investigators. (Schulberg's break with the party came in 1940, when he was summoned to a party tribunal and told to rewrite his first and most famous book, *What Makes Sammy Run?*, so that it more closely followed the then current party line.) Schulberg was also unrepentant about his action and, like Kazan, he remained a man of the left. But on their first meeting the two men discovered that they had more in common than their politics. For it turned out that the writer had also spent some time developing a script about working life on the Port of New York's docks, basing his story on a series of articles about union corruption there, for which a newspaper reporter named Malcolm Johnson had won the Pulitzer Prize, and to which Schulberg had acquired screen rights.

Kazan liked Schulberg's screenplay – with reservations – and while the director was busy with other projects Schulberg supplemented Johnson's work with research of his own. Actually it was much less of an arm's length process than that, for he drank and yarned and buddied up with New Jersey longshoremen in a search that was not so much for facts as for psychological and behavioral authenticity. Eventually, he introduced Kazan to a man named Tony Mike deVincenzo, who had once been a hiring boss on the piers, until he objected to the corrupt practices of the dockyard racketeers. Fired and blacklisted by the mob, he was reduced to selling newspapers on a street corner. Subpoenaed by the Waterfront Crime Commission, he testified against the hoodlums. When Schulberg took Kazan to meet him, Tony Mike was carrying a gun.

Kazan immediately drew an analogy between the experiences of Tony Mike after he testified, and some of his own experiences after 'naming names' – he was not physically threatened, of course, but he was shunned and excoriated by former friends. Here was the core to the story he had been looking for. Schulberg, who lived in the country, had been less afflicted by the response of others to his choice and, in Kazan's words, 'regarded our waterfront story with greater objectivity'. But, as he also put it, 'I did see Tony Mike's story as my own, and that connection did lend the tone of irrefutable anger to the scenes I photographed and to my work with actors. When Brando, at the end, yells at Lee Cobb, the mob boss, "I'm glad what I done – you hear me? – glad what I done!" that was me saying, with identical heat, that I was glad I had testified as I did. . . . I'd not forgotten nor would I forgive the men, old friends some of them, who'd snubbed me, so the scene in the film where Brando goes back to the waterfront to "shape up" again for employment by men with whom he'd worked day after day – that, too, was my story, now told to all the world. So that when critics say that I put my story and my feelings on the screen to justify informing, they are right.'

All movies, all fictions in any form, that have the initial impact and the lasting resonance of a work like *On the Waterfront* are animated by some personal passion of the kind Kazan describes, even if the passion is, as his was, a somewhat narrow one (and in the minds of some, rather dubious), and even if the work in question finally transcends that passion, as *Waterfront* did. Indeed, it is fair to say that, in this particular case, the movie would never have been made if Kazan and Schulberg had been moved by lesser motives. For Kazan's old friend and suporter, Darryl Zanuck, having encouraged them for months, did an abrupt turnaround ('Who gives a shit about longshoremen?') when a final script was delivered to him.

87

Thereafter, in quick succession, most of the other studios passed on the project.

But Schulberg and Kazan happened to be staying at the Beverly Hills Hotel, and they happened to be quartered across the hall from the legendary freebooter, Sam Spiegel, in those days operating under the transparent alias of S. P. Eagle. Emboldened by strong drink and strong anger, the writer-director team hailed him, hauled him into their suite and started pitching their story. For reasons that remain baffling, except that Spiegel was also a legendary player of long shots, he was interested. In a matter of weeks he had the financing together (the negative cost the astonishingly small sum of $880,000). Most important of all, it was Spiegel who brought Brando to the project.

Not without his usual shenanigans, of course. He had first thought of Frank Sinatra, a native of Hoboken, who was in some respects right for the part – right enough for Kazan to agree to the casting and to meet with Sinatra regarding wardrobe. Both men believed a commitment had been made. Whereupon Spiegel began talking to Brando, who at first said he would not work with Kazan, because of his testimony, then began to weaken under Spiegel's persuasiveness. With Brando in the lead, Spiegel could get more money from Columbia, the studio that had finally agreed to back the project, for, despite Sinatra's recent success in *From Here to Eternity*, Brando's was a more bankable name. Finally, with the acceptance of a condition – that he could leave the set every day at four so that he could keep an appointment with his pyschiatrist, a therapist to whom he had been introduced by Kazan – Brando agreed to take the part, permanently alienating Sinatra from all concerned.

Once Brando had signed, Spiegel insisted upon rewrite after rewrite, so many of them that, at one point, Schulberg's wife was awakened late at night by the sounds of her husband getting dressed. Where was he going? To New York. Why? 'To kill Sam Spiegel.' But Kazan believes that Spiegel's insistence on keeping the story moving, on the relentless building of tension, was one of the factors that made the picture work, and he also admits that he and Schulberg would have been satisfied with a lesser script.

That said, the producer's cheapness once shooting began infuriated everyone, especially since the locations were the docks and slums of harsh Hoboken, which offered no amenities; the season was a bitter cold winter, with temperatures hovering around zero much of the time; and the community, populated by dock workers who still owed allegience to the mob, was by no means welcoming. Spiegel did not help matters by visiting the set in his limousine, wrapped in a rich overcoat, delicately stepping around puddles so as not to damage his exquisite alligator shoes.

There are plenty of anecdotes about the shoot, most of which stress the camaraderie of the company, bound together by the difficult conditions they shared, perhaps by their unanimous hatred of Spiegel (who, by setting up an 'Us versus Him' situation, made what often turns out to be the only useful contribution a producer can offer a shooting company), possibly by the fact that the principal cast was composed entirely of actors in the Stanislavskian tradition, from Group Theater veteran Lee J. Cobb to Eva Marie Saint, an Actor's Studio student making her film debut. There was no compromise with the marquee in any of the casting.

Nor was there any compromise with reality. Kazan had been trying to free himself from studio sets since he began making movies (he had done so less notably, but with educative results, in *Boomerang* and *Panic in the Streets*), and now that effort paid off spectacularly. Similarly, he had been experimenting with the use of non-professional actors in small parts and as extras, and now his 'atmosphere' had an authenticity rarely approached by an American director. (This, in fact, was something else he had to thank Spiegel for, since the director's aesthetic needs coincided so neatly with the producer's desire to pinch pennies). In other words, *On the Waterfront* was, if nothing else, the culmination of a stylistic trend in American film, a trend that Kazan had been leading, which had been gathering force since the end of the war.

But, of course, *Waterfront* was something else. Its greatness cannot be contained within a techno-aesthetic definition any more than it can be explained by its working out of the political philosophies of its primary creators. It is as a narrative, spare but unsparing, of an unlikely young man coming to moral consciousness, that it achieved not only its initial impact but its lasting value. By now, the question of what constituted correct political behavior in the McCarthy era has lost its urgency, and the issue of union corruption has lost power along with the unions. What abides is the relentless, really quite unsentimental story of how Terry Malloy ceased to be 'a bum' and became a good man.

The details of that story are now too familiar to require detailed recounting. When we meet Terry, a former small-time boxer, he is hanging around the docks, existing on favors thrown him by mob boss Johnny Friendly (Cobb) and by his brother Charley (Rod Steiger), who is a lawyer for the racketeers. One of the errands he performs for them consists of unwittingly luring one of the mobsters' opponents into a death-trap. Later, meeting the dead man's sister, Edie (Saint), the first glimmering of conscience begins to dawn – as does love, of course. Encouraged by a waterfront priest (Karl Malden), Terry moves painfully into opposition to the mob, which kills Charley when he cannot buy his brother's silence. Ultimately, Terry bears witness against the criminals, is ostracized by other dockers, then savagely beaten by mob goons (perhaps the most famous of Brando's ritual beatings, with Kazan even composing one shot as a pietà). But, staggering from his wounds, he leads the contingent of longshoremen who witnessed his anguish past Johnny Friendly and his cohorts, thus claiming one free dock for free men.

Reduced to outline, it is a not entirely original movie story, except for its setting. What grants it its singularity is its playing. The hint of sexual heat underneath Saint's prim Catholic schoolgirl demeanor; the unctuously patronizing manner of Steiger's Charley, not quite covering the clammy fear in which he has lived his life; the awkwardness of Malden's priest when he tries to be a regular guy, not quite disguising his zealot's fervor – all of this is marvelous work, and all of it is stylistically of a piece, which is a great rarity in American film. And the star is completely with them, in no sense set apart. The delicate blend of untutored courtliness and boyish cockiness with which he woos Edie; the grief that plays across his face as she questions him about her brother's death, and the full realization of what he has done, and what it now may cost him; the gentleness of his famous final confrontation with Charley, full of pleading and puzzlement, as he tries to come to grips with his brother's betrayal – these are among the most privileged moments in our movie heritage. 'If there is a better performance by a man in the history of film in America, I don't know what it is,' Kazan wrote in his autobiography, and what reasonable person would disagree with him?

And yet there is this curiosity about the performance. Search though one may, it is impossible to find any detailed comments about his work from Brando. This possibly betokens, of all things, satisfaction with it. For as a friend of his was to tell Truman Capote, 'Marlon always turns against whatever he's working on. Some element of it. . . . Not always because of anything very rational, but because it seems to comfort him to be dissatisfied.' But not this time. There were a few gripes about the working conditions, an allusion to some personal unhappiness that upset him at the time, but no self-criticism, and no criticism that the project had failed to live up to its promise, no cynicism about his own low motives for taking it on. Just silence.

His co-workers were more forthcoming. Eva Marie Saint, for example, was voluble about her affection for him. 'I'm on a one-woman crusade to right the wrongs said about Marlon Brando,' she told a reporter later, in an interview full of anecdotes about his kindness in seeing that she was wrapped in blankets against the cold, or giving her back-rubs to relieve tension. He seems to have indulged in a certain amount of jokey, arm-punching camaraderie with Kazan, but the latter is careful to say that his best direction, as far as Brando was concerned, was non-direction – letting him find his own way into a scene. One famous bit of business, picking up a glove dropped by Saint in one of their early getting-acquainted scenes, was, he says, an improvisation that arose when it slipped out of her hand by accident. The back-seat confrontation between Brando and Steiger, which had to be shot on a stage, with stage-hands rocking the shell of an auto to simulate movement, because Spiegel was too cheap to provide them with a real car, was worked out by the actors with no guidance from Kazan, according to the director. And it worked out so well in the playing because the mechanics of the scene were simple and controlled, thus undistracting to them.

But of the sources of Brando's greatness in this movie, no one present at the creation has spoken, even speculatively. It may be that Brando saw in Terry Malloy's coming to awareness of his power to do right an analogy to his own coming to awareness of the power of his gift. After all, they were both raw kids who were lucky enough, each in his way, to find tutelege, and direction, at a point when many had given up on them. One may also speculate that now, in his sixth movie, he had fully absorbed the screen actor's craft, was free of constraining insecurity as he had not been before. Possibly, too, the experience of working for the first time in a movie in New York, back among his own kind, with actors and craftsmen who were part of the tradition that had formed him, may have had a liberating effect on him. But none of that quite solves the mystery.

All one can certainly say is that *On the Waterfront* represents a kind of apotheosis for the American theatrical tradition to which its leading creators owed allegiance, a consummation they had long awaited. For it represents the first entirely successful and thoroughly embraced translation to film of The Group Theater's aesthetic to the screen: the presentation of 'real' (i.e. working-class) people within an authentic representation of their milieu in a narrative that requires them to come to grips, whether they know it or not, with abstract social and political ideas which quite definitely engage and concern the audience.

And just as its theorists had long since proposed, it was the acting manner that The Group had propagated which both assured the illusion of reality and, at the same time, permitted it to transcend the particulars it was dealing with, granted its characters a humanity, a universality, if you

91

will, that to this day remains recognizable and emotionally riveting.

'Gadge', whom they had once somewhat patronized, but who had even before this become their most successful, therefore somewhat resented, envoy to the larger world, had done it. And he had done it employing the young actor whom another apostate, Stella Adler, had found and tutored, but whom they now had no choice but to see as their champion. There was irony enough in that. But that was only the beginning. What must have been more deeply galling was the fact that *On the Waterfront*'s political subtext was anathema to many of the old Group soldiers and to their newer recruits as well. Worse, it was precisely because the Stanislavskian ideals of performance were so perfectly realized by a company that contained representatives of their oldest – and youngest, as well as in-between – generations that this subtext was rendered palatable. By the end of *On the Waterfront* one really didn't give a damn what the film was saying. One took it to heart in a way that one never could the more crudely rendered stories about people accommodating themselves to respectable, indeed, conservative moralities in other Fifties movies.

For *On the Waterfront* was more than an unrestrained critical and commercial triumph. It became the occasion on which the show business establishment at last extended full-scale acknowledgement of the ethic and the aesthetic of its former opposition. The picture won three of the four prizes offered by the New York Film Critics and went on to win seven Academy Awards, among them best picture, best actor, best supporting actress, best screenplay. Brando, on the Oscar telecast, allowed himself some awkward horseplay with Bob Hope, and afterwards he is said to have bestowed a kiss on Louella Parsons (formerly known to him as 'the fat one', to separate her from that other aging representative of all that he justifiably loathed about Hollywood, Hedda Hopper, who was 'the one in the hat'). His acceptance speech was all a Middlewestern parent could hope for, brief and modest: 'This is a wonderful moment, and a rare one – and I'm certainly grateful.'

It was also, perhaps, the moment of maximum power both for Brando and the tradition he exemplified. What remained of opposition to the Stanislavskian ideal was not perhaps swept away away, but henceforth it would be on the defensive. From this moment on actors and serious observers of the theatrical enterprise in this country have had no choice but to define performance and the judgement of performance, within the terms of the fractious, often schismatic movement that had developed around the Russian's theories.

But, as a modern philosopher has observed, 'The moment of maximum power is the moment of maximum danger.' For if the performances contained in the film assured the ascendency of an acting style, the film itself did not predict a further development of the realistic trend which had been the most interesting and promising development in post-war American film, a true expansion of its range. Quite the opposite: it would soon become painfully clear that *On the Waterfront* represented a one-off culmination for that style of movie-making, at least as far as the mainstream producers were concerned. No one attempted to imitate its manner, build on its success. In other words, Brando – and all the actors who were already beginning to crawl out from under his overcoat – would be, for the remainder of this decade and much of the next (until the arrival of younger directors like Martin Scorsese), largely bereft of the stylistic context their approach to their art, their manner, required. They would become characters in search of *auteurs* who did not exist, or could not function consistently, in the movie world as it was now being reconstituted. And Marlon Brando, as the leader of that school, would feel the impact of the movie industry's fear and cautiousness in the later 1950s first. And hardest.

AGE OF ANXIETY

D arryl Zanuck's final rejection of *On the Waterfront* was only partially based on its lack of glamor. At least as important to him was the project's unsuitability to Cinemascope. Zanuck deemed the anamorphic lens largely responsible for the vast commercial success of *The Robe* in 1953, and announced that henceforth all Twentieth Century-Fox productions would be filmed in color in the new wide-screen process. For a time he had been willing to make an exception for *Waterfront*, but then thought better of it. In his final discussion with Kazan and Schulberg he became almost lyrical in his hopes for a new Cinemascope venture, *Prince Valiant*, to be based on the comic strip. His auditors were outraged.

They didn't know the half of it. For Zanuck's decision affected more than their hopes for *On the Waterfront*, more than the immediate future of Fox. It signalled a major shift in the entire industry's course. Clearly, it would have consequences, both direct and indirect, for Marlon Brando's future as an actor.

Zanuck was not acting whimsically. He was responding (by his lights responsibly) to a crisis the outlines of which can be perceived in a set of dismal statistics. Between 1945 and 1948, ninety million Americans had gone to the movies every week. By 1950, just two years after network television had established itself, attendance was cut by one-third. By 1953, the year Zanuck decreed his all-Cinemascope policy, attendance had dropped to forty-six million. In a matter of five years then, the audience for movies was virtually halved (its downward trend would continue until the mid Sixties, when it would start to stabilize at around 20 million per week). Gross revenues, buoyed by higher ticket prices, would not take such a severe beating, but profits would; by the mid Fifties they would be only about a quarter of what they had been right after the war. By the end of the decade the number of movies produced in the US was also halved. Considering that all this took place against a background of glowing prosperity everywhere else in America, this was more than a disaster. It was the beginning of a major and irreversible shift in the way most citizens passed their leisure time.

Hollywood's problems included more than a severe loss of customers. In their 1948 settlement of the famous anti-trust suit brought against them by the federal government, the studios agreed to divest themselves of their theatre chains, leaving them bereft of a very substantial and stabilizing cash flow. Losses of revenue abroad, where the importation of films and the exportation of profits therefrom were restricted by nations struggling with the problems of postwar recovery, also took their toll.

There was a hidden issue, too – age. The men who had created Hollywood's ruling oligopoly – the Mayers and Cohns and Warners – no longer had the energy and flexibility of youth. They were settled and defensive, unable and unwilling to adapt to new challenges. By the early Sixties most of them would be either dead or deposed, and their successors were not exactly visionaries. What was true of the moguls was also true of their most valuable assets, for the first generation of talking picture stars were also aging, thus less and less plausible (and compelling) as romantic figures. Some of them, too, would be gone by the early Sixties – Bogart, Cooper and Gable among them.

In this context, Zanuck's idea of relying on wide-screen spectacle made superficial sense, and soon enough all his competitors adopted some variant on it as well. For television in those days was studio bound and rather tatty-looking, so it was not unreasonable to imagine that spectacle, which TV had neither the technical capacity for nor the money to mount, might prove to be effective counter-programming – especially since Cinemascope, among other wide-screen processes, offered the means to give it (quite literally) new dimensions.

This strategy had its occasional successes. In the late Fifties and early Sixties a few big screen spectaculars (*The Ten Commandments*, *The Bridge on the River Kwai*, *Ben-Hur*, *Lawrence of Arabia* among others) did become what we would now call 'events' – must-sees that from time to time reassembled the old mass audience for movies in something like its former numbers. But the more general truth is this: once the novelty of widescreen wore off, and production in color became the norm, the new, technologically dictated screen manner did not significantly arrest the industry's long-term decline.

What we must also say now – though surprisingly few people said it at the time – is that expanded imagery did not necessarily betoken expanded vision. Rather the opposite: both genre films and films that aspired to a more self-conscious artfulness or social relevance (precisely the kind of movies in which Brando had been working) were harmed by the new technologies. Both kinds of films seemed to rattle around within the new aspect ratios, less forcefully shot, less energetically edited, than they had been. As Fritz Lang is supposed to have said, Cinemascope was good for shooting snakes and funerals and not much else.

You can't blame everything that went aesthetically wrong with the movies on Cinemascope. Technological constraints were reinforced by the emotional and intellectual constraints of what is perhaps the most cautious period in the America's 20th Century social history. Economic depression had been banished, the Second World War was a rapidly receding memory (and for most Americans a not entirely unhappy one). The world, despite The Bomb and The Red Menace, was for 'The Lonely Crowd' (to borrow the book title that became a catchphrase of social criticism in the fifties) a demonstrably better place than it had been. In this decade an air of certitude – perhaps one ought to say a pall of certitude; oh, all right, call it smugness – settled comfortably over the social and economic center of America. For in the largest material sense things finally seemed to be working out very comfortably for the American middle class. So its prissy sensibility, its joyless cultural, intellectual and moral pretentions, often previously the source of satire for the movies, was finally having its un-obstructed way with them.

This social climate discouraged principled confrontation everywhere in our public lives, and encouraged psychologically-based 'understanding' and amelioration in our private lives. Everywhere the wisdom and the benignity of large institutions, public and private, was stressed. Everyone talked about how class issues were disappearing (the nation was on its way to being a one-class – ie, middleclass society) and how conservatism was becoming more liberal, liberalism more conservative. Put it this way: the great wet blanket of prosperity had descended on America and in the best of circumstances (which, as we have seen, Hollywood was not enjoying) the movies would have found it difficult to avoid being smothered under it.

Comedy lost its quick, thrusting satirical edge to the ponderousness of the wide screen's rhythms, and it lost, as well, its romantic flair, because a slight liberalization of screen censorship now permitted giggly, squirmy sexual innuendo of a particularly vacuuous sort. Melodrama, too, lost the sometimes crazed sexual heat that repression had imposed on it while the great innovation of the 1940s, *film noir*, the glorious style of which naturally depended on black and white cinematography, virtually dis-appeared. So did the realistic air that directors as diverse as Kazan and Billy Wilder had imparted to a wide range of topics when they had taken their cameras, loaded with black and white film, into all kinds of streets, all over America.

Let me be specific. Here's a short-list of good American dramatic movies, 1945-55, randomly recalled; *Out of the Past, White Heat, All the King's Men, Sunset Boulevard, All About Eve, In a Lonely Place, High Noon, Ace in the Hole, From Here to Eternity, The Big Heat*, and, of course, *On the Waterfront*. Some of them have their roots in traditional American genres, some are based on popular literature, some are without any real precedent in film history. But all support this observation: that the visual style of the most interesting late Forties and early Fifties movies reflected (and reinforced) a certain tough-mindedness, not to say cynicism, about the American reality. This was perhaps a reaction against the sentimentalization of the common man and the common good during the war years and possibly an acknowledgement that vernacular movie making could encompass more than it had in the way of sharply observed human (and class) behavior as well as expand the form's melodramatic possibilities beyond its previous limits.

If all of these movies were in some way cautionary, none of them was cautious. Like the best pictures of the thirties (which, on the whole, were more comic and romantic in tone) they were anti- (or at least non-) bourgeoise in their attitudes, and they were energized by their own feeling, adventurousness, their makers' sense that they were doing something that had not been done before. And then, suddenly, at some point in the mid Fifties, they were no more. Perhaps one might want to mention *Invasion of the Body Snatchers* and *The Sweet Smell of Success* (1956 and 57 respectively) as movies that matched their predecessors in the sharpness with which they attacked their subjects, worked their metaphors, and continue to reward us when we look back at them. But still a generalization that must be insisted upon is that after 1955 American movies grew fat and soft, lost wit, style and èlan. The characteristic movie of the latter Fifties and early Sixties was something inspirational and elephantine, a Biblical spectacle or perhaps a lunky adaptation of some Broadway hit or recent bestseller.

It is curious, the lack of contemporary comment on the dulling effect that economic crisis, technological change and social and political conservatism had on film style and content. Only a few critical cranks like Manny Farber, writing in the more obscure film journals, noticed that, to borrow his phrase, 'movies aren't movies anymore.' Partly this was because genre film making did not, at that time, attract the critical and academic loyalties it now does. Reviewers were so used to beating up on Hollywood for its lack of conventional cultural and literary ambition that, despite the painfully obvious change in the way movies looked (an argument could be made that the shift to widescreen production had an impact every bit as forceful as the shift from silent to sound production), it was not generally perceived by mainstream critics. Or by the rest of us to be perfectly honest.

All concerned were caught up as we always are, in the flow of production, the flow of events, unable to pull ourselves up on the bank of the river and get a view of where the rushing current may be carrying us. This was (and is) true of both the people who make movies and those who go to them. The former, if they are production executives, are preoccupied with reading the market place, or, if they are engaged in the exacting business of creating a particular picture, soon lose any large perspective of it, so absorbing are the details of the task. As for the audience, we are mostly there for the story, hoping for disengagement from our reality, but not necessarily for profound engagement in another reality, especially if it includes grappling with difficult aesthetic issues.

I don't mean to imply by these remarks that those of us who constituted what remained of the reliably loyal movie audience (we were essentially the yuppies of the time, although, of course, that term had not yet been invented) bought the slogan 'Movies Are Better Than Ever' with which the industry was promoting itself. If anything we tended to mutter the phrase satirically as we brushed the fragments of the latest bomb out of our minds. But I don't want to suggest, either, that we recognized what was generally true, that American movies were actually *worse* than ever, enduring their most dismal historical passage.

We had many excuses for our lack of vision. Take me for example. I was awfully busy back then. I had graduated from high school in 1951. I had graduated from college, moved to New York and got my first jobs on magazines in the middle of the decade, at just about the time the movies ceased to be the movies as Manny Farber and his generation had known them. By the end of the decade, after trying psychiatry and writing fiction, I was helping to start a new magazine. None of these ventures were particularly successful, except as graduate education, but in the month Kennedy was elected President my first book was published, and a month later I was engaged to be married.

It was very preoccupying – this business of starting out in life – especially since I was an ambitious young man, determined to make my mark (or marks, since I wanted to be a writer) in the world. It didn't leave much time for critical observation – of society or the movies. One lived busily in the former, and went habitually to the latter of course, but not very alertly.

In other words, in those years I stood in relationship to the movies as

98

most adult Americans did (and do) – distractedly. I was moving out of the impressionable years, that period roughly between the ages of ten and twenty when certain movies stamp our memory so indelibly that it is fair to say that we internalize them as fully as we do first love, first triumphs, first humiliations, and find it difficult ever to return to these rite-of-passage films with any critical objectivity. But I was also a decade (more or less) away from professional involvement with the movies and so was under no compulsion to pass elaborate judgements on what I saw. Nor was I consciously preparing myself for what turned out to be my future career; it never occurred to me that I would end up reviewing movies or writing books or making documentary films about them. I was a dispassionate civilian, someone who had fallen into the habit of going to the movies once a week when I was a kid, allowed it to become a two-or-three-times-a-week habit in college, and saw no reason to kick it when I moved to New York, where, at first, I had few friends, no television set and many an idle evening at my disposal.

Like everyone else, especially those everyone elses who also read the up-scale, liberal-minded press, I had my gripes with the movies – mostly over their false and unfulfilled promises. But essentially my relationship was an affectionate one. That was true, I think of most people who were roughly my age, and it's easy to explain. We were, as moviegoers, entirely the products of Hollywood's golden age. We had no memory of silent film (they seemed impossibly primitive to us), which set us apart from our parents, and we had no memory of a world in which there was no such thing as movies, which set us apart from our grandparents. In other words, there was almost no wariness, no suspicion, in our attitudes toward movies as we had come upon them as children. Sound films, with all their conventions and 'codes' were one of the gifts of our lives. We were grateful for the many vicarious pleasures – romantic, heroic, comic – the movies had previously provided for us, and for all the valuable misinformation they had cheerily heaped upon us. It was far more attractively put, and perhaps on the whole more morally inspiring, than the misinformation regularly supplied by our other great sources of that commodity politics, religion, journalism.

So habit and affection conspired to render us critically passive before the increasingly larger screens of the Fifties. So did anxiety. For the industry's troubles were a large and continuing story in the press, which in this period took to treating it as an ailing patient, taking its temperature, reading its pulse, asking it how it felt this morning. And that encouraged the rest of us to follow suit. One read reviews and evaluated the experience of a film with this novel concern somewhere in mind – and perhaps with a larger tolerance for the flailings and failings of a chronically ill, but very game, friend.

Finally, some of us, a minority within a minority, had borne in on us, with the force of revelation, the news that the movies, this expressive form that, all childhood long, we had been told was a waste of time, perhaps even dangerous to our health ('Why do you want to sit in a movie on a nice day like this?'), was actually an art. An art as worthy of our serious attention as any other. An art whose time had finally come.

A few people had known this since the days of D. W. Griffith, but now, finally, they had acquired enough converts to achieve critical mass. Put it down as one of the unintended consequences of post-war mass higher education. Or, if you will, attribute it to the ending of cultural isolationism in the wake of political isolationism's demise. In any case it was suddenly, conveniently possible to see stirring examples of film-making traditions quite different from the American one. Between the mid Forties and the mid Fifties, while some 4,000 theaters showing American features shut their doors, some 500 'art' houses – a tenfold increase – opened.

These theaters, few though they were in number, had an outsized historical influence. As early as the post-war Forties many of us began to learn a new set of lessons from the Ealing comedies no less than the Italian Neo-Realism they programmed; from Carl Dreyer and from Devid Lean; from *Children of Paradise* and *The Red Shoes*; from everything they showed us that spoke to us in a different language, by which I mean not so much a foreign tongue, but a different imagistic and psychological language. These were lessons that would be enlarged upon throughout the Fifties, by The New Wave and the Japanese cinema, by Bergman and Fellini, by *Rififi* as well as by *Pather Pachelli*. Ultimately these theaters permanently expanded the cinematic expectations and the responsive range of the most influential segment of the movie audience – sometimes comically so, but mostly inspirationally so.

In our innocence a lot of us believed that, given its present destabilized state, and its need to find new directions, it might be possible for a film artist to function in Hollywood in something like the manner he or she did elsewhere in the civilized world. We may not yet have heard of the *auteur* theory, but something like its promise was vaguely stirring in our minds as we contemplated current, possibly pre-revolutionary conditions in Hollywood, which as such conditions always do, stirred hope in equal measure with anxiety.

I don't want to project our attitudes on to a figure who was as wary as

Brando surely was in those days. But given the films he had completed prior to 1954 – all of them filmed in black-and-white in the traditional aspect ratio, all of them made by men whose spirit was not mainstream Hollywood, all of them in one way or another examples of the better nature of late Forties, early Fifties American film-making – Brando had every reason to suppose that he could continue as he had: dropping in on the industry every year or so to do something at least potentially gratifying, something he (and his followers) could justify his presence in, no matter how it finally turned out. He did not see that, with fewer pictures being made more was staked on the economic performance of each individual movie, making production executives increasingly cautious, more desperate to hedge the large bet each of them represented. And he could not discern that the kind of film-making he had done was in the process of disappearing (at least for the moment; it would reappear after roughly a decade). Certainly he did not realize that his own stardom, sealed by the success of *Waterfront*, was in itself limiting, preventing him from taking the chances that a younger (and, yes, this must be said, less greedy and more vocationally committed) actor might have taken. Finally, he could not possibly have seen that new controversy in which he found himself embroiled was predictive of things to come.

But it was. And here Darryl Zanuck took a direct, rather than an indirect role in determining Brando's fate. As of 1954, the actor owed Fox a picture, and Zanuck was adamant that Brando report to work in the one the studio, in its wisdom, had chosen for him. This obligation was essentially an accidental one, an add-on to Brando's old *Viva Zapata* contract. (Remember that Zanuck had not really wanted him for that picture, and this call on his future services had been one of the things that had induced the producer to agree to Brando's casting). At the time Brando had been reluctant to sign away even such a relatively small piece of his autonomy, but it seems the ever-practical Kazan prevailed on him to do so. After all, Fox had never asked Kazan to make anything but seriously intended films, and he could not imagine Zanuck making an untoward imposition on an actor like Brando.

Kazan reckoned without Hollywood's mid Fifties crisis. That is to say, he reckoned without enterprises like *The Egyptian*, which was based on a best selling historical novel and suited the new dispensation perfectly, both because of its source (Hollywood was then much taken with the fancy that adaptations of commercially successful fiction lured a 'pre-sold' audience into theatres) and its subject matter (it held possibilities for exotic spectacle and spiritual uplift). Brando – not unreasonably – thought it was tosh. But he left New York for Hollywood just days after completing *Waterfront* for costume fittings and rehearsals, determined to fulfill his obligation as painlessly as possible. Then, suddenly, he decamped for New York. It seems likely that the ferociously demanding Michael Curtiz, a crude man but often an effective director (*Casablanca* and *Mildred Pierce* are among his estimated 178 titles), scared Brando off. Putting it mildly, he was not a man known for his ability to communicate with actors about the nuances of their performances. It is also said that Brando detested the prospect of acting with Zanuck's current 'protégée', Bella Darvi (whose screen name combined the first three letters of Zanuck's given name with the first two letters of that of his long-suffering wife, Virginia). Fox sued for $2 million, claiming that was the sum it would lose on pre-production costs if Brando continued to renege on his contract.

While this wrangle proceeded, Brando was suddenly presented with an authentic crisis. His mother, while visiting her sister in Los Angeles, had collapsed, desperately and, as it turned out, terminally ill, apparently from the accumulated effects of her alcoholism. He returned to Los Angeles to be with Dodie during her final illness, which she bore with great gallantry (Brando would later tell friends that she had taught him how to die).

Stella Adler thought he took his mother's death very well – 'There was no falling to pieces, he was strong and controlled when it happened' – but she also predicted, correctly, that the death of this 'heavenly, girlish, lost creature' would change her son. 'She was the symbol of many important things – her passion for purity, her attitude toward animals, earth and music . . .' In this, Adler was correct. There was, now, a new cynicism in his comments about routine movie work and, as we will have occasion to observe, an upsurge in his commitment to good causes outside the realm of his art.

It must be said, however, that other factors contributed to the restlessness and lack of focus he began to demonstrate during this passage. By this time Marlon Sr had become something more than the man who handled his allowance. He was a full-scale business manager, whose chief investment on his son's behalf was a cattle ranch in Nebraska. It was a constant drain on his resources and a constant strain on his relationship with his father, which, though outwardly pleasant, was never to be resolved in affection. Finally, there were romantic problems. While he was making *Viva Zapata* he had met the Mexican actress, Movita (Castenada), who had played – curious irony here, considering subsequent events – Clark Gable's Tahitian love interest in the first *Mutiny on the Bounty*. They had been keeping more or less steady company ever since, though that term is, putting it mildly, a relative one where Brando is concerned. The number of women with whom he was linked in these days is quite uncountable. Apparently, though, while he was shooting *Waterfront* she began insisting on marriage. This occasioned a breakup that was very troubling to Brando, who had obviously found in the older woman – she was nine years his senior – some sort of stabilizing influence. Now, though, he was involved with a much younger woman, Josanne-Mariana Berenger, a nineteen-year-old French model whom he met in New York and took back with him to Los Angeles. Eventually, much to the titillation of the press, they would announce their engagement, though they would never marry.

Clearly, there was much on his mind at this point, and he did not need the continued enmity of Darryl Zanuck. Nor did he need the expense of settling his dispute with him, so a compromise was arrived at. Brando was forced to commit to yet another future Fox film. In the meantime, *The Egyptian* would go ahead with Edmund Purdom. Yes, Edmund Purdom. And Brando would play Napoleon in *Desiree*. Yes, *Desiree*. The mind reels. Or at least does a little jig.

For one cannot quite understand what Zanuck was thinking of. He was often a bully, and he particularly liked giving outlanders little lessons in Hollywood power politics. He may well have been making sure Brando understood the mores of a community of which the production executive was one of the unquestioned grandees. (It is said that he gave Brando a lecture about being one of the troops, destined to go over the top when he was ordered to do so, whether he wanted to or not, which was obviously the wrong approach to their problem.)

On the other hand, Zanuck was rarely a fool. Indeed, he was, arguably, the shrewdest studio chief in town, the man who, in the 1930s, had established the tough, urbane and profitable Warner Brothers style; had subsequently merged his own Twentieth Century Pictures with Fox, rescuing the latter from bankruptcy with a schedule cleverly blending sentiment, nostalgia and social conscience; had, after the war, placed in production many of the era's more sharply realized commentaries on contemporary life and issues. He was not a man who would, in normal circumstances, waste an asset like this – the services of a hot young star – on something as inappropriate as *Desiree*. One has to believe he was operating out of panic, determined to impose his color-cum-Cinemascope strategy at any cost.

Desiree, too, was an adaptation of a best-selling historical novel, its eponymous heroine (Jean Simmons) being a young woman who meets and falls in love with Napoleon when he is a young officer, and whose sister marries his brother, Joseph. Desiree moons about after him for the rest of

103

the movie, even entering into a loveless marriage with an agreeable and civilized brother officer and, latterly, courtier, General Bernadotte (Michael Rennie), in order to stay close to Napoleon. Occasionally Napoleon returns her interest in the rather distant and diffident manner Brando affects in the role. Ultimately it is Desiree who persuades him to make his final surrender, and accept exile.

It is a ludicrous film, entirely characteristic of the kind of big, slow-moving machines that were beginning to lumber across the movie landscape. Moreover, Brando was for the first time directed by one of those stolid professionals who have ever been the backbone of Hollywood mediocrity. Henry Koster was no Curtiz in manner. A civilized, gently spoken émigré, he had directed Deanna Durbin; he had directed numberless mild and sentimental little comedies; for some reason he had directed *The Robe*. *Desiree* was his reward for his success with the previous picture, which, unfazed by whatever problems the new technology presented, he brought in on budget. As it turned out, he was something of an amateur Napoleon scholar, too, though Zanuck had not known that prior to giving him the assignment.

Brando was agreeable enough with Koster and the rest of the company when work was not at issue. And there were no temperamental outbursts, no signs of overt rebelliousness. His mood was, rather, devilish – like that of a high school kid enduring study hall and cutting up just enough to make his impatience known, but not so much that more time would be tacked on his sentence. An anecdote seems to characterize his spirit. It finds Brando staring soulfully, unspeaking, into a fountain on one of the sets. What is it? What's the matter? Koster inquires. Silence. Entreaties. More silence. Until, finally, the actor confesses he is wishing for something. What? the director asks, eager to get his star back on his feet and his shot made. 'I wish this fountain were full of chocolate ice cream soda,' comes the sober reply. Why. Long pause. 'Because I like chocolate ice cream sodas.' Another pause. And a general bust-up.

The camera got nothing so amusing from Brando. Kindly, one might suggest that he seems to have modeled his performance on one of those solid English character actors who had often been found in Hollywood historical epics over the years. He is crisply spoken, technically unimpeachable and utterly absent emotionally. Cedric Hardwicke or Claude Rains could not have taken the money and run more professionally. Unkindly, one might propose that Brando merely sulked his way through the role, staying just this side of legally actionable insubordination. But, for whatever reasons, this is perhaps the least fiery Napoleon in screen history; he has about him more the air of an absent-minded scholar than an imperial conqueror. 'I had an idea about how Napoleon should be played,' Koster later recalled. 'As a real extrovert, as a loud-mouthed dictator . . . no subtlety about him.' The latter quality should come out in him, he felt, only when his aim was romantic, not worldly, conquest. He met endlessly with Brando off the set, argued patiently. And got nowhere. Koster assumed that Brando was simply too 'introverted' to play the role – and it certainly seems that Brando stressed the 'shy' side of his nature in his dealings with the director.

Sometime later, Koster happened to see the picture in Germany and discovered that the actor who had dubbed Brando's voice for that version of the picture 'had spoken powerfully, and the Napoleon was sort of better than the one Brando had originally created.' It is possible, of course, that a more abrasive director, someone like Curtiz, might have jarred the actor to life.

Koster was the first director Brando had encountered who was settled in the ways of Hollywood, unquestioning of its routines and unquesting about trying to exceed the apparent limits of a project. Zinnemann, Kazan, Mankiewicz, even Laslo Benedek, were men of higher gift and spirit. So Koster was the first, but by no means the last, director to be tested and to a degree victimized by Brando's need to define their relationship. It must be understood that almost all stars make these tests, that a power struggle is almost always inherent in the actor-director collaboration, for a movie company is a sort of temporary family, with the director as father figure, the performers his fractious children. Brando could not tolerate menacing reserve – anything that smacked of own father's style. On the other hand, heedless hackery and easy amiability were also anathema to him.

Kazan unquestionably knew best how to deal with him. In manner, he was more sympathetic elder brother than father, a collaborator who was neither a dictator nor a patsy. Everything that Brando is, Kazan has said, 'is available to a director – if he agrees with you.' The director's job is to engineer that consent, by carefully psyching out the actor, determining, often through indirect means, where he is coming from, where he thinks he is going. Above all – and this applies to all seriously trained modern American actors, not just to Brando – he must listen and listen and listen to the actor's interpretive ideas, take them seriously, incorporate what he can of them into the film; otherwise the actor's careful psychological preparation, from which he derives his sense of professional identity, is rendered meaningless.

Deep in his heart the director may regard this as nonsensical, a waste of time, even an infringement of his own authorial prerogatives, but he had better create the impression that he is playing along. Now, of course, decades of experience have taught directors this trick of their trade. But in the Fifties and Sixties it was a new one, and many of them were old dogs; they had trouble with it. And with Brando. Nevertheless, as we will have reason to observe time and again, the men who later worked with him most happily – Arthur Penn, Francis Coppola, Bernardo Bertolucci – all mastered it. The others have endured much misery at his hands, and have brought out the worst in him – the kind of behavior that would eventually make studios shy away from him as a trouble-maker, give him a not entirely justified (or for that matter unjustified) reputation as an actor who endangers schedules and budgets.

For the moment, however, no great harm was done, either to *Desiree* or Brando's reputation. Its critical reception was predictably patronizing, though *Desiree* actually outgrossed *On the Waterfront*. And, by and large, everyone forgave Brando; we all understood that there were things that actors in Hollywood had to do, for mysterious reasons to which none of us were privy. If anyone was unforgiving of Brando it was Brando himself. For, in interviews about the movie, that note which would soon become characteristic when he discussed movies made under conditions that offended him – a note of defensive cynicism – crept into his conversations for the first time:

'Most of the time I just let the make-up play the part.' And: 'Movies, to me, are a way of making a living. Any satisfaction one gets beyond that is gratis.' And: 'The successful actor in Hollywood is not the actor who is . . . interested in good parts. He is interested in two or three good cowboy pictures a year.' And: 'I don't mean to say . . . that I'm not interested in making a good living. It's all right to be impecunious in Bora-Bora [interesting choice of words, considering later developments]. But to be impecunious here in Hollywood is damn near criminal.' And so on. More – much more – would follow over the years.

From afar, Stella Adler commented: 'Marlon was discovered as a personality before he discovered himself as an actor.' To which one might add: he was discovered as a personality before he had a personality, that is to say, a firm sense of his own identity. The muddled boy, that curious combination of the hard and the yielding, who had come to New York in search of himself only a decade earlier, had not resolved any of his primal conflicts. They had merely been subsumed by the agreeable persona of the aspiring actor – earnest, idealistic, embracing poverty as he purely pursued his art. It had served him quite well for a time; it was both good copy and a sufficient explanation for his behavioral oddities as he rose to fame.

But the usefulness of that persona in sustaining him as a star of the magnitude that he had now become was obviously limited. For one thing, it defied the logic of his new fame and (as it seemed to the press, if not to him) his growing prosperity. Evidence of the fact that he was beginning to understand that himself surfaced even before the *Desiree* mess, on his summer stock tour in *Arms and the Man* in 1953. He had recruited for it a company of his old theater pals (among them William Redfield), most of them serious players, eager to do the best possible work under the circumstances. Brando, however, quickly discovered that, so far as audiences were concerned, he was no different from other stars out in 'packages', picking up the small change of celebrity, and he behaved accordingly. Redfield recalled that he was good perhaps once or twice a week, when something in the performance or the audience rubbed him the wrong way and got his juices flowing. The presence of a celebrity of his own stature in the house was also stimulating to him. But most of his performances were, at best, erratic. When Redfield took him to task for his lack of discipline, Brando replied: 'Man, don't you get it? This is *summer stock*.'

From that point it was but a short step to the realization that movies were just . . . well *movies* – vehicles that paraded performers past larger and yet more uncomprehending audiences, audiences equally incapable of making careful observations, fine distinctions, about what they saw. To oversimplify slightly, his pattern was this: the actor – not the star – would accept a role that seemed to offer him certain opportunities to try something new, extend his range; then, in the usual way of movie-making, the promise of the part would be vitiated, to a greater or lesser degree, by the process of putting it on the screen; whereupon the actor, his own most severe (if not always precise) critic, would sulkily withdraw his emotional commitment to the part, sometimes in mid-performance, sometimes as the picture came to the screen, sometimes afterward, when he would be at pains to agree with his critics.

In time, of course, all his old, pre-Hollywood suspicions about the possibilities of doing anything worthwhile in the movies, now reinforced by what he saw as embittering experience, would surface, along with many a dismal comment about the childishness and social inutility of acting as a profession. His defenses eventually came down to these; a man has to make a living somehow, and sometimes, however inept it is as art, a movie can do some good in the world. In other words, the not entirely misplaced bleatings first heard at the time of *Desiree* would grow louder and more commonplace as the years wore on. It should be added that much of the reviewing that greeted his work from this point on in his career did him no favors, perhaps precisely because it arose from the same source as his self-criticism, which was unreasonably heightened expectations of him.

Guys and Dolls, the film he went into very quickly after *Desiree* wrapped, provides an excellent case in point. He was probably charmed into taking a job in the movie adaptation of Frank Loesser's truly wonderful Broadway musical by this ingratiating telegram from Joe Mankiewicz, who had, after all, seen him through another anxious reach: 'UNDERSTAND YOU'RE APPREHENSIVE BECAUSE YOU'VE NEVER DONE MUSICAL COMEDY. YOU HAVE NOTHING REPEAT NOTHING TO WORRY ABOUT. BECAUSE NEITHER HAVE I. LOVE, JOE.'

Brando would later be quoted as saying that producer Samuel Goldwyn's offer came at a moment when, understandably, he wanted 'to do something in a lighter color.' He also confessed that he was scared of attempting to sing anywhere outside the shower, but then added, unexceptionably, 'I think its part of an actor's job to do new things.' Very reasonable, very sensible.

And aside from a certain tension between Frank Sinatra, who played Nathan Detroit, proprietor of New York's 'oldest established permanent floating crap game', and Brando, playing that highest-rolling gambler, Sky Masterson, production went smoothly. The singer was still aggrieved by the fact that he had lost the *Waterfront* role to Brando, and since he was notoriously an actor who was best on the first take while Brando still needed his several groping, mumbling read-throughs, there was an explosion after their one long scene together, in which Detroit is required to consume a slice of cheesecake while attempting to con Sky into a sucker bet. At the end of a day of many takes, Sinatra cried: 'These fucking New York actors – how much cake do you think I can eat?' For his part, Brando was dubious about Sinatra's choices as an actor. Too romantic, he thought, too ingratiating, not enough toughness and street smarts. At one point he urged Mankiewicz to speak to Sinatra on this matter. 'You first,' said Mankiewicz. Or words to that effect. Brando, it is said, lost some of his regard for the director because of this refusal. Still, he and Sinatra worked in parallel sub-plots, which rarely merged, so their animosity did not often affect the production.

But Brando was right about his co-star's work, and so was Stephen Sondheim – no less – when he came to review the picture for an obscure and sober-sided film journal. 'Sinatra's lackadaisacal performance,' he wrote, 'his careless and left-handed attempt at characterization, not only harm the

picture immeasurably, but indicate an alarming lack of professionalism.'
He also got at the other major flaw of the production, its design, which was
the work of the very distinguished Broadway designer – and very inexperienced Hollywood designer – Oliver Smith. 'Samuel Goldwyn, Joseph
Mankiewicz and Mr Smith apparently couldn't make up their minds
whether the scenery should be realistic or stylized. As a result they have
the disadvantages of both.' There is a bit more to it than that. For its basic
Broadway set an obviously painted backcloth is used, very like one that
might be used for a theatrical presentation, but very jarring on the screen.
Worse, the practical sets in front of it – the street itself, various interiors –
are at once (and paradoxically) cramped and underpopulated. They are
flatly over-lit and, in the Goldwyn manner, far too neat and clean (the fastidious producer hated dirt, and this was not the first urban drama he had
tidied up too much). On the whole, the picture lacks the raucous energy of
its source. Cautious when it should cut loose, prim when it should be jazzy,
it lacks the bustle and jostle that any portrayal of urban lowlife, however
stylized, must have.

But Brando is marvelous in what is probably his most underrated performance this side of *Mutiny on the Bounty*. It is Sky's function, in the
scheme of the story, to seduce Miss Sarah (Jean Simmons), leader of the
Salvation Army-like 'Save-A-Soul' mission (he has a bet with Nathan that
he cannot get her to accompany him to Cuba), and Brando plays the gambler with great delicacy. There is just the slightest roughness to his tone,
but he enunciates with the thoughtful precision of a man who needs to
think about the niceties of grammar and pronounciation. His movements
and gestures also have the studied grace of a man learning to mind his manners. There is something touching about him, and precisely because there
is nothing studdish about him we can see why that genteel lass might take
him to heart. In other words, he makes an essentially unbelievable relationship believable. He is more than a diamond in the rough; he is a
diamond in the midst of a self-polishing process.

His dancing is minimal, more a question of choreographed movement
than sets of combinations; but his singing, much criticized at the time, is a
revelation. His voice is light, but true, and in fact reminds one of those
other splendid non-singing singers, Fred Astaire and Gene Kelly – making
up for its lack of theatrical resonance with its authenticity of feeling. It is
movie singing, not stage singing, and the more effective for being so. The
same is true of Simmons (she and Brando had taken a liking to each other
on *Desiree*, and they had fun together). Sondheim said it nicely: 'Both
could give lessons to most of the more polished voices in Hollywood on

how to *act* a lyric.' Indeed, Brando's 'Luck Be A Lady' number, in which he bets $1,000 apiece for the 'souls' of the entire Broadway gambling fraternity (if they lose they have to report to Miss Sarah's mission and participate in a revival meeting, thus redeeming the pledge he made to her in order to lure her to Cuba), is the only production number in the show with something like the vitality and tension of the stage production.

Despite its decidedly mixed critical reception, *Guys and Dolls* grossed some $9 million on its initial release, and was the top moneymaker of 1956, its year of release. Here was further evidence, as far as the industry was concerned, that Brando might be, next to William Holden, then the beau ideal of middle-class masculine virtue, the most important male movie star, and perhaps Holden's necessary opposite.

He went next to what is surely the most appalling movie he made in this decade, and one of the two or three worst pictures he ever made, *The Teahouse of the August Moon*. It is easy to see what attracted Hollywood to it: based on a popular novel by one Vern J. Sneider, in John Patrick's adaptation it had been a great Broadway success, and was thus another 'pre-sold' property. As for Brando, who campaigned for the role, it offered an agreeably liberal-minded, live-and-let-live message and the opportunity for radical off-casting. Hidden beneath a deep coating of make-up, speaking in a sometimes incomprehensible accent, he was Sakini, a comically sly Okinawan interpreter and handyman to the post-war American occupation forces. As David Wayne had done on the stage, Brando did a creditable job vocally (he got a Japanese friend to speak his lines into a tape recorder and then mimicked him), and with movement – there is a nice scuttle and scurry about him as he simultaneously obliges and subverts the soldiery, and their plan to bring western-style democracy to a venue not entirely appropriate to it. 'Okinawa very fortunate. Culture brought to us. Not have to leave home for it,' he says at one point, and that pretty well captures the vacuous flavor of the film.

The movie is full of that sort of pseudo-comic pseudo-wisdom, as Sakini takes in hand a bumbling Captain Frisbe (Glenn Ford), who has failed at all his previous assignments in military government, and helps turn his wayward and childish native charges – they are patronized unmercifully by the unwittingly racist script – into what a Pentagon plan wants them to be: incipient capitalists. Of course, this is accomplished by nefarious means: stills and a network bootlegging potato brandy are rigged up, and the institution of the title, a Geisha house, is set up. First the hopelessly square Frisbe embraces their free-spirited example. Then a dotty psychiatrist (Eddie Albert), and finally even the commanding officer, Colonel Purdy

(Paul Ford, in his patented, and usually enjoyable, specialty as a Babbity blowhard), are won over.

Hard to say which is more painful: Sakini's aphorisms ('Pain makes man think, thought makes man wise, wisdom makes life endurable'); the smarmy Fifties air of the piece, which holds that all problems are genially soluble, all differences (racial, cultural, social) minor since we are all fundamentally the same under our different-colored skins; or Daniel Mann's flat direction. Perhaps, finally, it is Glenn Ford's playing. He was a sort of second-string William Holden, often cast as a beset middle-class figure, but without Holden's incisiveness or capacity for dangerous anger. He was also a sort of fake method actor, muttering and mumbling, stumbling and stammering, as he mimed thoughtfulness. His was truly a manner without substance, though the critics were generally far easier on his fraudulent style than they were on Brando's authentic one.

Brando despised him – and Mann – and reverted, apparently, to flat affectlessness on the set, as he had on *Désirée*. In the end, his performance is hard to judge, partly because its context is so overwhelmingly banal. He is lively in the takes Mann finally printed, and as insinuating as he can be in the circumstances, but one is conscious only of technique. His Sakini is, ultimately, a kind of parlor trick, an impression of a foreigner, not a true performance as one. Needless to say, he got generally more favorable reviews of his work here than he had for *Guys and Dolls*, largely because most critics had nothing to compare it to, except, perhaps, other Oriental impersonations by western actors in, say, the Charlie Chan series. It was possibly better than those, but still overrated, because radical revisions of a precious star image, making yourself fatter, older, dumber, crazier or otherwise different from your usual self, always wow the impressionable; it is acting made visible instead of invisible, which is what the best acting nearly always is. It's a wonder Brando didn't win an Academy Award for Sakini – and no wonder at all that eventually he did win an Oscar for what was essentially the same trick (more subtly managed in quite a different context) in *The Godfather*.

Brando addressed the issue of race from the opposite perspective in *Sayonara*. It was based on a novel which the director Joshua Logan encouraged the endlessly decent-minded James A. Michener to write. (Logan had, of course, been the co-adapter and director of *South Pacific*, drawn from a book of Michener short stories.) He had in mind something that would help Americans appreciate Japan's traditional performing arts, which might serve as the basis for another musical. What Michener turned out was more a plea for racial tolerance, with special reference to the

111

American armed forces policy of discouraging marriage between the occupation forces and Japanese women and Japanese disapproval of such matches. Michener, who was himself married to a Japanese woman, crafted a story in which an American jet pilot, Lloyd Gruver (Brando), an ace in the Korean war, meets and falls in love with Hana-ogi (Miiko Taka, a Nisei, discovered in Los Angeles). She is a dancer in the Takarazuka Opera Company, an all-female music hall troupe, whose management assiduously promoted the idea that its members led a convent-like existence, denying themselves all congress with the opposite sex – especially the Occidental opposite sex – the better to devote themselves to their art. A parallel story, involving an enlisted man, Kelly (Red Buttons), living with a Japanese woman (Miyoshi Umeki) ends in tragedy – mutual suicide, because they are prevented from marriage and he is about to be shipped home (which was the informal method the military had devised for punishing interracial fraternization).

Trouble afflicted the company before it arrived in Japan, some of it arising from Brando's dissatisfaction with the script. He did extensive rewrites, most of which were not incorporated in its final version. Once in Japan, the situation deteriorated further. The Japanese entertainment conglomerate that had promised Logan permission to shoot with its No, Kabuki and Banruku puppet companies, suddenly insisted on renegotiating its deal. The Takarazuku people remained adamantly opposed to the project, and there was much criticism in the Japanese press, which feared that the Americans would travesty revered cultural institutions. The casting of Ricardo Montalban as a Kubuki star did nothing to reassure critics.

In the event, Logan was forced to recruit players from outside these institutions, and the Takarazuka Company become the fictional Mitsubayashi Company. As far as a westerner can judge, he treated Japanese theatrical traditions respectfully, though, of course, they function mainly to provide atmosphere, a touch of exotic spectacle, helping to justify the length of what turned out to be an interminable movie. Michener's original plot underwent one significant change, too. Instead of parting in the final reel (hence the title *Sayonara*) Gruver and Hana-ogi defy custom and marry, thus providing a happy, exemplary ending instead of a downbeat, but possibly more realistic one.

The film, as it was finally released, is pretty, bitter-sweet, 'moving' on some simple, tear-jerking level. Brando's performance, however, is remarkable. He insisted on supplying Gruver with a soft Southern accent, with the implication that the racial prejudices love encouraged him to overcome were profound. But what's best about his work is its curious blend of amiability and discomfort. His Gruver is, at heart, a good ole boy, eager to please and perhaps as surprised as anyone to discover that he is causing displeasure. But he is also a West Point graduate, his nature stiffened and stifled by discipline (Brando said he drew on some of his more gung-ho Shattuck classmates for aspects of his characterization), and Brando plays this conflict with great subtlety. When we meet him he is engaged to marry the daughter of an air force general. She is a nice, spirited girl, and her parents are comfortable, middle-class people, none of them visibly deserving of disapproval or even disappointed hopes. Brando's scenes with them are marvels of awkwardness, of eye contact avoided, of sentences swallowed half finished, as he strives not to hurt them unduly, yet to communicate his shift of heart. At one point, trying to explain what has happened to him, he picks up a throw pillow, studying it, picking at it as, haltingly, he attempts to say hard things in a soft voice. The scene is heartbreaking in its behavioral authenticity.

So are the scenes between him and the woman he insists on addressing with incorrect over-politeness as 'Miss Ogi'. He falls in love with her from afar, and wins her attention largely by sitting in a park and eyeing her longingly as she and her troupe trot back and forth between their dormitory and their theater. His struggle between discomfort and persistence is charmingly done. Somehow you believe that this modest (and protected) woman might, against *her* will, feel the force of *his* will, despite the distances separating them. When, at last, they get together, his innocent eagerness to learn, to enter her world, has both a boyish sweetness and a gentle masculine force. In other words, he surrenders standard American male attitudes – that guffawing resistance to otherness that particularly marks soldiers, athletes and others who derive their emotional sustenance from closed fraternities.

Unlike Kelly, however, he never attempts to embrace fully the customs of an alien culture. He retains the stance of a sympathetic observer, and he retains those aspects of his American maleness which are essential to his self-definition, which is, of course, why he avoids Kelly's tragic fate. His reaction when he discovers his friends' bodies – it was one of the several matters of debate between Brando and Logan, with the director in this case winning out – is a brilliant, and extremely effective, example of suppressed emotion, of throttled rage. It is of a piece with the long display of reasonableness that preceded it, in which he was seen patiently working through channels on behalf of their marriage, believing that common sense and common decency would win them their hearts' desire. (True to the developing spirit of his screen character, he does subsequently absorb one of his ritual beatings at the hands of a Japanese mob, outraged by the love-death of Kelly and Matsumi and looking for a foreigner to blame.) But given the tentative, compromising way he has played Gruver, there is just irony in this development, and, of course, it all helps give dramatic strength to his final break with convention, his marriage to 'Miss Ogi', which, because he is a war hero and she a theatrical star, receives media coverage, and thus becomes an exemplary moral act).

With its earnest effort to portray what was then an exotic culture re-spectfully, thus imparting to the film an air of expensive and 'beautiful' spectacle, with its careful attempt to preach racial amity in romantically approachable terms, with its stately pace and soberly 'thoughtful' manner, *Sayonara* is a paradigm of Fifties movie-making, Fifties American culture. But it is to a degree redeemed by Brando's performance, for which he re-ceived another Academy Award nomination (though of course it was But-tons and Umeki, so cute and so sad, who actually got the Oscars). It re-solutely refuses to inflate itself to the scale of its surroundings.

Typically, Brando was unhappy with it. He made his unhappiness mani-fest in the article, previously alluded to, written for the *New Yorker* by Truman Capote, which caused something of a sensation at the time and, perhaps more than any single journalistic item about him, revised public perceptions of Brando. In those days, the magazine and its middle-brow audience liked to affect an air of smug superiority to popular culture in general, to the movies in particular, and Capote was obviously determined to play to this attitude when he invaded Brando's hotel room in Kyoto on a night when the star was restlessly confined there with some minor ailment. In the manner that the 'new journalism' would soon make *de rigueur* in celebrity profiles, the novelist set a scene of slightly squalid indulgence. The overweight actor, who, it was carefully noted, had insisted on the pro-duction company underwriting the transportation and upkeep of an ex-tensive entourage, is discovered in an unkempt atmosphere, littered with carelessly discarded clothes, unconsumed snacks, 'deep-thought' books and the manuscript pages of a screenplay on which he is avoiding work. In the course of the evening he orders excesses of food, downs excesses of drink, indulges in excesses of self-pity and self-loathing.

Brando was dismissive of a project he had once found promising: 'This wondrous hearts-and-flowers nonsense that was supposed to be a serious picture about Japan.' But his contempt ranged farther and wider than his current work. Take the theater, for instance. 'What's so hot about New York?' the actor inquired rhetorically at one point. 'What's so hot about working for Cheryl Crawford and Robert Whitehead?' he asked, naming the theater's two best-known producers of serious plays. 'Anyway, what would I be in? There aren't any parts for me.' This, and Brando's satirical thrusts at Logan, who despite their similar professional backgrounds was no Kazan – since he refused to play actor games with his players, even sometimes gave them the line readings he expected – momentarily caused Capote to lose ironic distance. The writer took both Broadway and a director who had made a great name for himself there more seriously than he ought to have. For this was still the Fifties, still a period in which literary people like Capote felt obliged to regard Broadway as somehow culturally superior to the movies, whereas, in fact, their values had by this time more or less merged (as, in fact, Logan's own recent success in film, and the history of the *Sayonara* project itself, proved). In any event, Capote interrupted the flow of his article to list a number of suitable theatrical enterprises that he knew had been offered to Brando, making special reference to *Orpheus Descending*. Tennessee Williams had written this for Brando, whose refusal to play in it had sabotaged its chances, and sabotaged some of Brando's reputation with theater-minded people, who saw this as evidence of his final 'Sell-out' to Hollywood.

This, in a sense, Brando indirectly confirmed. In his first press conference in Japan he had made a very winning speech, saying he had undertaken the picture because 'it strikes very precisely at prejudices that serve to limit our progress toward a peaceful world'. Since he was able to decorate his remarks with references to Oriental religion, which he had indeed studied, and even to such cultural traditions as flower arrangement, he had been helpful in easing some of the tensions surrounding the production. Now, to Capote, he insisted on applying his justification for appearing in *Sayonara* to his entire movie career – and to his abandonment of the theater as well. 'You can say important things to a lot of people. About discrimination and hatred and prejudice.' And so on.

Here, for the first time, a new theme in Brando's public reflections about his art surfaced. Perhaps movies could not, in their nature, offer him satisfaction as an actor. But they could be, as he put it, 'a factor for good', for 'moral development'. For the moment, he indicated, this potential was sustaining him as he toiled on *Sayonara*. He had formed his own production company, Pennebaker (his mother's maiden name, and considering what her ideals meant to him, a not insignificant choice), intending to produce films that would 'explore the themes current in the world today'. His salary from the present silly venture would, if nothing else, provide money 'to put in the kick' for Pennebaker's more purely intentioned ventures.

Capote got some sport out of the fact that, together with someone known only as Murray, Brando was occupying some of his spare time in Japan writing the script for what he intended to be his first independent production. Capote was amused to discover this was to be, of all humble things, a western titled *A Burst of Vermillion*. It seemed not to occur to him that the form had long since proved itself to be metaphorically capacious, capable of handling all sorts of pointed themes, often more subtly and interestingly than films which attacked important topics more directly. He was, of course, dismissive of Brando's claim that the project would, indeed, address the subject of racial prejudice in its own way.

Read now, the sniggery-Brahmin tone of the piece sets one's teeth on edge, and considering the pathetic end to which Capote came – society's rejected pet, drugging himself into oblivion while promisng the same kind of great things he satirized Brando for proposing – one is, perhaps perversely, sympathetic to Brando's rather innocent idealism. But it is as a prediction of troubles to come that Capote's work is valuable. For, from here on, almost all of Brando's professional problems, problems that would by the early Sixties vitiate both his powers of choice and his powers as a performer, all stemmed from his insistence that his movies should make some usefully uplifting statement about matters of high concern. When he was thwarted on this point he would become balky and unreachable in a manner that far exceeded anything such failed father figures as Koster or Mann or Logan had endured. In other words, he would act on, act out, the attitude Capote observed – perhaps in part because others, too, responded as the writer had, patronizingly, sneeringly.

He worked ceaselessly in these days, and moved on quickly to another prestigious, 'serious' and morally upstanding project, the adaptation of *The Young Lions*, Irwin Shaw's best-selling attempt to encompass the entire experience of the Second World War within a single volume. It was a novel both sober and slick, an attempt by an esteemed writer of short stories (and of a sensational anti-war play of the 1930s, *Bury the Dead*) to realize one of his literary generation's great ideals, 'the big book' – something their *lieber meister*, Ernest Hemingway, died still trying to accomplish.

The story traces the lives of three young men: a poor American Jew, Noah Ackerman (played in the film by Montgomery Clift); an ambitious entertainer and politically uncommitted show business figure, Michael Whiteacre (Dean Martin, who played the part perhaps less interestingly than cool, quick Tony Randall, who was the first choice, might have); and, as Shaw originally wrote him, a Nazi true believer, Christian Diestl (played in a controversially different spirit by a blond-haired Brando). Their lives are coincidentally, but not unpersuasively, intertwined. Diestl meets and flirts with Whiteacre's girlfriend at a Swiss ski resort, where he is an instructor, in the last days of peace. Ackerman and Whiteacre meet at their draft board, where the latter is trying to get a deferment. They will soldier on through the war together, and just after liberating a concentration camp, they will confront Diestl in combat.

All three are, as a result of their wartime experiences, changed men by that time. But the movie Diestl is also a changed man from the character as Shaw originally envisioned him. He had portrayed him as a man mildly sympathetic to Nazism in peacetime who becomes more and more committed to Hitlerism as the war proceeds. The idea was to contrast his shrinkage of conscience with the developing moral awareness of his American counterparts (particularly Whiteacre) under the impress of battle. A lesson in the differences between the possibilities offered by a free society and those presented by a totalitarian one was thus proposed. The movie entirely reverses Diestl's development. He is like Shaw's original in the early passages, but as the film develops, he grows more and more disenchanted with Nazism, with war in general. In other words, his moral growth, instead of being contrasted to that of his American counterparts, parallels it.

Brando has often been accused of imposing this change on the movie. But the film's director, Edward Dmytryk, and its screenwriter, Edward Anhalt, both thought that with the war over a decade past it was perhaps more fruitful to make the film less of an anti-Nazi tract, and more of a conventionally anti-war piece. Besides changing Christian's character, they also changed the climactic combat scene. In the novel the Nazi kills the Jew and then the Wasp kills the Nazi. The movie permitted Ackerman to survive, and leaves in doubt whether he or his friend killed Christian, who, in this version, fires no shots at them at all.

Brando, who had been recruited to the project because it would enable him honorably to repay his post-*Desiree* obligation to Fox, agreed with these revisions, and he became their chief public defender. For example, when the production was on location in Germany, he told a press conference: 'Irwin Shaw wrote his great book while war hatreds were white hot. We hope they have cooled. The picture will try to show that Nazism is a matter of mind, not geography; that there are Nazis – and people of goodwill – in every country.'

It can be argued that there was some reasonable justification for the filmmakers' tamperings with the novel. But it is also true, as Shaw's biographer, Michael Shnayerson says, that though the changes may have been 'well-meant', they also represented 'a shocking liberty' to an author who was at the time rather nervously defensive about his reputation in literary

117

circles, which, because this book was commercially successful, was beginning to be discounted.

In any case, Shaw was infuriated by the revisions, and he came to Paris as shooting began, arriving not long after a waiter in a restaurant spilled a scalding pot of tea in Brando's lap, causing third-degree burns around the genital area, and briefly hospitalizing him. When he came back to work he was not in the best of moods – especially for a television interview that David Schoenbrun of CBS set up with him and Shaw. 'Any problems with the characterization?' the correspondent asked, not entirely innocently. No, said the actor. Yes, said the writer. Shaw then accused Brando of changing the role because he wanted to appear sympathetic on the screen. Brando replied that Shaw knew nothing about the character. 'It's my character,' Shaw replied hotly. 'I gave birth to him. I created him.' 'Nobody creates a character but an actor,' Brando replied. 'I play the role, now he exists. He is my creation.'

The conversation deteriorated still further. Shaw called Brando 'stupid', and raised his fists to him. Then, in Schoenbrun's account, Shaw gave vent to the following feelings, utterly typical of most writers, especially those who had, like Shaw, attempted to write for the screen: 'Well, it serves me right, sitting down with a stupid fucking actor. An actor doesn't have any fucking brains; if he had any brains he couldn't be an actor. An actor is an empty fucking inkpot, you have to pour ink into the goddamn fool to get anything out of him.'

Subsequently, Shaw was chastised by Hemingway himself for caring so volubly about the matter. 'What you do,' said Papa, is sell your book to the movies, go to the bar, and take a drink. You don't think about the movie, you don't look at the movie, you know it's going to be a piece of shit. The idea of selling a book to the movies is to make money.'

A valid, if snooty, point. As for Brando, it may not have been entirely accurate of him to tell the author, 'I just read the script and knew what the guy was like and played it straight. I had absolutely no problem. It was a great role.' Apparently he liked Dmytryk, whose manner is similar to Kazan's: quick, smart, unpretentious – and unfatherly. He got Brando to speak up and speed up sooner than most, and with no backsliding, either.

Brando's interest in Montgomery Clift's performance was also revealing in its way. He had always been uncomfortably aware of him. (Clift, too, was born in Omaha, had trained with a schismatic Stanislavskian and was as aware as Brando was that they were rivals for a generation's loyalties.) Legend has it that, in addition to meeting when Clift was briefly a candidate to replace him in *The Eagle Has Two Heads*, Brando once vroomed up to Clift on his motorcycle, introduced himself and said, 'People tell me I remind them of you.' 'Oh,' said Clift. 'Yes. But I don't see it,' with which Brando wheeled away. One might have thought that by this time, with his own career in the ascendency, and with Clift's beginning its decline (this was his first picture after the auto accident that had shattered his face and his confidence the previous year, and he was drinking heavily), Brando might have shown a certain compassion for his colleague in this difficult moment. But that was not so.

The story and the shooting schedule kept them apart, except for the concluding sequence, and Clift, not unnaturally, kept company with Dean Martin, his more frequent scene partner, and an affable drinking partner, too. Indeed, each was in need of the other's support, for this was Martin's first serious dramatic role, and Clift was understandably anxious about resuming his acting career. Even so, when they were finally in proximity on the set, Brando, despite his increasingly professed contempt for the actor's art, was caught lurking behind a camera, attempting to study Clift at work. 'Tell Marlon he doesn't have to hide his face when he's watching me act,' Clift whispered to Dmytryk. Clift, who was on Shaw's side in the battle over the script, and restored as much of the novel's dialogue to his scenes as he could, later expressed contempt for Brando's work. 'Sloppy' was his judgement; not a one hundred per cent effort.

The conflicts attending this producton now seem rather academic. *The Young Lions* is, finally, a popular fiction. Its characters are archetypes in a schematized story, and its best quality is its relentless narrative pressure. To the degree that the movie kept that up – and it pretty much did, though it has some wandering passages – it served the novel reasonably well. Since its story could sustain with equal logic either the author's moral or the one which replaced it on the screen, it really does not make much difference what the movie actually said, so long as it did not endorse manifest immorality, which it did not.

Moreover, all concerned had reason, in the end, to thank Brando. This is not sloppy work. It is, in fact, more interesting than Clift's, which is a version of his performance in *From Here to Eternity* – another sensitive barrack-room outsider. In Brando's long absences, while the Ackerman-Whiteacre story is pursued, one misses him. His performance in the opening passages, with Whiteacre's fiancée (Barbara Rush), is very good, soft and tentative, and patient in his attempt to avoid conflict, get on with his seduction. 'I sink ve should not discuss zis,' he says as politics rears its ugly head at a New Year's Eve party, 'because I don't know all the answers, you don't know the answers. Political discussions go 'round and 'round.'

This is a character unformed when we meet him, therefore with somewhere to go emotionally as the film proceeds. Building this kind of a line was something Brando was often more attentive to than his scripts were. Yet this line, which leads toward his reformation and ultimate martyrdom, is walked ambiguously. Indeed, it is possible to see what happens to Diestl more ironically than the arguments about this character might lead one to think. At the start of the war, you can sense his pleasure in his fine new uniform ('A young golden god of war' is how another character describes him). You can sense his confusion when a Frenchwoman rejects his advances: he is not, as he sees it, personally responsible for the ugliness of occupation, and he is genuinely puzzled to be a victim of prejudice. When he protests against totalitarian methods ('I don't think it's possible to remake the world from the basement of a dirty little police station') it is a 'good' German, correct and fastidious, speaking, not a political radical.

You can sense his confusions beginning to reach a resolution when he is ordered to participate in a massacre on the African front, but you can also sense a desire to compromise those confusions, to retain an outward show of loyalty, whatever levels of disgust he is reaching inwardly. He does, finally, toy with the idea of desertion, after his friend Hardenburg (Maximillian Schell) is grotesquely wounded and inveigles Diestl into providing him with the means to commit suicide. But even then, confronting his comrade's slatternly wife with news of her husband's death, there is a marvelously Germanic rectitude about him. This character may eventually turn his back on the evils of Nazism, but he is always loyal, humanly and rather touchingly so, to the larger cultural tradition that formed both the light and the dark sides of a national character. Even in his final moment, when he aims his gun at Ackerman and Whiteacre, you feel it is possible for him to shoot out of that larger, good-soldier's sense of duty. He does not, instead firing a shot in the air, which reveals his presence. This may or may not be an act of suicide, but it is surely an irony, and one that is in keeping with the tormented and never quite emotionally resolute character Brando has given us.

Something Schell said about Brando after working with him applies to this performance. 'He knows that in these times an actor can't say "I love you" openly to a girl he loves, but has to cover up his feelings with some gesture.' It is what Brando does throughout this movie, and not only when he is confronting women, of course. He half-hides his commitments to principles in the same way. How conscious he was of so doing we cannot know. It may well be that these gestures were entirely spontaneous and unconscious. It is, in fact, what he did in *Waterfront*, in *Sayonara*, in every movie where heavy make-up was not an option, but some kind of emotional disguise remained, as it always was for him, a necessity. In any case, as Schell seems to have recognized, it is one of the bonds he forged with us, his devoted audience, in the Fifties. For we were all, consciously or not, modernists. We understood that the point of a scene, a life, was not to be approached directly, not to be summed up, QED. That was for politicians, ideologues, all the venal windbags of our public life who were so sure of what was right and wrong, so sure of what they were doing, so determined to drag us along on their ill-conceived adventures.

Does an irony present itself here? I think so. The hunger Brando had expressed to Capote, and would go on expressing, for moral leadership or, anyway, for film roles that would instruct the world in right behavior, ill became him. He was, if anything, the poet of our ambivalences, the not-so-secret sharer of our dubiety about all those cocksure voices, amplified by the media bullhorn, who always seemed to know what they were doing and what we should be doing – about the Cold War, about mental health, about family life, about what did and did not constitute a good society and what programs were required to create one.

What, then, was he doing? Groping for words, I think, metaphors for his inchoate discontents. And not finding the right ones, finding exactly the wrong ones. When he finished *The Young Lions*, Brando paused in his career. It would be over two years before he appeared on the screen again. It is appropriate for us to pause as well, and reflect on his recent accomplishments. He had appeared in five movies since *On the Waterfront*, an average of one a year. All five had been major commerical successes. But all five had been based either on a best-selling novel or on a long-running Broadway play. That is to say, all of them had been in their origins mainstream works, and, in their adaptations to the screen, examples of Hollywood's current conventional wisdom about how to re-attract the mass audience. All of them were produced in a wide-screen process, four of them in color, and all of them, save *Guys and Dolls*, had embodied sincere, but comfortably stated, essentially incontrovertible, messages: against war or racism, in favor of peace and tolerance – something of which we could unquestionably approve, but which did not unduly stir us. Setting his ridiculous Napoleon and his unfortunate Sakini aside, Brando's work in three of them, whatever their overall creative failures, whatever his own dissatisfactions, whatever his own trouble-making on the set, was, finally, worthwhile.

The great thing about all these performances was that the line he had established in his first films, the factor that had first distinguished Brando's work from most of the movie star acting that had preceded it, derived from his insistence on letting his characters grow. His comings to consciousness, even in these big mainstream movies, continued to be more interesting than those of other movie protagonists precisely because, in the films' early passages, he was unafraid to portray foolishness, moral blindness, even stupidity. He made sure we understood that most heroism begins in anti-heroism. Or at least non-heroism.

And yet, increasingly, what he was doing was discomfiting to many of us, and not just those who shared his theatrical generation's ambitions for him. One had the feeling that he had been taken prisoner in an undeclared war, and was putting on shows for his captors – earning privileges by amusing them in vehicles that had passed their censorship, and were certain not to fan any rebellious sparks that might still be glowing in the auditorium.

I think he felt what we felt, but could not, any more than we could at the time, articulate his disappointment at what he was doing. Moreover, though his native intelligence and his intuitions are first-rate, he is not a man who is much good at formulating formal arguments for or against a course of action, nor does he seem to have any capacity for the kind of ana-lytical thinking required to bring a movie from idea to script to finished form. Or to criticize it coherently. Finally, we must not forget to apply Schell's observation: it was not in Brando's nature to express his feelings directly. In effect, when he expatiated on the subtextual matters he thought his movies should be taking up, he said 'politics' when he meant to say 'lostness' or 'loneliness' or possibly even 'existential pain'.

This is possibly a point at which it is useful to remind ourselves once again that Brando was the child of alcoholics. In recent years psychologists have put a good deal of effort into studying the effects of that experience on adults and, as it turns out, Brando uncannily fits the profile they have devised: a man who learned early to tread warily and speak ambiguously, so as not to stir the unpredictable emotions of the most powerful figures in his life; a man to whom placatory and ameliorative behavior became second nature precisely beause so much erratic emotion had been visited on him; a man mistrustful of love, though obviously searching for it; a man finally given to excesses of self-denigration, quite unable to recognize, let alone take pleasure in, his own achievements.

All these elements were constituents of the 'feminine' side of his nature, of which Kazan spoke, and all of them redeemed, made touching, the re-bellious and angry side of his screen character. Whether we are discussing Terry Malloy or Sky Masterson, Lloyd Gruver or Christian Diestl, it had served him superbly as an actor. But as a man trying to take charge of his

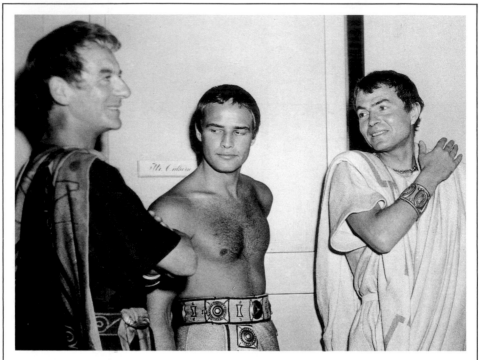

On the set of *Julius Caesar* (left to right) John Gielgud, Brando and James Mason.

PREVIOUS PAGE Cecil Beaton's portrait of Brando.

Brando as Mark Antony.

Awaiting his cue to lead a cavalry charge.

With his sister Jocelyn on the set of *The Wild One*.

OPPOSITE A classic image: Brando in *The Wild One*.

Johnny (Brando), the leader of the Black Rebels.

Brando's father, producer Sam Spiegel, and mother with him on the set of *On the Waterfront*.

Elia Kazan, director of *On the Waterfront* with Brando.

OPPOSITE Brando plays Terry Malloy in *On the Waterfront*.

Brando with Horace Hough and Elia Kazan (right).

OPPOSITE With Eva Marie Saint in *Waterfront*.

Eva Marie Saint with Brando on the *Waterfront* set.

Michael Rennie, Jean Simmons and Brando on the set of *Desiree*.

OPPOSITE Taking a break during the filming of *Desiree*.

Brando as Napoleon and Jean Simmons as Desiree.

Frank Sinatra as
Nathan Detroit and
Brando as Sky Masterson
in *Guys and Dolls*.

With Josianne
Mariani-Berenger who he
had planned to marry
in 1954.

Joseph Mankiewicz (left) with Brando and Samuel Goldwyn (right).

Jesting with M.C. Bob Hope at the 1955 Academy Awards ceremony.

With the Oscar he won for *On the Waterfront*.

Marlon Brando speaking to an actors class at Universal Studios. The class includes Clint Eastwood and David Janssen.

Marilyn Monroe and Marlon Brando attend a Hollywood premiere.

Brando being mobbed by fans and press in Japan.

Glenn Ford, Machiko Kyo and Brando in *The Teahouse of the August Moon*.

own destiny, trying to help define a character at the script stage or suggest unwritten implications through improvisation on set, his inarticulateness, his inability to state his case firmly, his desire to mediate and accommodate, not to mention his fear of his own anger, which generally led to prodigies of suppression, served him badly. To people involved in his movies of the later Fifties it read as sulkiness, childishness, star-tripping.

And now he wished to serve as his own producer, to act decisively and forthrightly on his own behalf, risking that which was the hardest thing to risk, open wrathfulness on the part of others when he dared to manifest his wishes and needs openly. It puts it mildly to say that he was not really a good candidate to exercise the kind of creative autonomy that some other stars of his stature had begun to wield in this decade. But it was also obvious to him that he had to try, as, indeed, his work on the 'western' that so amused Capote and Pennebaker's acquisition of other properties indicated. (Two of these the company actually co-produced: *Shake Hands with the Devil*, with James Cagney starring and Don Murray in the role Brando might have played – that of an idealistic American medical student, turned Irish revolutionary, turned, finally, pacifist; and *Paris Blues*, with Paul Newman taking Brando's jazz musician role after he – and Marilyn Monroe – lost interest in the project.)

When he finished *The Young Lions* in late 1957, Brando meant to get serious, at last, about independent production. He was, however, distracted by, of all unlikely occurrences, marriage. Just weeks after finishing his picture he suddenly wed Anna Kashfi, in a match that was a disaster from the start and would have consequences that reverberate to this day, since Christian Brando is their issue. Eddie Dmytryk takes some responsibility for their meeting. Kashfi had worked for him on *The Mountain*, when she expressed an interest in meeting Brando. The director gave her the name of producer A. C. Lyles when she asked for contacts in Hollywood, and Lyles, a friend of Brando's, innocently introduced them. Their courtship, however, was desultory until she was stricken with tuberculosis and Brando – characteristically – took pity on her helplessness, becoming a devoted visitor at her bedside. ('Care-giving' is also one of the salient characteristics of the children of alcoholics.) She was surely Brando's type: a small, dark, exotically attractive woman who claimed to be of Anglo-Indian background. Unfortunately, as soon as the press announced their marriage, her father, a man named Callahan, living in England, stepped forward to proclaim that she had been born there, had no Indian blood and had not, to his knowledge, ever set foot on the subcontinent. She stuck to her story, but Brando was outraged by her duplicity, and, though she was pregnant, they separated. There was, it seems, a brief reconciliation when the child was born, but thereafter their relationship deteriorated into scandalous animosity. Hers was an addictive personality, and a vindictive one, and their battles over custody of their child persisted for years, and included dramatic abductions. No outsider, of course, can calculate what harm may have been done the boy by this miserable chain of events, but it cannot have been minor.

Be that as it may, Brando was surely even less focused than usual when he addressed the problems of creating a screenplay for the film that was eventually to be known as *One-Eyed Jacks*. Aside from the fact that both scripts contained characters of Mexican extraction, there seems to be no relationship between this western and the one that so amused Capote in 1956. It does seem likely, though, that Pennebaker was able to charge its development costs, which Brando estimated at $250,000 – probably an exaggeration – off against the new project, which was at least initially based on a novel by Charles Neider called *The Authentic Death of Hendry Jones*. The novelist did a first-draft screenplay for producer Frank Rosenberg, who submitted it to Brando, who, in turn, committed to it in a matter of days – unprecedented decisiveness for him. Of course, there would have to be rewrites. . . .

And then the fun began. Having liked, for obvious reasons, Stanley Kubrick's great pacifist film, *Paths of Glory*, Brando eagerly agreed to him as director. Calder Willingham, whose novel about military school life, *End as a Man*, may have recommended him to Brando, was signed on as screenwriter. Now, for months on end, they met virtually every day to work on the script at the handsome, but not overwhelming, home Brando had recently purchased on Mulholland Drive, near Coldwater Canyon. (It is interesting to note, considering the reclusive uses it would be put to, that the place had once belonged to Howard Hughes.) Brando, it is said, called meetings to order by striking a large Oriental gong. In time, Willingham was dismissed, to be replaced by Guy Trosper, and finally, when disputes over casting arose, Kubrick decamped. (It is just possible that the director, fearing his career could be lost in this morass, contrived his own dismissal, for he almost instantly signed for *Spartacus*.)

'We've spent six months on this film and I still don't know what the story is about,' Kubrick had cried at some point in their deliberations. Or words to that effect. 'It's about $350,000. . . .' Brando had replied with a sigh, referring to his current estimate of development costs. It might have profited all concerned to consult Capote's article, which had appeared by this time, for in it Brando had insisted that he only meant what he said about forty per cent of the time, and he had also offered an estimate of his attention span – seven minutes. There is no reason to doubt either figure, and both were relevant to these discussions. Hollywood people are accustomed to assume that whatever the star says is definitive, not to be trifled with, and so rush to do his bidding, which in this case must surely have resulted in many a spitballed idea getting written into this or that draft of the script – or at the least leading to many wasted, confusing hours of discussion. The limit of the star's ability to concentrate must, similarly, have led to the abandonment of promising lines of attack before they were fully explored, as well as the failure to resolve many an other issue presented by the story line. No, writing, communal writing in particular, with its many opportunities for distraction, was not the ideal occupation for Marlon Brando.

Yes, of course, his hand was all aces in a game where the deck was inevitably loaded in his favor. And the script, if we can judge it by that portion of it that finally made it to the screen, surely reflects many of his preoccupations. Essentially, *One-Eyed Jacks* is a revenge western. Two gunmen, the Rio Kid (Brando) and Dad Longworth (Karl Malden), make a fine living robbing Mexican banks. One day, however, they are ambushed by mounted police. One of their horses is lamed, and they flip a coin to determine who will ride away on their remaining mount in search of another. Rio loses and Dad never returns. Rio spends five years in the Sonora jail. Escaping, he and his confederates learn of a 'cheesebox' bank on Monterey, where coincidentally Dad, having gone straight, is the sheriff. As it turns out he is married, and with a beautiful stepdaughter named Louisa (Pina Pellicer). Rio, pretending that he too escaped capture, claims no grudge against Dad. But, of course, he intends to rob the bank, kill Dad and seduce the girl. However, he kills a man who is mistreating a bar girl, and Dad administers a brutal flogging (the most sadistic of all Brando's on-screen beatings) and then breaks his gun hand. Rio and his gang retreat to a picturesque fishing village up the coast where he recuperates. He returns to rob the bank, is jailed and sentenced to hang. But Louisa smuggles a derringer into him, and he escapes, finally kills Dad, and promising to return to the girl, who is now carrying his child, he rides off.

Dad. Dad. Dad. A smooth, well-spoken, pious man. Highly respected in the community. Yet a man with a secret life. A betrayer of trusts. And unconscionably cruel to his Kid. Who is inarticulate. A young man putting a hard face on his sensitivities. A young man who, despite his rough manners, is quick to defend the defenseless. Eventually Kid kills Dad. What could the uncredited author of this screenplay have been thinking about? One resorts to irony only to avoid belaboring the obvious – and imputing classic models to this essentially modest and very personal enterprise.

It must be judged a perfectly serviceable, even enjoyable, tale as far as the unknowing public was concerned. And if *One-Eyed Jacks* only incidentally took up the kind of obvious moral issues that Brando had so often insisted he wanted to address in movies, it did take up, metaphorically, the kind of psychological issues that were of moment to Brando, satisfying that agenda that he had hidden from himself, or, at any rate, had not dared to speak about. It might well have been, in the end, a satisfying experience for him, and one that might have opened opportunities to express himself in his own way on the screen.

But then he decided to direct the picture himself. The job *was* open. Rosenberg demurred. And it seems likely that his backers at Paramount entered some questions about the idea. Brando was not, after all, an unknown quantity, and what Hollywood saw as his dilatory nature and blithe disregard of schedules when he was shooting were well known. He was a type that had always, and not incorrectly, frightened production executives. As early as *Desiree* one of them had remarked, 'The only good thing you can say about the twerp is that he doesn't smoke marijuana.' Less colorful comments had issued from similar sources during and after most of his more recent films.

But . . . well, he was a star. Look at those grosses. So greed came into play. And also hope: maybe if we give him a good cameraman . . . a smart AD . . . a solid production manager. And a darker thought: chasten his arrogance, teach him a lesson. How much can it cost? He whom Hollywood would humble, it first indulges. It is, perhaps, the most basic law of the business.

Brando didn't see any of that. 'I've got no respect for acting,' he declared. And: 'Acting is the expression of a neurotic impulse.' And: 'Acting is a bum's life in that it leads to perfect self-indulgence.' And: 'You get paid for doing nothing and it all adds up to nothing.' Heigh-ho, the director's life for me.

A two-month shoot stretched to six months. A two million dollar budget went to six. A million feet of film were exposed, 250,000 feet printed – six times as much as usual in the first instance, more than three times as much as usual in the second. The rough assemblage of the work ran close to five hours. Brando was meticulous – you'd have to give him that. He gave motivations to the extras. He waited hours for the right light, or for the cloud formations to reach their most photogenic proportions. He dislocated a shoulder showing Malden how to handle a bullwhip. He covered every sequence from every imaginable angle. But eventually, it is said, cast and crew were standing around on the set, helping him decide on an ending by putting alternatives to a democratic vote.

And when Brando got all this stuff back to the cutting-room, he despired of it. No more than a script conference is an editing room a place for a man with a seven-minute attention span. Cutting a film, especially one with this much exposed footage, requires the patience of Job, and the concentrated eye of a pointillist. Brando, in fact, abandoned the task and took another acting job. Costs, of course, continued to mount as post-production crept along for months more than was customary.

One may put it kindly. The directorial temperament is not, usually, the actor's temperament. Good, bad or indifferent, a director has to be decisive, keep things moving. Actors, by constrast, like to examine alternatives, let someone else decide what to keep, what to throw out. Or one may put it unkindly. He was having his revenge on a system that had administered to him all the hurts and slights, large and small, real and imagined, it automatically visits on 'talent', which is always regarded as feckless, childish. Indeed, reports of directorial larkiness abound.

In the end *One-Eyed Jacks* did not return its negative cost, let alone the additional nine million dollars it cost to place it in release. And yet it is an achievement of sorts. It *is* a beautiful film – the decision to shoot the last half of the western by the seaside in Monterey is both original and productive of wondrous imagery. Much of the dialogue has a gritty, period quality to it. Malden, given a chance to do evil – an opportunity not vouchsafed him before – relishes it. Brando himself is marvelously broody; this is perhaps the juvenile delinquent he didn't get to develop fully in *The Wild One*. Yes, the movie is self-evidently self-indulgent. And, yes, it has its *longeueurs*; and, yes, in effect, it has two climaxes, the first of which, the flogging and its aftermath, is by far the stronger. Brando's chief objection to the finished film, an ending in which he and Louisa do not die, is irrelevant. There was no tragic inevitability implicit in this script; no reason, therefore, why a little hint of eventual romantic reunion, after the Kid has outrun the posse pursuing him for the shooting of Dad, is unacceptable.

But, of course, Brando made his post-partum blues public. Directing, he now said, is 'like being an emotional traffic cop.' And: '*One-Eyed Jacks* is just a product . . . Movies aren't art.' And (ludicrously): 'I'm a businessman. I'm a captain of industry – nothing else. Any pretensions I've had of being artistic are now just a chilly hope.'

Certainly any hopes he had of being a director were, for the foreseeable future, frozen. And it is too bad. *One-Eyed Jacks* was for a time a cult film, granted that status by those of us who remained faithful to Brando's promise, however he or the industry or the reviewers (who for the first time, but not the last, mostly reviewed his budgetary failures, not the work on the screen) regarded the finished work. With the passage of time, it seems better than that. The western was the one traditional genre that prospered in the Fifties, a place where a certain toughness of mind and spirit could still flourish, and where certain archetypal figures and situations were allowed a spaciousness they could not find in the movies' cramped contemporaneity. *The Gunfighter* and *High Noon*, *Winchester '73* and *Shane*, *The Searchers* and *Rio Bravo* – whatever their defects, these films exercise a claim on movie history and our affection. *One-Eyed Jacks* belongs among them. And in its quirkiness it is not the least of them.

The work for which its star-director deserted it need not detain us long. *The Fugitive Kind* is the movie version of the Tennessee Williams play, *Orpheus Descending*, which Brando had long been criticized for not doing. Now it was to be brought to the screen with Anna Magnani, the very actress he claimed 'would have wiped me off the stage', cast opposite him. Williams insisted that the work, despite its roots in classical myth, was emotionally autobiographical ('You will find the trail of my sleeve-worn heart in this play'). Certainly he had been persistently loyal to it, since it was a reworking of his first produced work, *Battle of Angels*, which closed out of town in 1940. It is a high-pitched melodrama, in which Val Xavier, a guitar-pickin' singer wearing a snakeskin jacket, symbolic of his freedom from convention (did it inspire Presley, or more recently David Lynch, when he made *Wild at Heart*?), finds an underworld on earth when he wanders into a small town and takes up with a storekeeper's lusty, middle-aged wife, enjoys a flirtation with a nymphomaniacal heiress, and comes to a brutal end.

Brando is miscast in this role, despite Williams's long-standing passion to place him in it. And that may account for Brando's equally long-standing resistance to it. For he is, in effect, the Blanche Dubois of the film, a delicate soul set upon, ultimately martyred by the cruel world. Since his sensitivity, played as unworldly innocence, is established at the outset, the pleasure of seeing him come to consciousness – a movement that defined all of his best previous work – is denied us, and denied the actor as well.

In any case, *The Fugitive Kind* is a work from which a sensible director would keep a stylized distance, and it just barely worked, or perhaps just barely didn't work, when Cliff Robertson and Maureen Stapleton (cast in a supporting role in the movie) played it in a not-quite-realistic 1957 New York production. But the film's director, Sidney Lumet, decided to get (as they say) up close and personal, and aside from a well-written opening courtroom monologue, which outlines Val's background and character, and which Brando does with poignant (if mannered and self-imitative) simplicity, the movie is most of the time one of those insanely miscalculated ventures that at first creates laughter and then an appalled silence. It is said that Williams was hissed as he left the New York premiere, and its grosses were said to be not just minor, but humiliatingly so. It is also said, however, that Brando received a million dollars for his services – if so, it was the first time any actor received a seven-figure salary for making a movie, thus a significant milestone on the way to Hollywood's present wildly inflated pay scale. It was obviously enough to return Pennebaker to a semblance of solvency. In addition the work repaid whatever debt Brando may have been thought to owe to Williams and to the theatrical tradition that had formed him. It also provided an excuse for avoiding it in the future.

Was Brando's movie career now in trouble? Not really. The largest expense to him was that work on this film, together with his delays in finishing his western, prevented him from taking the leading role in *Lawrence of Arabia*, which Sam Spiegel offered him – certainly proof of his continued viability. Both *One-Eyed Jacks* and *The Fugitive Kind* could be regarded either as indulgences or as temporary deviations from common sense. One might even imagine the mogul community imagining that he had learned valuable lessons from these experiences. All he needed to do was return to what industry leaders still believed was the main line. If not *Lawrence*, why not *Mutiny on the Bounty*? Superficially, it represented the same wisdom. Based on a beloved best-seller and a movie that everyone remembered as wonderful, it offered spectacle and romance, action and exotic adventure. And a fine part for a man with a rebel's image: Fletcher Christian, leader of the morally defensible mutiny against the sadistic Captain Bligh; Clark Gable's old role. Best of all, from its point of view, MGM, which was financing the project, owned all rights to all three of the Charles Nordhof-James Normal Hall historical novels about the *Bounty*; there would be no huge charges for story acquisition. Or so it was fondly imagined.

Brando was interested. And he offered producer Aaron Rosenberg a little suggestion. Might not the work be made more meaningful to modern audiences if it went on past the point where the first film had stopped, showed something more of the mutineers' life on Pitcairn Island, where they attempted, and failed, to found an Edenic colony, free of the world's pressures and temptations? He spoke, later, about the eternal theme he discerned in this aspect of the story, 'the struggle of black versus white, of the urge to create and the urge to destroy. If man cannot find happiness on an island paradise, where can he find it? Rosenberg agreed to accommodate the star's ideas.

It was his first mistake. But not his last. The trouble with Brando's plan was that it destroyed the structural unity of a story that climaxed dramatically with the successful mutiny. There the original film had left them, leaving the miserable concluding passages of this history unspoken. That redoubtable craftsman, Eric Ambler, the espionage novelist, took a first crack at the story. His work was deemed unsatisfactory. Thereafter, five other writers were employed on it, running up a bill for story costs alone of some $237,000. Eventually, the company set forth for the South Seas without a finished script. And without a finished *Bounty*. The shipwrights working on the authentic reproduction fell some six weeks behind schedule. That was only the beginning of the technical difficulties that plagued the production. The weather and the seas were more changeable than they were supposed to be, so there was trouble matching shots in sequences. And, since the seas were also running high, many sequences were slow, dangerous going.

The lack of a finished script didn't help matters. With approval over its finished form, Brando wrangled endlessly over it with the director, Carol Reed. At their first meeting, it seems, Brando had disconcerted the gentlemanly Englishman by proposing that they scrap the *Bounty* and tackle instead the story of Caryl Chessman, the convicted rapist who had become something of a literary hero as a result of his long, brilliantly conducted campaign to evade the gas chamber, which included a number of books. That idea came to naught, of course, and Brando apparently developed a certain respect for Reed, who was a superb craftsman.

Still, he was a director who had never before undertaken a production on this epic scale – though it is doubtful whether even a tough, resourceful veteran of large-scale action films could have handled the combination of problems presented by the importunate Brando, the incomplete script and the untamable elements. In the confusion, needless to say, bored and anxious actors began to fall out. Richard Harris, playing John Mills, Christian's co-conspirator, and Trevor Howard, playing Bligh, both became testy with Brando – to put it mildly. He remained, for the most part, in good spirits. This was his introduction to the South Seas, and though he was living in a lordly style that did not enhance his popularity with his fellow players, he was genuinely enraptured by the handsome natives (he began an affair with Tarita, who was playing Movita's old role, and he would eventually have children with her, and marry her as well) and by a lifestyle that suited him (shall we say?) philosophically – languid and unconcerned with getting, spending and celebrity.

Still, twentieth-century reality, or at least the motion picture industry version of it, was always near at hand. And troubling. When a production manager put together a revised schedule, indicating that after months on location the picture still needed 139 days to complete, the picture was shut down and the company returned to Los Angeles to work on interiors and backlot sequences. Rosenberg, Brando and Reed were called into executive conference, and when Reed, now ailing from kidney stones and exhaustion, could not in conscience promise to finish the film in the hundred days the studio now mandated, he was asked to leave (or perhaps volunteered to – the record is unclear). In any case, most of the footage he shot was scrapped.

Brando was outraged. He had had his differences with Reed, but for the most part he had been a good and patient father figure. To replace him, Rosenberg signed Lewis Milestone. He had made great films in his day (notably *All Quiet on the Western Front*), but his reputation had diminished over the years. This was principally because he had not always been wise in his selection of stories, for his craftsmanship, even on rather ungrateful projects, remained bold. (He had begun as an editor, and he knew how to set up for stirring cuts; he was also excellent at lighting.) The trouble was that he was now in his late sixties, not in entirely good health and, even in the best of circumstances, not someone who enjoyed talking things over with his actors. Confronted by a star in an advanced state of the sulks, Milestone responded in kind. Very quickly they were communicating solely through intermediaries – if at all. This was Milestone's recollection, some years later: 'Right or wrong, the man simply took charge of everything. You had the option of sitting and watching him or turning your back on him.' The production routine, as Milestone remembered it, was that mornings were spent with Brando and a writer closeted in the star's dressing-room, working over the day's script pages. After lunch Brando would emerge and direct the picture while Milestone went off and read the paper.

The return to Tahiti was no return to paradise; it was production hell. The same troubles that afflicted the company on its first visit – the weather and the seas – recurred, and this time large numbers of people were hurt (and one was killed) in a sequence in which a small boatload of deserters is pursued, on Bligh's orders, by a party in native war canoes. Before the picture was wrapped, Milestone quit and solid George Seaton shot the concluding sequence, Christian's death. For this the actor bedded himself on two hundred pounds of ice – it was a variation on the dousing he took when he was supposed to have stumbled out of the freezing sea in *Truckline Cafe*

131

– so that he could duplicate authentically the death tremors he had witnessed at his mother's bedside.

By the time it was finished, the *Mutiny on the Bounty* negative cost some $20 million, double the original budget, and with another $7 million tacked on for prints and advertising, it was bringing MGM dangerously close to bankruptcy. In the long months between completion of principal photography and release of the film, stories about the troubles on set, already widely rumored, began leaking to the press. And, somehow, Brando seemed responsible for all of them. That he had caused some delays is unquestionable. That he had been difficult for Milestone and some of his fellow players to work with is beyond doubt. But the fact is that the really costly mistakes of this production – those stemming from the unfinished script, the delay in ship construction, the ill-scouted and at best very difficult location – could not fairly be blamed on him. Rather obviously he was being scapegoated by studio executives who were laying off the blame for an ill-prepared production, and using the supine showbiz press, as they often did, to help them. The journalism finally reached such a level of viciousness that Brando felt obliged to bring a libel suit against one publication and its writer.

The public had long understood Brando to be a difficult chap, and, in any case, a simple story about an actor on a star trip plays more conveniently for journalists and readers than complicated tales involving technical problems, in which there are no clear-cut villains. Public knowledge that the star was being paid what was in those days a huge sum, $1,250,000 against a percentage, did not increase sympathy for him inside or outside the industry. When the picture was released, it was not Brando's performance that was reviewed, but his reputation, and most of the notices were negative, if not downright defamatory.

The distrust and dislike of Brando felt by older, more conservative critics and audience, and *haut* Hollywood, until then silenced by his success, could now safely spew forth. Why, the man had brought an insititution (MGM), which people had not previously known they revered, close to extinction! It was even implicitly argued that Brando and his kind – undisciplined, with no reverence for tradition – were what was wrong with the movies, perhaps with all of society.

At first, prejudiced glance, Brando's performance as Fletcher Christian seemed to prove their point. For it was manifestly not Clark Gable's. And everyone was feeling sentimental about him, since he had just died prematurely, killed, as rumor would have it, by the exertion of working with another difficult exemplar of the new Hollywood order, Marilyn Monroe.

It was true, Brando was no Gable. In this role, he was much better. Gable's Christian had been a stolid, no-nonsense, very American sort of hero. Brando first appears as a drawling fop, with a dandy's red cape swirling about him, a handkerchief tucked in his elegant sleeve, handsome ladies on his arm, talk of a swell country weekend on his lips. He infuriates Bligh, an officer up from the ranks, and sensitive to class slights. Since the *Bounty*'s mission is to collect samples of breadfruit, thought to be useful in feeding the masses, Brando is languidly contemptuous – 'halfway 'round the world on a grocer's errand'.

It is a delicious performance, wonderfully comic, and socially acute (his accent is perfectly placed, he is clearly of the squirearchy); and its beginnings – once again – leave the actor somewhere to go. Indeed, what can eventually be read as rebellion begins as upper-class needling of a lower-class – let us use the anachronistic term – nerd. That Bligh has a corrupt side and a sadistic streak comes almost as a surprise to Christian, and the principled opposition to the captain that develops in him, as evidence of misconduct piles up, comes as a surprise to him, too. It is, at first, unimaginable to him that he might become the leader of a mutiny. He conducts it, when finally he must, with impeccable manners. And he seeks most earnestly to convert it into something else, not just an end to wretched conditions, but a beginning of a better alternative. (In a way, Brando's later attempts to live on his own private atoll in the South Pacific, and to develop aquafarming techniques there, represent in some measure an example of life trying to imitate art.)

Indeed, Brando's playing of the tragic last passages on Pitcairn, with his shipmates falling into moral disarray, his hopes coming at last to nothing as the *Bounty* burns in the harbor, completes the thoughtful arc of his performance. His own line is almost strong enough to compensate for the fact that the dramatic line he insisted on for the movie remained essentially intractable, imposing on it a whimpering conclusion. Yet he does not lose our sympathy. 'I did what honor dictated, and that belief sustains me,' he says, before adding, still with something of the wicked dandy about him, 'except for a slight desire to be dead.' If the rest of the actors – giving much more conventional performances – had been up to him, and if his directors had imagined a way to key this elephantine enterprise to his eccentric work, they might yet have pulled off an artistic coup. Or anyway a cult classic.

It would have been useless at the time to point any of this out, such was the hue and cry about Brando's brave and original performance, which, taken together with the stories that had preceded it, and the commerical failure that followed, did irreparable harm to his career, and perhaps to his self-regard. What might have been seen as the great climax to this phase of his career was instead seen as its nadir, the bad end which so many had for so long predicted. He would be many years recovering from this fiasco.

But let a good and wise director, soon to enter Brando's life, have the final, and more nearly accurate, word. Said Arthur Penn, some years later: 'Hollywood loves to elevate someone to stardom and then start tearing him down. When you have someone like Brando, who is a superbly creative human being, I think they are terrified of him and I think that was probably the case on *Bounty*. Personally, I thought his performance was a terrific work of art.'

SIX

FOOLISH SEASON

I n 1966, Pauline Kael, considering Brando at mid passage (he was then 42), summoned no less an authority than Ralph Waldo Emerson to help her define the issues her favorite actor – she has been his most faithful critical supporter – was then confronting. 'Thou must pass for a fool and a churl for a long season,' the Transcendentalist sage had advised the American artist a century before. Kael added this gloss: 'We used to think that the season meant only youth, before the artist could prove his talent, make his place, achieve something. Now it is clear that for screen artists, and perhaps not only for screen artists, youth is, relatively speaking, the short season: the long one is the degradation after success.'

The piece is a typical Kael performance, full of sharp, discrete observations which she is unable to marshall into a fully sustained, entirely persuasive argument. What she seems to be saying finally is really rather banal: that the sometime 'Byronic Dead End Kid', a fellow who clearly awakened in her certain – shall we say? – sub-critical responses, and a man who surely had the potential to redefine our ideal of heroic acting, had been seduced and betrayed by Hollywood – same as everybody else in the overarching mythology by which literary people comprehend life upon the wicked sound stages.

She likened the development of his career to that of the typical hero of a typical movie, at first discovered to be in some way atypical, either more idealistic or more cynical than the norm, then forced by the mechanisms of the plot to be either raised or lowered until he seems to share the values common to the audience. Brando's entire public life, says Kael, follows that line, except that, desperate to escape from ordinariness, he had chosen 'to become an eccentric, which in this country means a clown, possibly the only way left to preserve some kind of difference.' She adds: 'When you're larger than life you can't just be brought down to normalcy. It's easier to get acceptance by caricaturing your previous attitudes and aspirations, by doing what the hostile audience has been doing to you.' She cited John Barrymore and Bette Davis as people who had preceded him in this strategy.

One trouble with that argument is that Brando always *was* a wierdo, long before anyone ever heard of him. Surely his 'eccentricity' deepened with the passing years, but the overall evidence is that he consciously chose to stress that side of his nature less, not more, in his Sixties work. Kael to the contrary notwithstanding, he is *less* self-consciously witty, *less* self-satirizing, than he was in the fat Fifties movies she was at pains to deplore, when his spirits were up and he carried with him the feistiness of success. He is also much less sexy than before, much less volatile than he was in his previous on-screen encounters with women. Indeed, it is impossible to recall a single romantic scene that had either the rapacious menace of *Streetcar* or the insinuating seductiveness of his scenes with Eva Marie Saint in *Waterfront*.

This is peculiar, almost perverse, given the movement of the decade's larger social currents and even trends within the movie industry. After all, black comedy was increasingly 'in', in all the better cultural circles and there really was a sexual revolution going on somewhere. And both were matters that should have interested Brando the actor and Brando the screen character. That they did not may have been a function of the increasingly restricted choice of roles presented to him, or it may have been a function of the increasing sobriety with which he confronted a world now visibly living up to his worse expectations in terms of racial relations and its incapacity to attack the hunger and sickness and ignorance – a condition he claimed was borne in on him on his many visits in this period to Third World nations. Most of the time, apparently, he didn't feel like being funny or sexy in public. It is also likely, as we shall see, that his response to roles was dulled by his inability to connect consistently with directors who would create for him the kind of atmosphere which he needed for his work. Time and again we find him beginning movies in good spirits, contributing good moments to them, then withdrawing from them emotionally.

If one had to pick a single word to characterize Brando on screen in the Sixties, it would not be 'eccentric'. At best, this quality is the occasional saving – but never totally sustaining – grace of his work. When it is completely absent (in, say , *The Appaloosa* or *The Countess from Hong Kong* or *The Night of the Following Day*) he – and we – are in trouble.

Curiously, there are times when 'professionalism' seems the right word for him. He often has the air of a man making the best he can of a bad job – that is to say, mobilizing a certain amount of craftsmanship, but nothing like his former free-wheeling inspiration, as he toils his way through the decade. But professionalism – which we might define as practiced moves presented with bland conviction – is not a rare quality among star actors.

Their reliability is one of the qualities that make them stars, but it was not enough for Brando, and it was not enough for us.

From him we wanted a sense of danger, the possibility that he would fall flat on his face attempting some high-risk, previously unknown turn. And that he did not give us. Considered purely as an actor, shorn of the promises he had made previously, he was mostly, well, OK in his Sixties films. OK – it's the last term we ever expected to apply to him. And perhaps the last term he ever expected to have applied to him. Toward the end of this period one began to see this passage as a long ritual beating of the kind he so often absorbed (and continued to absorb) in his films, and to see him as a man stoically accepting them – just desserts for an actor who never quite believed he was entitled to the good fortune, or the acclaim, that had been visited on him.

Finally, though, the word that seems most nearly to characterize his work in the period is . . . 'depressed'. The word carries with it all sorts of clinical connotations that are reflected in his screen work: lack of sustained concentration, inexplicable anger, low libidinal energy, infinite distractability.

It is convenient to blame his troubles on Hollywood crassness and insensitivity – never in short supply – and on a malevolence particularly directed at Brando, which had begun to gather in the Fifties and visibly surfaced in the Sixties, when people began to feel it was safe to set loose. Depending on your point of view, Hollywood is either a closely knit community, jealously protective of its own rather conservative social standards, or it is tribal in a harsh and primitive sort of way, quick to banish individuals whose weaknesses seem to endanger the tribe's welfare. Its behavior is particularly vicious toward box office leaders who become laggards – especially if, like Brando, they were not, when they were on top, notably sensitive to local standards of *politesse*. One does have to take tables at charity functions, pay elaborate tribute to prominent dolts and nincompoops, 'put back in' (as a favorite local saying has it) to an industry that has treated you generously, with *pro bono* activites. All of which says nothing of its natural fear of singular and rebellious talents.

His enemies, however, may not have been as important in shaping (or rather misshaping) Brando's career as his friends were. This is a point Kael was bound to miss, since one of the most basic tenets of her criticism is the belief that Hollywood is the world headquarters of evil genius, the typical movie deal essentially a pact with the devil. 'Corruption' is a word much used by her. 'Whore' and 'whoring' are also favorites. It sounds like tough-minded realism, but it is really dark romanticism, a kind of bedazzlement with Hollywood's otherness. In fact, Hollywood's business style is a curious mix of the avuncular, the confrontational and the careless – all quite transparently obvious. The genius of this system lies not in subtlety, but in its notable lack. What happened to Brando was not that anybody asked him to 'sell out.' Or forced him to. It was that attempts to rescue his suddenly faltering career by perfectly well-meaning people produced dismal unintended consequences.

It happened like this: in the wake of the *Bounty*'s disastrous voyage, it was apparent that Brando required a safe harbor in which to lay up and repair damages. And MCA, his long-time agents, were now in a position to provide one. In 1959, the agency, in a complicated deal mainly predicated on its need for production facilities for the television programs it was then packaging for its clients, had taken control of Universal Studios. Subsequently required by the federal government to choose between production and the agency business, its executive opted for the former, on the grounds that the money would be better. Their business plan was to use TV as a source of profits steadying the company against the higher risks inherent in feature production, and as a place where new talent could be developed, old talent pastured. They determined, as well, to make their theatrical films on a carefully cost-controlled basis. No *Mutiny on the Bounty* for them. And no *Cleopatra* (the 1963 Fox release was the most expensive in history to that date and it became, for the industry, a cautionary film).

Brando's trusted agent, Jay Kantor, became a highly placed production executive at Universal, and he offered the star a one-picture deal for the modestly priced Pennebaker production of *The Ugly American*, as Brando's first picture after *Bounty*. Soon thereafter Universal bought Pennebaker for a reported $1 million, in a deal that obliged Brando to make a certain number of films for the studio on a non-exclusive basis.

Brando was by no means the only one-time MCA client who found a home at Universal, but he was probably the one least likely to succeed at a studio committed to cost-conscious, genre-oriented production. On the other hand, the studio had no desire to sabotage him, and had every motive to return him to success. Then, too, Brando may have imagined he could make his arrangement with the studio work for him in another way, since it provided him with financial stability while leaving him free to embark on other more ambitious or more 'personal' projects. One can discern, in at least half the films Brando did in the Sixties and early Seventies, reasons why an actor of his background would take them on. Some of them aspired to make the sort of political statements that would interest anyone who had imbibed the Group Theater tradition, others carried the potential to challenge him as an actor. That almost all of them failed, often ludicrously, to fulfill their promise does not invalidate his enthusiasms. Neither does the fact that some of his directors failed to fulfill their promise to provide him with the creative atmosphere he required, failed to listen to him, take his ideas seriously.

Let me reiterate, for emphasis, a point made earlier: even as he turned forty, even in his huge fame some part of him was still clinging to the only identity that had ever made sense to him, that of the young actor, maintaining his 'integrity', seeking 'good experiences', in his work. No one was ever going to accuse him of 'whoring'. For that matter, no one was going to accuse him of being 'a movie star', though of course many in the business, those with no eye for motivational distinctions, did.

It was now possible to impute to his renunciations, and ultimately his degradations, a certain martyred nobility. But even so, for us, his core audience, the disappointments were acute. It was not just that he was working in bad pictures; we could understand that as the luck of the draw, even as a sort of inevitable balancing out of his average, given the good luck that had attended the early phases of his career. It was that for the most part he was working in *cheap* bad pictures.

For, with just a couple of exceptions, his Sixties movies did not have even the commercial ambitions of his second-phase films. They were mostly – to the degree that the old-fashioned term was still applicable to the new Hollywood – program pictures. Whether at Universal, where much of his work was perforce done, or elsewhere, his films were routinely made, generally by directors – even some who had good reputations at the time – turned out not to be first-class; by other craftsmen of no great distinction, with supporting casts of the most modest attainments. No one would mistake these films for events, except insofar as Brando's presence in anything made them so for his loyalists. They were designed primarily to keep studios and distribution systems humming – well, no, busied, since Hollywood could not be said to have been humming in this period (box office receipts reached their all-time low in 1962; attendance was cut in half, and fell below 20 million per week, for the first time, in 1967).

Finally – and this was perhaps the most grievous of all defects in a time when Brando himself, and most of his natural, middle-brow audience were galvanically politicized by the Civil Rights struggle and the war in Vietnam – only two or three of them were endowed with any sort of contemporary social or political relevance. Now, at a moment when one might have expected Brando's social consciousness, if not his artist conscientiousness, to be rewarded with the kind of work he (and we) had the right to expect, he suddenly seemed in every respect irrelevant, a back number.

It was intolerable, this dismissal. Intolerable, that is, to those of us who had chosen him as our Paladin. We could comprehend this passage only as one of those trials by which, traditionally, heroes are tested in myth and literature. 'Marlon Brando: An American Hero' was the title of Kael's essay. In the early Seventies, I wrote an article about him that went even further, rather grandly trying to fit Brando's career to the pattern of Joseph Campbell's heroic 'monomyth'. To wit: a first act in which the hero endures the drama of departure and then isolation from the community that nurtured him (i.e. the theater specifically, culturally aspiring middle-brow society in general); a second act in which he undergoes a series of trials (we are at the dark center of that act at this point in our story); a third act in which a victory is achieved and he returns in triumph to reintegrate with the society he left behind in youth (this he seemingly achieved in 1972, with the almost simultaneous release of *The Godfather* and *Last Tango in Paris*).

They seem silly now, these ponderous critical impositions on the poor man during a hard time. But they do, at least, measure our extraordinary commitment to him. If to justify our faith in his genius we had to impute to Brando a valiance that embarrassed him and made us look a little foolish, too, well so be it. Had he not taken much larger risks on behalf of his art? This high regard also measures, I think, a degree of self-pity, as well as pity for the actor's circumstances. We just couldn't believe that our champion could sink as low as he did in the Sixties. And we with him.

For, like many of us in this period, Brando suffered not merely from career confusions, but from personal and ideological confusions as well. His private life, not to put too fine a point on it, was a mess. He divorced Kashfi in 1959, and finally married Movita at a secret ceremony in 1960, because she, like Kashfi before her, was pregnant. (Brando claimed in court that after they conceived their child they never again slept together.) In 1962, they, too, separated, more or less amicably. But there was nothing amicable about his relationship with Kashfi. Their custody battles over their son, Christian, continued on into the 1970s: throughout this period they were in and out of court, asserting their claims on the boy, accusing one another of innumerable violations of various agreements about where (and how) he should spend his time. There were frequent raids on one another's homes in attempts to reclaim Christian, and these sometimes ended with the police intervening. To complicate matters still further, by 1970 Brando had fathered two more children with Tarita.

It seems worth recording his remarks to Capote a few years earlier on the subject of love: 'What other reason is there for living? Except love. That has been my main trouble. My inability to love. . . . I can't love anyone. I can't trust anyone enough to give myself to anyone. . . .' It was not an uncommon confession from a man of his age and background, especially one who was, as he was at the time, in the midst of a twenty-year course in psychoanalysis. Nor was his relationship with his children unique, just rather more complicated than most, given their varied maternal backgrounds and his unique status in our celebrity hierarchy – the latter a point Brando has more than once advanced in discussing Christian's case with the press in 1990.

Like a lot of successful, preoccupied men, Brando appears to have been an affectionate and indulgent father, but often a very distant one. As his family grew he seems to have looked at it, perhaps understandably, in somewhat unconventional terms, perhaps as a little United Nations, with himself as a sort of benignly neglectful Secretary-General. In one of her court actions, Kashfi raised a not entirely unreasonable question about Christian's exposure, in his father's house, to a succession of lovers and a variety of half-siblings. To which Brando replied blandly that he expected his children, regardless of who their mother was, to play together as brothers and sisters. Very nice. Very naive. And not entirely forthright. Christian, for example, seems to have had everything he needed, except the things a child needs most – emotional and geographical stability. In those periods when Brando did have custody of him he was often left in the care of Brando's women friends or of his sister Fran and her husband in Illinois. There were spells in boarding school, too. How could his father expect the boy to grow up untroubled? Or to accept his siblings without strain? Or they him. The ideal was fine; the practicalities of the situation were daunting.

This was especially so because Brando now embraced political activism, becoming more than ever a restless wanderer on behalf of the causes that stirred him. This was not entirely uncharacteristic behavior, to put it mildly, among artists of all sorts, performers in particular, during this period. And, of course, there was nothing especially compelling going on in Brando's career, nothing to make him want to keep his nose pressed against the grindstone.

He travelled widely in support of the civil rights movement, abandoning his reclusive ways for extensive public appearances. Among them, prominently, were the Selma, Alabama and the Washington, DC civil rights marches of 1965. After Martin Luther King's assassination in 1968, he walked through Harlem with New York mayor John V. Lindsay, in a

successful attempt to calm riotous unrest. A month later he was in Berke-
ley on a more controversial mission – an appearance at a memorial service
for a member of the Black Panthers, slain by police. In this tragic year, he
went everywhere, even into the jungle of the talk shows – the last place one
expected to find him – on behalf of the movement. He seemed to want to
take on himself all the guilt of the white race for all the inequities visited on
the blacks. At the ceremony for the black radical he said: 'The preacher
said that the white man can't cool it because he has never dug it. I am trying to dig it. That's why I'm here.' Significantly, he added: 'You've been
listening four hundred years to white people and they haven't done a thing.
. . . I'm going to begin right now informing white people what they don't
know.' This, for a time, he earnestly tried to do. He even tithed a percen-
tage of his income to the Southern Christian Leadership Conference.

At the same time, he worked for UNICEF, even attempting to make a
documentary about starvation in India. Later, in the mid Seventies, his
concern for the fate of American Indians brought him to Wounded Knee,
to the Menominee Uprising in Wisconsin, to many a fund-raiser for the
cause, and, at the height of his involvement, to stage-managing his famous
non-appearance at the 1973 Academy Award broadcast at which a surrogate rejected his *Godfather* Oscar as a frivolity not to be countenanced
when most native Americans were discrimated against, kept in dire
poverty and, as well, grievously misrepresented in film and television.

Until this later period, when his passions seemed to run away with him,
Brando the activist was almost as singular as Brando the actor. But in the
opposite way. For unlike many of the other performers who thrust themselves forward as spokespersons for this or that cause, he caused almost no
controversy. In the Sixties, he took positions, contributed his presence, but
almost never made pronouncements. He did not strike revolutionary poses
in public, nor did he offer radical criticism of the society that had created
the conditions about which he protested. His manner, instead, was very
much that of less famous liberals, quietly, self-effacingly bearing witness to
the things he believed in, seeking redress of specific grievances and appealing to conscience in the most polite and reasonable terms. Nor did his involvement with the Civil Rights movement lead him, as it did so many
other celebrities, to noisy opposition to the war in Vietnam. To put it
simply, he was no Jane Fonda. Certainly he stirred none of the exaggerated
outrage she did in this period.

To some, of course, political posturing by persons who have gained fame
in non-political pursuits is always an anathema. Contemptuous talk about
selling political ideas through celebrity endorsements, as if they were so

much detergent, has abounded in high-minded circles since the 1930s. But since it has become an ineluctable fact of American public life, it seems idle to debate the practice further. It is not idle, however, to analyze a little further Brando's style in this realm.

In 1969, Renata Adler wrote a short essay that remains the best analysis of the way the Fifties generation responded to the politics of the Sixties. Some of us, she wrote, 'dropped a generation back, to lead a student movement that belies everything we are,' and some of us quietly took positions 'in society as it was before we came and as, in the years of its most annihilating smugness, it nearly killed us off.' But some of us, knowing 'what there was of our alienation privately, and not yet as a claim or a group experience,' could not bring ourselves to make common cause with either of these groups any more than we could, finally, with Sixties youth. We tried, some of us, but, as Adler says, 'the rhetorical and inarticulate' had no appeal for a crowd that had long since learned that the most comfortable place to stand was 'at a certain humorous remove from our own experience.' Ironists we were, and if any cause summoned our souls it was clarity. We became, as Adler put it, 'the last custodians of language', because 'lacking slogans, we still have the private ear for distinctions.'

And here – talk about ironies! Marlon Brando in his curious way continued to serve us, though that was not entirely clear to us – and was probably not clear to him – at the time. Formerly, he had implicitly challenged, with his behavior on and off screen, middle-class smugness; now he implicitly challenged radical chic embraced by many in this class. At any rate, he maintined a certain reserve, a certain distance, from it.

To trace Brando's course through the Sixties is to trace a course many of us followed, albeit less colorfully: from political engagement via support for the Civil Rights movement, which was our kind of revolution (belated, necessary, well-spoken and, in its tactics, morally unexceptionable), to disengagement when its fervor, but not its capacity for making careful distinctions beween allies and enemies, was taken over by the anti-war movement. A spirit that, for a moment, held the promise of erasing many class distinctions, was transformed, through violence and the crudest kind of media manipulation, into a spirit that exacerbated those distinctions, how ever unexceptionable the cause it tried to advance. In the later Sixties, many of us who were older than the college-age activists, withdrew in disgust from our newly redefined political life. Or at least, narrowed our focus, concentrating on this or that specific issue – ecological or consumer matters, for instance, or the needs of a particular social group. It was at this point that Brando's involvement with the Indian rights movement became his primary public issue. By then no one was paying much attention to Marlon Brando, and until his re-emergence in the Seventies as a leading spokesman for, and a significant contributor to this movement, he kept quite a low profile. There was a moment when, devastated by the murders of Martin Luther King and Robert Kennedy, it was rumored that he might abandon acting altogether and devote himself entirely to quasi-political activity. On the other hand, there was also speculation that he might withdraw from *all* forms of public life. He has himself said that he was, by that time, 'paralyzed with hopelessness', but he attributed that to the hunger and misery he had seen on his travels in the Third World. It also seems likely that the disarray of his career contributed to the distinct air of withdrawal that hung about him in the last two years of the Sixties and the first two of the Seventies.

Whatever his reasons, it was in 1968, that watershed year in recent American politics, that, after a search that had taken him to Mexico, Bali and Thailand among other locales, he bought Tetaroa, a circular atoll consisting of thirteen small islands thirty miles north of Tahiti. He had first glimpsed it during the making of *Bounty*, and now he imagined that it might be a place where he and his family could achieve self-sufficiency and survive the holocaust which recent events had convinced him would soon come. As late as 1976, he still thought world devastation was likely. He told a journalist visiting him on Tetaroa: 'The end is near, if not at hand.'

One may reasonably speculate that he was over-dramatizing, justifying a decision that was not in some respects very practical. Tetaroa may be a great place to lie low, but it also, quite literally, lies low, about five feet above sea level. His hopes for a vacation hotel were spoiled by flooding – and importunate guests. With a shudder he would recall 'Middle-aged ladies from Peoria telling me, "Mr Brando, we loved you as Napoleon" for Christssake.' And a colleague described his days as a hotelier thus: 'He'd hide in his hut all day, until the dinner bell rang. Then he'd run like hell up the beach, like Bigfoot or The Abominable Snowman, and disappear into a clump of trees.' In more recent times he has devoted himself to experiments in aquaculture, and the island is also, apparently, a notable sanctuary for tropical birds.

How typical this now seems, this arc of activity. How many of us, over these years, passed from self-absorption to public activism to, finally, a more private exercise of our social commitments – his generation, my generation, the next generation. The question was always this: how to maintain one's sense of self (perhaps a better phrase might be one's tradition of self) while at the same time participating usefully in the life of confusing,

144

not to say wrenching, times.

If we look more closely at Brando's movie work in this period it becomes obvious, however, that within the increasingly limited options available to him (and no matter how disappointing the finished product turned out to be) it was the actor in him, not the political idealist, that he was usually trying to satisfy. By and large his choices only make sense if we look on them as opportunities either to stretch his gift or to find an environment in which it could function comfortably. In particular he appears to have agreed to the majority of his projects because the directors already attached to them promised to create the kind of working conditions he required. This, I believe, is the hidden theme of his professional life in the decade following the *Bounty* debacle.

On the surface, the first of these films, *The Ugly American*, seems to defy this argument. As it worked out, however, whatever interest the film has derives not from its rather commonplace 'message', but from Brando's performance in it. The former was rather standard liberal big-think. The latter was, at least for a while, wittily subversive of liberal big-thinkers.

Based on a best-selling novel of no literary merit whatsoever, but thought at the time to be 'controversial', *The Ugly American* tells the story of an American ambassador's eduction in Third World politics. An intellectually arrogant newspaper proprietor, Brando's Harrison Carter MacWhite, is appointed US ambassador to fictional Sarkhan, in Southeast Asia. He is questioned at his Senate confirmation hearing center on his friendship with a Sarkhanese named Deong, who served with him in the guerrilla war against Japan during the Second World War and has emerged as leader of the opposition to the American-supported government. He looks like a Commie to the Know-Nothing solons. MacWhite responds with a bland lecture: Americans have got to begin seeing issues in the non-aligned nations in terms other than black and. . . . red. Deong, he is sure, represents a third force in Sarkhan, one we must carefully, with reason and dignity, woo away from Communism.

Arriving in Sarkhan, and reviving this friendship, MacWhite begins to feel less sure about Deong. They fall out when, against Deong's advice, MacWhite reroutes his pet project, the so-called Freedom Road, financed by American dollars, so that it aims directly at a section of the country controlled by Communists. Just as his friend predicted, this does not look like economic development to the Reds; it looks like a counter-revolutionary threat. The Communists launch an attack on the road's dedication ceremony destroying in the process a children's hospital managed by the wife of the road's construction chief. (The couple are played by Jocelyn Brando and Pat Hingle). The ambassador is now convinced his friend is behind the attack, but no, the government tells him Deong is targeted for assassination by the Communists, who need him for a martyr. They do kill him, but his dying words are anti-Communist, pro-American. Even so, the guilt-ridden, and thoroughly chastened MacWhite resigns. He is last seen delivering one more lecture – this time on American television – urging Americans to aid in the development of Third World nations, not because it is a way of fighting Communism, but because it is the humanitarian thing to do. He believes, he says, that 'If the Cold War disappeared right now, the American people would still be in the fight against ignorance and hunger and disease, because it's right. It's right. And if I had one appeal. . . .'

At this point the hand of an unidentified viewer is seen reaching out to click him off – not unjustifiably. MacWhite *is* something of a bore – partly because throughout the movie he has nothing original nor radical (which seems significant, given Brando's avoidance of radical stances in his political activities) to add to the discussion of American foreign policy. His line was standard issue among enlightened liberals at the time, endlessly set forth on all the better editorial pages and Sunday morning discussion programs.

What's worse, though, is that the movie never escapes its origins in social science fiction (one of its authors was a political scientist). Its character and situations had been invented to make an essentially abstract point, and so never achieved human interest. Quirks, frets, crotchets – the element of surprise – were alien to them, and the film as a whole does not address this defect. Directed by a Brando pal, George Englund, who was one of his partners in Pennebaker, in a rather academic style – correct, distant, lifeless – it is visually monotonous.

It is also unconvincingly acted, except, on occasion, by Brando. He plays MacWhite, especially in the early passages, as an Ivy League twit – all drawling nasality and condescension in his hearing room appearance, all false self-confidence when he arrives in Sarkhan and attempts to fire up his weary and cynical diplomatic staff, all false *bonhomie* when he tries to re-establish his friendship with Deong. A dapper, smooth and above all vain man, he is often fussily busy with his pipe, smugly tamping and stoking it as he offhandedly delivers his high-minded opinions. He has, however, one quite deliberately cultivated oddity, a pencil-thin mustache, more suitable to a shoe clerk than to a member of the Foreign Policy Association. At first one reads it only as a signal of misguided vanity, but it can also be read as a signal of an individuality, mostly suppressed, from a man who has carefully taught himself temperateness. But whatever the facial hair signifies – and it

146

does seem worth stressing that it is a very sly mustache, not a boldly flaunted one – there it is: a quirk. Something to catch in your mind while the rest of the movie drones witlessly on.

At the time the performance drove Andrew Sarris crazy. Obviously aware that Brando's company was the producer of record, the critic made the not illogical point that the film was 'designed to make Brando the center of attention at all times.' He guessed that weakish actors were deliberately cast so that Brando could effortlessly outshine them. He observed, for example, that Brando could steal a scene from Sandra Church – Broadway's original *Gypsy*, who had made a comic-touching virtue of modesty on stage – 'simply by breathing', and that the Japanese actor, Eiji Okada (of *Hiroshima, Mon Amour*) had such a weak command of English that he could not hold his own in contention with the star.

Fair comment. Especially about a man who may have felt a need, at that moment, to reassert his star power as forcefully as he could. On the other hand, he sometimes has about him the air of a man rather desperately trying to save the show. That is to say, one can imagine the actor looking at a dull script and dailies and saying, 'Uh-oh, somebody better do something,' and getting busy. Perhaps too busy. There is more here than the send-up comedy Kael perceived in the film, and more than mere egocentricity, too. But whatever motivated Brando, one must insist that if *The Ugly American* has any interest at all after almost thirty years, that interest – intermittent as it is, since finally the plot's bad coinage outweigh the good coinage of Brando's work – derives from Brando's canny observation of a social type and his attempt to portray a man losing misplaced confidence and coming to fuller, truer consciousness of himself and the world. In other words, for whatever reasons – perhaps good, perhaps bad – in *The Ugly American* he was an actor acting. And an actor thinking.

Against the accumulated wisdom of the ages, I maintain that Brando sustained that attitude even unto his next film, *Bedtime Story*. 'Say it ain't so, Marlon' was the common response to this venture at the time, and it has passed into the annals as the common consent nadir of his career, mostly, it would seem, because no one has the heart to retrieve the body from cold storage, lay it out on the table, and conduct a responsible autopsy on it. One might have thought that the comparative success of *Dirty Rotten Scoundrels* in 1988 would have encouraged this activity, since it is, until its new, improved cinding, virtually a scene-by-scene (often shot-by-shot and line-by-line) remake of *Bedtime Story*. But that hasn't happened.

Too bad. One has to be careful not to make too bold a claim for this movie. But this much should be said for *Bedtime Story*: it's a pretty solid

147

farce, full of lively, original comic invention, and it is directed with more conviction than a lot of Brando's other movies – even if (ahem) Ralph Levy had little experience outside television. More important, precisely because he had never played farce before, and was intrigued by its techniques, it energized Brando. He admired his co-star, David Niven, for his graceful comic ways, and was on record as thinking he could learn something from *movie* actors of his kind (Tracy and Grant were mentioned), men who know how to hold back and then 'dart in' to make their points. He often deferred to Niven as they worked out scenes together. His other co-star, Shirley Jones, reported the set to be a happy one, with Brando having 'a good time', despite worries about a recent weight gain (the first of many), which led to more than usual concern about his lighting and make-up.

His commitment shows in the movie. Even one who admires his generally under-valued work in *Bounty* and *The Ugly American* must admit that there is a certain tightness about him in these films, something occasionally too studied, too self-conscious in the pursuit of his effects. Here he is relaxed, cutting loose, overtly rather than covertly clowning, and perhaps sending a plea to his audience: lighten up, gimme a break – something like that.

Why didn't we? In part, I think, because this comedy didn't suit the style of its time, even though it was written by Stanley Shapiro, who had successfully scripted some of the Doris Day comedies, which had, as much as anything, set that style. As opposed to the great tradition of romantic or screwball comedy, these movies were single-issue comedies. In the earlier films the threat (or temptation) of sex outside marriage was usually just one of several problems a girl faced, and usually faced down with a show of wit or spunk. In Fifties and Sixties comedy, sex was the only issue, with Day, or someone like her, sweetly evading every threat to her virginity until Rock Hudson or Cary Grant or whoever gave up and agreed to meet her at the altar.

These films were very much the product of a slightly liberalized production code, which now permitted open smirking about sex – an attitude that somehow seemed more adult to people who had never once had an adult idea about sex. It seems likely that even Stanley Shapiro, who had made a good thing out of exploiting this opening, was fed up with it by 1964. For *Bedtime Story* is much rougher in tone and development than his earlier work. Its vulgarity is bumptious, not sneaky, and much the better for it. Brando is Freddy, a GI stationed in Germany but with a sideline in conning young women out of small change, usually with a story about needing funds to pay for an emergency operation required by his 'Grosse Mutter'

(Brando puts a nifty comic spin on that phrase). When he invades the Riviera turf of Lawrence (Niven), a much more elegant operative, preying on much richer – and older – women, that fastidious fellow reacts defensively. Freddy is a potential competitor, of course, being younger and more obviously sexy. But he also lowers the tone of the neighborhood and, indeed, threatens the good name of con artists everywhere.

Pretending to bring Freddy into his business as an apprentice, Lawrence in fact tries to abuse him into voiding the field. In one particularly swell sequence, Brando is required to play Lawrence's mad younger brother, helping him to get rid of a lover determined to marry the latter and bring him back to Oklahoma with her. Love me, love my brother Ruprecht, says Lawrence, who then brings her to a cell where Brando, affecting an underslung jaw, is soon tossing food around and swinging from the rafters like a demented ape – and an awfully good impersonation it is. Soon both men are in pursuit of Shirley Jones's Janet, believing her to be the heiress to a soap chip fortune, which it turns out she is not. In aid of his effort, Brando is next pretending to be a paraplegic, traumatized by a disastrous love affair (as if that cross-reference to a past triumph is not enough, he also has a line in which he carefully refers to himself as 'a bum', with just a hint of Terry Malloy in his tone). He's good at the physical comedy in this passage, and at comically turned self-pity.

Set aside for the moment the thought that this is not the sort of thing people expect to find their great actor playing at. It was also not the sort of thing we were supposed to think was funny – and still aren't. Lonely women preyed on for their money are a subject for pathos, not laughs. Nor are crazy people and cripples comfortable subjects for jokes. Nowadays, all of these minorities have lobbies, branches of that greatest of all lobbies, which defends the interests of the humor-handicapped. But even back in the Sixties, we knew it just wasn't – well, you know – tasteful – to base comedy on these unfortunates.

The spirit of farce has, of course, been strangled in these toils; it's an anarchic form which requires treating the pitiable with the same contempt it visits on the powerful. *All* things human must be alien to it, or else it loses its animating force and (depending on your point of view) descends or rises to satire, which is a form of special pleading. Certainly *Bedtime Story* was strangled in the several varieties of nice-nellyism with which people responded to it, and as a result comedy – at least comedy that announced itself as such – was effectively denied Brando thereafter, though he has gone on looking for chances to play it.

True, Pauline Kael thought he was funny in *Morituri* (meaning 'those who are about to die' – there was also a more explanatory title, *The Saboteur – Code Name Morituri*, hastily devised after the film opened poorly in a world weak on Latin tags). But he's going to the same well he went to in *Bounty* and *The Ugly American*, giving himself some room to grow by coming on in the early sequences in less than heroic guise. He's not a fop or a twit this time, but he is amusing at first glance as Robert Crain, an epicine pacifist, and a German living above World War Two's battles in India.

When British Intelligence, represented by Trevor Howard, first tries to recruit him, he responds, in the flutiest of tones: 'I think I have all I could possibly want. I have my books and my music and my mother's art collection, and a visit from a beautiful lady from time to time. And what I value most, my privacy.'

No dice. He is told he'll be turned over to the Germans if he doesn't sail aboard one of their freighters to make sure it does not deliver its cargo of rubber to Europe. The captain (Yul Brynner) is an anti-Nazi merchant seaman; the first officer is a devoted party member, a familiar kind of war movie fanatic; the crew is composed of criminals, some of them political, some of them the usual menacing riff-raff. Crain's main assignment is to disarm explosives which have been placed so as to destroy the ship in case it is about to fall into Allied hands – which he does in the film's only deeply suspenseful and entirely successful sequence.

The problem with the movie is that it aspires to being something more than a thriller. Brando is burdened (or perhaps burdened himself) with more than one speech of this nature: 'All wars are idiotic. I'm not concerned about this war. I don't care who wins or loses it. I am concerned about the Gestapo. You have no idea what they are capable of.' Worse, though, is its heavy traffic in heavy irony. It belabors the fact that Crain must befriend the Nazi first officer in order to advance his mission and pretend contempt for his natural ally, the civilized captain. And then it heads toward an even heavier irony. For the ship takes on, from a Japanese submarine, a group of American POWs and a young Jewish woman, Esther (Janet Margolen), who is being returned to Germany, and certain imprisonment in a concentration camp. When Crain's cover is blown, his only hope is to foment a mutiny and he seeks Esther's aid. This poor damaged creature has already been forced by Nazis to have sex with her brother and with seventeen soldiers – 'hour after hour, while you were listening to your Mozart' (which is, alas, an all-to-representative example of the screenwriting). Trying to help out by recruiting the American prisoners to Crain's side, she is forced to submit once again to gang rape, which drives her to insanity (eventually, mercifully, she is killed in the fight for control of the ship). This is simply too much. Irony has now darkened to horror, and the modest genre base of the movie simply cannot sustain those notes.

We may understand that in wartime groups of fighting men may permit themselves the descent into bestiality, even if they are on 'our' side. We may understand that fate sometimes forces people like Esther to endure unspeakable brutalities. But a movie that wishes to take up such matters must do so in a context of high seriousness. It can't casually pick them up and put them down in the course of telling a little suspense story. The viewing mind reels, disoriented.

Brando may have felt this. Reports from the location, which most of the time was a rented tramp steamer moored off Catalina, have him staging a near-mutiny of his own – possibly because he was dealing with an irony of his own. He had accepted this project, which was not a Universal film, in part because its director, Bernard Wicki, was the sort of person people were telling him he should work with — young, artistically ambitious (he had just done *The Bridge*, a much-admired German anti-war drama), unbeholden to Hollywood habit. As so often happens, people had mistaken a gloomy manner for authentic artistry. Brando unloosed one of his colorful metaphors to summarize his feelings: 'Making this movie has been like pushing a prune pit with my nose from here to Cucamonga.' Oh well, at least he was able to secure small roles for his old pals Wally Cox and William Redfield.

Undaunted, Pauline Kael was still advising him to look for directors of this ilk *after* seeing *Morituri*. Equally undaunted, Brando continued to follow that advice, signing to make *The Chase* with Arthur Penn, who was the most interesting American director of the Sixties. He had worked in live television, made a name for himself in the theater with his productions of William Gibson's *Two for the Seesaw* and *The Miracle Worker*, made a particularly intense film adaptation of the latter as well as the lively, original *Mickey One*, which was less a gangster movie than a commentary on the genre. He was just two years away from making that great touchstone movie of the era, *Bonnie and Clyde*.

Penn was not the only attractive aspect of *The Chase*. Lillian Hellman, to many a great lady of the theater (and certainly one with a taste for high, hot melodrama), was adapting the piece from a novel and a play by Horton Foote, who was one of a group of promising younger playwrights live TV had helped bring to prominence and whose writing was particularly attuned to actors of Brando's generation. The producer was Sam Spiegel, who had now added *The Bridge on the River Kwai* and *Lawrence of Arabia* to *Waterfront* and *The African Queen*, making him possibly the most successful independent of the time – a crude man who somehow made 'classy' pictures while maintaining a relentless and excessive style of life, all chartered yachts and rented country seats. Finally, an interesting cast was chosen. It was not exactly all-star, but it included three strong younger women (Jane Fonda, Angie Dickinson, Janice Rule), solid supporting players out of a variety of traditions (E. G. Marshall, Henry Hull, Miriam Hopkins and, once again, Brando's sister Jocelyn) and three promising male newcomers (James Fox, Robert Duvall and, in his first important movie role, Robert Redford).

In short (and on paper) *The Chase* was everything *Morituri* was not – a big, 'important' movie that attracted large anticipatory interest from press and public. It promised, as well, a serious examination of significant contemporary issues. For when Bubber Reeves (Redford) escapes from prison, and makes his way back to his home town in Texas – where Brando is the sheriff and the audience's surrogate, a decent, liberal-minded man trying to keep the lid on everyone's unreasonable passions – he awakens, in a single night, all sorts of class and sexual enmity. The story offered the possibility of a metaphorical examination of a topic much on everyone's mind in the wake of John F. Kennedy's assassination – the American propensity for violent outcomes. For Bubber, like the murdered president, is finally killed for no good reason, except that he stirs inchoate anxiety and envy and (perhaps) because he happens to be in Texas.

That metaphor was, Hellman insisted, an imposition. Her original intention had been 'a modest picture about some aimless people on an aimless Saturday night'. One somehow doubts this protestation, given Hellman's Stalinist past, and some aspects of the film itself, which makes much of the way the town's leading citizen – a banker, of course, with a decadent family – instigates the tragedy by trying to protect its interests and respectability.

But there is certainly plenty of evidence that the script was 'mauled about and slicked up', as Hellman put it, for three other writers were called in to work on it by Spiegel. And we know such massive intervention usually adversely affects the spirit of a production: everybody gets nervous and the producer, whom the writers are trying to satisfy, becomes the film's *de facto* author. That was the case here. 'What happened . . . was, of course, the center of the film . . . moved out of my hands and clearly into Sam Spiegel's hands,' Penn said recently. Thereafter, 'I was essentially in the position of a functionary . . . nicely paid to work with all these wonderful actors.'

152

This he did very earnestly. But, as he also says, 'I'm not sure I was ever able to coherently tell you what I thought the film was about . . . there was no way of saying, "Wait a minute, what does this all add up to?" . . . I was simply caught up in the components, making each of those as good as I could.'

Still, one of the components was Brando, and to Penn he was a revelation. One of the reasons the film has remained an embittering experience for the director, who said he was 'disfunctional' for a period after it was finished, was that 'Marlon improvised some wonderful, wonderful stuff . . . scenes that he improvised with Angie Dickinson, scenes that he improvised with this great company of absolutely superb actors . . . are just not in the film.' This was because 'the literal authorship of the film was in high dispute,' and Speigel just could not bear to add further confusion to the issue by adding this material. This is doubtless one reason he broke his contract with Penn, which called for editing to be accomplished in New York, and took the negative with him to London, where the film was cut with no directorial supervision. The producer knew, of course, that Penn would fight to insert these improvisations into the picture.

What we have here are all the elements of a big picture disaster: bickering authorial egos; a producer (whose successes had all come when he ceded control to strong directors) intellectually incapable of forthrightly solving the project's creative issues and relying on his natural deviousness to solve its human issues; a good director working on his first mainstream production and not knowing how to assert command of it. The result is a film that is uncentered in every possible way – narratively, intellectually, emotionally – and which presented itself to audiences as an almost random succession of melodramatic sensations. (The broadest of these is Bubber's murder. Having been rescued from a lynch mob, he is killed as Brando's Sheriff Calder leads him into the jail, with the scene staged so as to imitate the footage of Lee Harvey Oswald's murder by Jack Ruby.)

There being no more interesting way to read the movie, one is forced to read it as Kael did: superior Northern liberals looking down their noses at the Southern peckerwoods. My dear, what can you expect from such . . . primitives.

The first New York screening of the film was a disaster, with a packed house in a Broadway movie palace hooting and hollering and talking back to the screen. The critics treated it with similar derisiveness. They did not focus their contempt particularly on Brando, and, indeed, his performance (or what's left of it) comes across as workmanlike; his developing belly, which he was at pains to let hang out, suited the part, he worked up a good

153

Texas accent, and he accepted another of his ritual beatings. Fine. What else is new?

No one paid a lot of attention to that aspect of his role which is un-questionably one of the things that drew Brando to it – the irony of a Southern sheriff going against mythic and media type and being the one representative of authentic liberal values in the piece. And no one knew what Penn and the other actors did: that Brando worked harder, with less complaint, public or private, on this film than he had on any other for years:

'It was just a delight to watch him sort of hunker down into a set. You know, he'd come on a set and slowly make it his own . . . this would move around here, and this would be here, and pretty soon it was his place and his environment. And it was just lovely to behold. And the other actors, actors of no small accomplishment themselves – Jane Fonda – would literally, really watch him work. It was going to school with one of the greats.'

There is irony and instruction to be found here. For this role and this film were not better – were in many respects worse – than material on which he had exercised far greater contempt in the past. To be sure, Spiegel was un-happy with him: he sneered that Brando needed to feel tortured in order to work, and now 'had to pseudo-torture himself to function.' And Brando, disgusted by the producer's, and the studio's, constant attempts to raise the film's quotient of violence was heard to mutter: 'Fuck 'em. If they're going to be so stupid, I'll just take the money and do what they want and get out. I don't give a damn about anything.'

We have observed before Brando's inability to say what he means, espe-cially when he is trying to articulate professional dissatisfaction; notably his habit of condemning a movie for its failure to take up serious issues when, in fact, what's bothering him is a failure to provide him with the working conditions he requires.

The capacity to insist on your due is an essential requirement of the movie star's profession: 'they' (corporate Hollywood) will run roughshod over you if it is lacking. All the great ones – Davis and Cagney in their bold ways, Stanwyck and Grant in their more subtle ways – have had it. But Brando just can't bring himself to assert his skittish ego on his own behalf – nice Middlewestern Wasp boys are not taught that skill; are, indeed, taught that people who have it are not 'nice'. This was especially true, perhaps, for him, effacing himself as best he could in order to keep the tenuous peace between his parents. In any case, he felt obliged to wrap his profes-sional unhappinesses in high-sounding principles: the unworthy self stifled and held blameless for asserting its needs; worthy abstractions seemingly served.

Now here he was in a movie that, more than most, failed its promise, failed it laughably, in the process becoming a textbook case in how movies should not be made and presenting Brando himself in the dullest possible light. And yet he said almost nothing critical about it. There can be only one reason why: the working conditions suited him. He became, in Penn's view, the great saving grace of *The Chase*.

'I think Marlon Brando is one of the most maligned guys in the history of movies. . . . Brando is an eminently fair guy. And perfectly accessible and decent and available. He has an abundance of gifts and he makes those purely and prodigally available. . . . He's not just saying the lines, he's never, never dogging it. He's out there working. He loves the work, he loves the process. He doesn't like the economics. He doesn't like the environment. He doesn't like being a star. . . . But he does love the work.'

Uncanny, isn't it? This perversity. But it was Penn himself, working with actors the only way he knew how – like Kazan before him, working the only way *he* knew how – who perhaps unknowingly created the atmosphere which brought out the best in Brando: letting him consult his instincts and find his way into a part, letting him fool with Hollywood's sacred text, the shooting script, a document which is, of course, often the end product of foolings-with by far less talented and concerned people.

This is, I think, at the heart of Brando's career problem: there just were not enough Kazans and Penns to go around, not enough directors who knew, understood – and shared – the values of the acting tradition that had formed him. To put it another way, his struggle was not so much to say what he wanted to say, but to say it in the manner he wanted to say it. One can add that he was paying the pioneer's price: the actors who have crawled out from under his overcoat – the DeNiros and the Hoffmans and the Pacinos – don't have that problem. Or at least they don't have it as often. There are plenty of directors now who share with the actor in the process of finding and defining a character. If sometimes the new mannerism is a drag, and expensive to producers, one must also note that in the realm of performance, if nowhere else, a consistently higher level of authenticity is available in movies than was formerly the case.

Be that as it may, Brando continued his search for sympathetic, empathetic direction. In his next two films, neither of which need detain us long, he went first with another young director whose early films seemed promising, and then to one of the most revered of the old masters for help. His reward was still more frustration.

155

Sydney J. Furie was a Canadian-born director who had made two stylish (or should one say 'mannered'?) films in the 'swinging' London of the early Sixties – *The Leather Boys* and *The Ipcress File*, the former a youth gang film, the latter an espionage thriller. They seemed, especially the latter, very hip, though there was nothing about them to suggest that he was just the right man to direct a western. Still, sometime in 1965 he and Brando found themselves in Utah, pretending it was Mexico and the Southwestern American border, and trying to make something significant out of a story about a man whose horse is stolen by a Hispanic bandido named Chuy – pronounced Chewy (to risible effect, though not more so than the constant repetition of the name 'Bubber' in Brando's previous movie). He was played by slick John Saxon, and Brando's character, a saddle tramp named Matt Fletcher, has a terrible time recovering his property from him, an effort complicated by his growing need to extract a young woman named Trini (Anjanette Comer) from the bandit's clutches.

This time Brando's ritual punishment for daring to exist consists of being tied to rope and dragged through a rocky stream and scratchy sagebrush by a galloping horse. More interesting, or anyway more memorable, is a hand wrestling contest Chuy obliges him to engage in – for this is one with a difference: there are scorpions on the table, waiting to sting the loser's hand. At one point this contest is photographed from the scorpion's point of view. But then Furie's search for the odd angle is, finally, the most suspenseful element in the movie: what will he think of next? Through the horse's legs, through a tequila bottle – these are routine views for his camera. At one point he blocks out 90 per cent of the screen with some shadowy foreground object. At lots of points he keeps Brando in the dark; he is often, quite literally, just a shadow of himself.

This searching for dubious visual novelty when they should have been searching for his character drove Brando crazy. He and Furie argued about his make-up. They argued about the line changes he insisted on making – usually at that moment when canny movie actors try to stage such discussions: late in the day, when the light is about to go, and if the scene is not finished the set-up will have to be expensively duplicated the next day. People on the set imagined that any day he and Furie would come to blows. They didn't. Instead, Brando sulked a lot: you can see him doing it on screen. *The Appaloosa* is one movie in which he is guilty as charged: he mumbles. It is the perfect verbal equivalent of Furie's visual murkiness. Together, they contrived to create a cinematic rarity — a claustrophobic western. It is one form, perhaps *the* one form of originality this spacious genre cannot accommodate.

All right, so much for what passed as the avant-garde in the commercial cinema. Let's try classicism. Charles Chaplin, for example, a man whose devotion to the eye-level long and medium shots was unsullied by any technique that had been invented during the half-century intervening between the time he had first appeared in such a shot and found it good and the day he walked on the set to direct the first day's shooting of *The Countess from Hong Kong*. 'Hollywood chi-chi' was his phrase for all the other ways a camera might look at a scene.

This manner had always worked for him as a performer, permitting the camera to hold in frame all, or almost all, of his favorite subject, which was, of course, himself. Not that Brando, devotee of silent screen comedy, cared about that. He said that it would be a privilege to read the telephone book under The Old Master's guidance. He apparently did not notice that the script Chaplin presented him with was somewhat less original than a new edition of the phone book. For Chaplin had drafted this story in the 1930s, imagining at one time that it would be right for him and his one-time bride, Paulette Goddard.

It is the tale of a Hong Kong 'dance hall girl' – she works in a house where all the ladies are given titles – who stows away in the ocean liner stateroom of one of her customers. From there, the Countess, played by Sophia Loren, hopes to smuggle herself into America. Needless to say, the comedy revolves around his attempts to hide her presence. She threatens to tell the captain she has been abducted if he exposes her and he can't afford that since (1) he is in the midst of an unpleasant divorce and (b) he has just been appointed ambassador to Saudi Arabia. Naturally, enforced propinquity makes their hearts grow fonder, Inevitably, there is much slamming of doors and hiding in closets as passengers and ship's personnel threaten their secret. Needless to say, the claustrophobia here is even worse, than it was in Brando's previous film.

It is perhaps necessary to add that verbal exchanges, the delight of 1930s romantic comedy, which often operated quite happily in similarly cramped quarters, were not within Chaplin's range. Brando was several times reduced to belching for laughs that didn't come. Perhaps necessary to add Chaplin had less of the onset manner Brando required than any director he had ever encountered. It was his solipsistic habit to act out, in detail, every gesture and expression he expected his performers to make and to require that they imitate him precisely. 'Chaplin's a nice old gent,' Brando told a journalist in London (where the picture was shot). 'We do things his way, that's all.' He made no public criticism of the director, who was then 77. Reviewers were not so discreet, though, of course, everyone wrote about the picture more in sorrow than in anger. For everyone, after all, felt a little guilty about Chaplin, who had exiled himself from America rather than face immigration service inquiries into his former political and sexual activism. Few blamed the stars for this failure; most seemed to think it was nice, even brave, of them to help the old man out.

An elderly 'classicist' (Andrew Sarris's nice word for Chaplin) having failed him as badly as the bright young things had, Brando now found himself in the company of a man who, at 61, should have been at the height of his powers, but was not. Early and late John Huston created a great body of work, but now, no less than Brando, he was groping for handholds during a slippery passage. At some earlier point Brando had turned down *Reflections in a Golden Eye* on the same grounds that several other stars had – the role was that of a suppressed homosexual. But when his old rival, Montgomery Clift, died on the eve of production, he allowed himself to be recruited to an Italian location (something to do with co-star Elizabeth Taylor's tax situation and her desire to be near Richard Burton, who was also filming in Italy at the time). It did not, on the face of it, appear to be any more sensible a career move for him than it did for Huston. The director was famous for doing what most people thought of merely as bold, dashing adventure stories told with a certain humor. Brando was best respected for the agonizing authenticity with which he found his way to his best self. An adaptation of Carson McCullers' literary curiosity – a Gothic tale placed in the plain geometric confines of a Southern army post and told in a spare, straightforward prose almost worthy of Hemingway – just had to be all wrong for them.

But Huston's best films – the ones that constitute the main line of his career – are rather special kinds of adventures. *The Maltese Falcon* and *The Treasure of the Sierra Madre* and *The African Queen*, to name just a few typical works, are largely quest stories, involving eccentrics, ill-matched outsiders pursuing improbable, if not totally impossible, dreams. Everyone in *Reflection* is certainly eccentric enough – not to say downright weird enough – to claim Huston's concentrated attention. And though no one every strays from the fort, there is a quest in it. To be sure, it is a devious and unacknowledged one, but, in effect, it is for freedom: escape from the sexual closets in which three of its major characters are trapped. As Major Weldon Penderton, Brando, married to Leonora, a general's flighty, sexy daughter (Taylor), but reluctantly, in great anguish acknowledging his attraction to Private Williams, a mysterious enlisted man (Robert Forster), thereby acknowledging his true nature, Brando, too, is pursuing a variation on his great theme. He is not moving toward the good, toward an embrace of generally approved values, but he is moving toward acceptance of a painful truth about himself. The other major figures in this drama balance the scales of desire with great delicacy: Colonel Morris Langdon, a blunt and lusty brother officer, funnily played by the marvelous Brian Keith, uncomplicatedly enjoying his affair with Penderton's wife; Mrs Langdon (Julie Harris) an hysterically neurasthenic and self-destructive woman; and Anacleto (Zorro David), the Langdon's openly homosexual houseboy, whose cheery embrace of his sexuality is the equivalent of Leonora Penderton's.

They are a horsy crowd, these military folk, and Leonora's white stallion, which only she can master, is the I-can-read symbol of natural, unfettered sexual power. And Penderton's attempt to ride him is the source of his ultimate humiliation. The scene is terrifyingly staged by Huston, and it is the turning-point of the movie. After the animal throws him, Penderton beats the animal savagely. Thereafter, though, he begins to own up to what he really wants sexually, and it is his discovery that the always-lurking Williams is interested, not in him, but in his wife, that finally unbalances him completely. This leads to the film's climactic murder – of the private, who is discovered in Leonora's room, watching her sleep.

This is, obviously, a dangerous movie, walking not along the edge of intellectually fashionable absurdity, but of unfashionable hysteria. (Instead of using full Technicolor, the original release prints were struck in muted gold tones, intended to soften the impulse to titter at the bold, primary colors of the film's emotional palette.) But yet, it is also a film that imprints itself on the memory because of its vivid resistance to the usual. When, almost reluctantly you return to it today, fearing that recollection has once again played you for a fool, you discover that it is actually better than you remembered. For the years have done what Huston's gold tint (long since banished from the video cassette) couldn't accomplish – cooled and distanced it, so that it can be viewed with a certain objectivity. Seen in this new light, Brando's performance, in particular, comes as a revelation.

It is, simply, one of his greatest. Begin with his accent. It is strangled southern. He seems afraid of its softness, its sweet languidness. So he clips its impulse to the languid, treating his own voice almost as if it were a raw recruit whose undisciplined civilian ways must be stamped out in basic training. Move on to his appearance: the plastered down hair, the uniform kept tightly buttoned even when he is off duty, the ramrod posture that is never granted permission to stand easy. Finally, consider the measured precision of his locutions when he lectures, dryly, on military tactics, his effort to reduce the passion of battle to abstract logic. There is also a curious vanity about the man. He is like a little boy playing soldier, and rather pleased by his own (as he sees it) successful impersonation of conventional, grown-up maleness (he has a lovely moment, saluting himself in a mirror). And all of that, for Brando, is only a beginning.

When the stallion runs away with him, his furious response has about it a curiously innocent quality, that of a child confronting first knowledge of the world's intractability and his own powerlessness in it. His lips widen into a pout and he blubbers like a three-year-old. There is no sadism in his behavior, nothing to suggest that complexity of forces that compose an adult's rage. So the sequence becomes a confrontation with his imperfect primal self, the self that all his posturings cannot hide.

But it is, at last, his acknowledgement of what he is, what he must be and wants to be, that is most painfully real, and touching. When he thinks Private Williams is coming to visit him, he is back at the mirror, cold-creaming his face like a happy teenaged girl. His moment of moments is so quick that one could miss it with the smallest glance away from the screen – a quick pat of his hair as he sits, almost primly, on his bed, thinking his dream lover is drawing near, never imagining that Williams is headed for the bedroom next door. There was not then an actor in America who would have dared these moments, though now, with his example before them, many would. What is Stanislavsky's phrase? 'Public solitude.' Yes. The ability to behave in public as we do when we believe we are unobserved.

Much good it did him. The film was too rich for most critics' blood – and the general public's, too. There *was* hooting and hollering, and listings on their 'ten worst' lists by critics with such fine critical sensibilities as Judith Crist. In every sense, *Reflections in a Golden Eye* failed miserably. And deeply. It seems unlikely that it can ever recover from the contempt initially visited on it, even though Huston stoutly insisted, to the end of his life, that it was one of his best works. Certainly the set, despite all the volatile temperaments gathered on it, was a happy and hard-working one. Moreover Brando never once said a word against the film – a sure sign, as we know, that he had been granted the time and space he required to work as he felt he should.

To do your best and to have it go unrecognized, treated as indistinguishable from your worst, is embittering. And now, truly, Brando bottomed out. His next films, both of which were belated and half-hearted attempts to catch hold of styles that were thought to be favored by the youth culture, were unredeemed even by honorable intentions. The first of them, *Candy*, appeared in 1968. It was based on a book by Terry Southern and Mason

Hoffenberg (the former a voguish black comic novelist). The novel had originally been published by the Olympia Press of Paris, whose list included a lot of hard-core porn and some fiction of merit (like *Lolita*), which, for one reason or another, mainstream publishers feared. Anyway, the piece titillated the literati. The title is, of course, a play on a more famous title, *Candide*. Candy is a female innocent, exploited sexually by various archetypal fakirs of our time. Brando was recruited to the enterprise by its director, Christian Marquand, whom he had met in Paris when they were both young actors. They had remained close friends and Brando had, in fact, named his son for him. In the film he played Grindl, an Indian guru maintaining the lotus position in the back of a semi-trailer truck until circumstances offered him the possibilities of Kama-Sutrian positions. His make-up was perfect. His accent was superb, his comic timing sharp. He was a great sight gag, and as such it could be argued, perhaps, that his cameo appearance was the best thing in a movie attempting – but failing – to achieve the jumbled, anarchic spirit of, say, an old Marx Brothers movie. But the argument must be resisted. The movie was god-awful, in that peculiarly Sixties, throw-everything-at-the-screen-and-see-what-sticks sort of way.

If Brando's appearance in *Candy* can be explained, feebly, by his friendship with the director, there is no explanation whatsoever – political, professional or personal – for his appearance in *The Night of the Following Day*, although it did discharge his final obligation to Universal. The film, directed by Hubert Cornfield, whose filmography contains such titles as *Lure of the Swamp* and *Angel Baby*, and who was basically an empty stylist, ostensibly concerns the kidnapping of an adolescent heiress (Pamela Franklin) by a gang that is both inept and cruel. Richard Boone, an old Actor's Studio friend, plays the chief sadist: Rita Moreno, an old girlfriend, plays a drugged-out accomplice; Brando, with dyed blond hair contrasting prettily with his black turtleneck, appears as a jive-talking chauffeur (not entirely coincidentally named Bud), who finally turns on the conspirators and rescues their victim, though he cannot be said to have played him in the full sense of the word. The film has a chic air about it; its pace and imagery are dreamy; and, indeed, at the end the whole story is revealed to be a (possibly precognitive) dream on the part of the victim. Probably someone was thinking Sixties psychodelia, but the movie doesn't have the courage even of that misplaced conviction. Brando came to despise Cornfield, and had Boone replace him for the last few weeks of shooting. He also offered the most colorful of the many bad reviews it received: 'It makes about as much sense as a rat fucking a grapefruit.'

Queimada, as it was known in much of the world, or *Burn!* as it was re-titled to make it seem more accessible in the United States (it didn't help), was also a failed attempt to catch on to the Sixties *zeitgeist*. When its North American distributor dumped the picture, without making any serious effort to publicize and market it, Pauline Kael said they were making a mis-take, 'because it plays right into the current feelings of the young movie audience.' But it was she who was wrong, making the same error as the film-makers. The idea that the middle-class Sixties college kids, playing at rebellion, were serious revolutionaries was proposterous. So was the idea that they would dutifully take history instruction from a film that schemat-ically fictionalized nineteenth-century colonial experience, even if it did painfully analogize it to the current agony in Vietnam. Somebody should have remembered rude, shrewd Harry Cohn's ancient, possibly apochry-phal dictum, which held that people don't go to see movies where guys wear knee britches and write with quill pens.

Be that as it may, *Burn!* did have aspirations more serious than Brando's two previous attempts, and, once again, the director, Gillo Pontecorvo, was reckoned to be just the kind of young genius with whom Brando should cast his lot. His reputation was based on *The Battle of Algiers* of 1965, and his technique in that film *was* astounding. Using hand-held cameras, grainy black-and-white film, amateur actors, and short, newsreel-like cuts, he veraciously, ferociously captured the spirit of urban guerrilla warfare as Arab revolutionaries and French foreign legionnaires struggled for control of the eponymous city (it was reported that black revolution-aries in the US used *The Battle of Algiers* as a training film). Pontecorvo showed, at least in this picture, a more authentic gift than most of the young directors Brando had linked with, and the actor agreed to work with him even before Pontecorvo finished pitching his (unwritten) story to him in Hollywood.

Pontecorvo's timing was excellent, for Brando had recently turned down – after first appearing to agree to do – Elia Kazan's adaptation of his own novel, *The Arrangement*. His excuse was that he was too preoccupied by the threat of racial violence in the United States, and, indeed, in 1968 his public activities on behalf of blacks reached a height. He went so far as to say that henceforth he would only do movies of 'appropriate significance'. Which *Burn!* clearly promised to be.

It is, however, one thing to agree to act (in both senses of the word) on your principles (and for $750,000) in your living-room on Mulholland Drive, with views of Los Angeles stretching in all directions; quite another to act on them on a jungle location in Colombia. It is one thing excitedly to agree, in the three languages he and Pontecorvo imperfectly shared, to do a work of high principle; quite another to attempt the specific, practical work a movie requires across the kind of language barriers existing between actor and director. That is particularly so when the director is required to supply the kind of patient emotional support needed by an actor like Brando. After a few weeks of good feeling, things started to fall apart. To make matters worse, Brando became ill with a tropical facial rash that required constant attention between shots and, of course, distracted him.

He also grew increasingly anxious about the performance of Evaristo Marquez, a local agricultural worker whom Pontecorvo had discovered and cast opposite Brando in the demanding role of a native revolutionary named José Dolores. Besides being utterly untrained as an actor, the man spoke almost no English, and so soaked up much of the directorial attention to which the star naturally felt entitled. Finally, Brando became convinced that Pontecorvo was exploiting and mistreating his native cast (if so, the hypocrisy of the showbiz Marxist is delicious). Things came to a head when the director required some forty-odd takes of Brando, in a scene where he was forced to stand in the hot sun while a sugar-cane field burned behind him.

Brando headed for the airport, but much of the company followed him there to plead with him to stay. He acquiesced. But a little later, pleading illness, he decamped for good. The production shut down for months while the lawyers wrangled, the upshot being that it was finished in a non-tropical Third World country, Morocco, of all places for a story that was supposed to be set in the Caribbean. Ultimately the film limped into the theaters with (in the US at least) twenty minutes of the director's cut missing.

What confronted those of us who could find a theater where it was playing – and one had to move quickly – was not entirely uninteresting. Brando plays William Walker, a British *agent provocateur*, sent to a Portuguese island in the Antilles to foment revolution among the natives, so the English can take over and assure an uninterrupted supply of sugar for their tea. (Originally the island was supposed to be a Spanish possession, but the Franco government was touchy about Spain's reputation as a particularly cruel colonial power, so the film-makers ceded the place to Portugal, which historically had no presence in this part of the world, but whose boycotts of films – and production companies – that offended it were not as costly as those of its Iberian neighbor.) Walker finds in José Dolores a likely front man for a revolution, trains him and his men in insurgency, and soon enough the Portuguese are forced out. Asked by his revolutionary friend where he's headed next, Walker replies: 'A place called Indochina. Ever hear of it?' (The movie is somewhat better than that heavy-handed dialogue may indicate.)

Ten years pass off-screen and Walker is next discovered fallen low and brawling in a London dive. The imperialists need him again. For Dolores has learned Walker's lessons too well, and has now gone over to the opposition against the British. Brando returns to conduct a scorched earth campaign against his former ally, who is ultimately captured. Brando tries to save him from execution, first by telling the island's rulers that a dead martyr is more dangerous than a defeated revolutionary on the run, then by pleading with Dolores to escape, and showing him how to do so unscathed. His sometime comrade in arms refuses; he, too, senses the power implicit in martyrdom. The film ends with Walker being assassinated as he is about to take ship from Queimada (which means 'burned' – past tense – in Portuguese, and refers to a previous firing of the island when it was first conquered by the Europeans, but also has a current colloquial meaning, of course). A smile, somewhere between the ironic and the beatific, plays on Brando's face as he expires.

It is, of course, almost impossible to judge a film as drastically truncated as this one was by its distributors. Crucial sequences are quite obviously missing, and so its continuity is often incomprehensible. But it can be said that Pontecorvo is not a natural formalist. The immediacy of the *Cinéma vérité* manner he affected in his earlier film, the sheer rush of its rhythms, is badly needed here, and only rarely in evidence. Mounted on tripod or dolly his camera is stiff, distant, distancing. Nor does he know how to fill the screen with the spectacle of historical warfare. Everything looks paltry as well as far away.

This air of abstraction extends to writing and performance, too. The film badly needs both a well-personified protagonist and a richly characterized antagonist, but from the local population it supplies no one but some squads of Portuguese soldiery in its first half, a committee of businessmen and planters in the second. Brando was right – Marquez lacks the technical facility to play a hero; he looks the part, but he can't act it. Brando might have filled the anti-heroic vacuum, but the film gives him no background, no motivation, nothing on which to build a full characterization. And he, for whatever reasons – surely his disagreements with Pontecorvo have something to do with it – invents nothing. There is a shadow of his Mr Christian in his William Walker, but only a dim one. In any case, that's not a great idea, for this figure needs to be dark and devious, and Brando manages, at most, a sort of upper-crust cynicism. And, of all things, likability. For while using Dolores, Walker comes to like him, like him better, certainly, than the local colonialists he's supposed to be aiding, better than his far-off imperialist masters. One suspects that Brando's natural sympathy for 'the wretched of the earth' (to borrow a phrase from Franz Fanon, the Marxist writer whom Pontecorvo surely consulted) interfered with his 'process' as he worked on this role. One is also sure that his disgust with the whole enterprise also daunted his imagination. *Burn!* was perhaps not a disgrace as a film, but Brando's performance was troubling in its lack of spirit.

Bad enough that this was his tenth consecutive commercial failure (and one of the worst), but now Brando seemed not even to be trying. Directors who wanted to work with him could not get permission from the studios to employ him in anything like a major film, even at cut prices. In 1971 he was actually fired (it was a first for him) by producer David Merrick – exactly the sort of erratic egomaniac he should never have been working for – from the Sidney Lumet production of *Child's Play*, which was exactly the kind of third-rate material (guilty doings in a Catholic boys school) he should never have been working in.

The alternative was not, on the face of it, much better. It was *The Nightcomers*. But for some curious reason it reanimated him. It is what has since come to be known as a prequel, a tale that tells what happened before a more famous story takes place. In this case what we have is an account of the previous history of Peter Quint and Margaret Jessel, the ghosts who haunt the children in Henry James's famous ghost story, 'The Turn of the Screw' (which previously had been dramatized, and turned into a movie, *The Innocents*). We learn how they died and why they exercise such a powerful hold on the imaginations of little Master Miles and his sister, Flora. Basically it is because Quint (Brando), a servant at Bly House, an English country house, likes to tie up girls – especially Miss Jessel (Stephanie Beacham), the sexually repressed governess to the orphan children. Miles, having spied on their love-making, induces his sister to emulate it with him. Quint, it must be admitted, has a certain rough and ready charm, and a willingness, which no one else has shown, to play with the lonely youngsters. Since he has love and pain, love and death all mixed up in his mind, he soon has the children nicely muddled, too. Afraid that their spoil-sport housekeeper will send their friends away, they murder them in the belief that their shades will hang about Bly house, and keep them entertained in perpetuity. All right, Old Artificer, over to you.

'Turn of the Screwy' would be a perfectly acceptable alternative title for *The Nightcomers*. And looked at from a purely literary point of view, it is everything James never is: coarse when it should be delicate in its language, broad when it should be subtle in its effects, openly sexual when it should suppress the impulse to reveal. (The old Production Code had given way to the new ratings system in 1968, and this movie, like many of its moment, partook of the new freedom zestfully and tastelessly; some of Brando's encounters with Beacham came very close to soft-core porn.) It is, in short, a movie of which it is extraordinarily easy to make fun. And yet Brando is frequently very good in it. Sporting his first Irish accent – it's a good one – he is often utterly disarming in his passages with the children. There is no obvious note of menace in his playing, which makes him all the more menacing. For despite his talk about the big subjects, he is like a child himself, unaware of the ramifications of what he is spouting, and unaware of the effect it is having on his audience. This, of course, makes his murder at their hands the more startling, and also gives it a curiously satisfying psychological (and moral) correctness.

But the main thing about Brando's work is that it is alive, bursting with energy. The director, Michael Winner, is a cheeky, egocentric movie maker, who was known in those days for his lack of inhibiting 'good taste' was sometimes perversely stirring. Anyway, his spirit appealed to Brando. And Brando appealed to the director. 'Immaculately professional' was his judgement, 'the most hard-working actor I've ever met.' Cheerful, reasonable, self-critical, a great sense of humor – these were some of the other descriptions Winner offered an inquiring reporter a couple of years later.

And, indeed, the set was practical jokey. Brando, for example, was now wearing earplugs to keep distracting noises out. People wondered if he could actually hear the other actors' lines. So Winner had Beacham mouth her words silently and everyone had fun watching Brando trying to keep up, for several takes, the pretense that he could hear her. Another time the lunch break was called when Beacham was tied naked to her bed. Until then Brando had used knots she could easily slip out of, but this time he trussed her securely, and left her to squirm for a few panicky moments before returning to free her. Well . . . maybe you have to have been there.

But good feelings, though they may help, do not in themselves produce good performances. Confronting this film, minor and silly as it often is, one also confronts what had been largely absent from Brando's work for years – going back even to the late Fifties. That was, simply, libidinal energy. Or, yet more simply, sexiness of the special sort he had once delivered. Heaven knows, that energy had driven a private life marked by the hundreds of sexual encounters neither space nor inclination has permitted one to take up here. We all know that besides driving his performances in all his best case scenarios it is the quality that made him a star in the full popular sense. We can even see that it is what drove his only truly great performance of the Sixties, in *Reflections in a Golden Eye*, where he mobilized his sexuality implosively rather than explosively, menacing only himself with it. But now, however perversely, however parodistically, however self-satirizing, it was out in the open again. He is not just acting sadism in his encounters with Beacham in *The Nightcomers*, he is pleasuring in it – not perhaps in the cruelty itself, but in the surfacing of a dark, but authentic, element of sexuality that is almost never represented in movies.

And in those moments we suddenly saw what had been missing in his Harrison MacWhites and his Sheriff Calders and his William Walkers. Somehow that which had first drawn us to him, that which had been the generally unacknowledged source of the anxiety he had stirred in older generations, had been tamed without anyone quite knowing it was happening – including, I think, Brando himself. Pursuing the significant, the 'appropriate' statement, he had himself been guilty of the sort of self-repression that was anathema not only to the artistic principles that had formed him, but to his best self. And, most ironic of all, he had done so in the very period when everyone, everywhere was embracing the very sexual revolution he had, in his early presence, predicted.

Bad advice? Bad instincts? Bad Karma? Or just plain bad pictures – a run of them without precedent in the annals of stardom? In the end it is impossible to say which was the most important factor in bringing Brando to the brink of being unemployable as the Sixties turned into the Seventies – and even for pushing him over the brink into being considered laughable in some unsympathetic quarters. Certainly one does not want to imply that *The Nightcomers* represented anything like a comeback, though reviewers, as if tiring of beating up on Brando, or just possibly aware that he had found something restorative in this role, were on the whole kind to him. But the movie itself was greeted with edgy guffaws that hard edged sex always elicits in the movies. In the US the picture was released sparingly.

But if *The Nightcomers*, a cinematic fringe-dweller if there ever was one, inevitably referred us backward to all the commercially hopeless enterprises to which Brando had given (lent is perhaps the better word) himself since his voyage on the *Bounty* had carried him to the remoter shores of the movie world, something in this movie, released exactly ten years later, also hinted at the possibility of energies gathering, spirits brightening, for a return journey. As it happened, that hint might safely have been broader.

SEVEN

MOMENTS OF TRUTH

ometime in 1971 Marlon Brando appeared in the office of Robert Evans, then chief of production at Paramount. Tanned, with his hair lightened almost to blond by the South Seas sun and pulled back in a bun, he looked fit and vigorous. He was here on business almost unprecedented for him; he was lobbying for a role, that of Don Corleone, in *The Godfather*. 'I know a lot of people in Hollywood say I'm washed up,' Evans would recall him saying, 'and I know you've heard a lot of stories about me, and some of them are true. But I can play that part, and I can do a good job.'

Before this meeting Brando had done something even more unprecedented for an actor of his stature; he had made a screen test. Of course, no one called it that; it was billed as a make-up test, determining whether the 47-year-old actor could impersonate a character who was supposed to be something like two decades older. It had been managed very discreetly. Coppola had taken a video camera to Brando's home, sat him down at a table on the terrace, a cup of coffee in front of him, and had him register a range of expressions – no dialogue. Brando darkened his hair with shoe polish, pencilled on a mustache and stuffed Kleenex in his mouth to broaden his face. It is said that, studying himself in a mirror before facing Coppola's camera he muttered to himself: 'That's it, that's it. Mean bulldog face, warmth inside.'

Did he really find his character that fast? Obviously not in all its nuances. But he had the right idea, and he liked it. One doubts the tale that when the tape was shown to studio executives they failed to recognize Brando; he required the coating of latex that gave his skin an aged quality and the prosthetic device that widened his jaw line, which make-up artist Phil Rhodes devised for the film itself, in order to lose himself fully in the role. But there is no doubt that he made a powerful impression on his select audience.

Still, hesitation was not entirely erased. Everybody admired Brando's reputation. The question was, could he still live up to it? And, more importantly, would he meet Hollywood's standards of discipline? The gusto of his performance in *The Nightcomers* was apparently lost on them. And no one had yet observed what we have seen: that the most important casting decision in a Brando picture – after Brando himself, of course – was settling on a director sympathetic to his way of doing things. At this point, naturally, the executives had no way of knowing that they had such a figure in Coppola, though with his test footage in hand, and with the beginnings already established of what was to prove an excellent relationship with his star, the director began pressing them very firmly on Brando's behalf. Having endured casting brainstorms that had ranged from Danny Thomas, the comedian, to Melvin Belli, the celebrated attorney, to Carlo Ponti, the movie producer (and husband of Sophia Loren), Coppola let it be known that the only alternative to Brando that he would consider was Laurence Olivier, who was at the time too ill to attempt the role.

The only reason Brando has subsequently advanced for letting his eagerness for the role show was this: *The Godfather* said something metaphorically about the corporate mentality of America. To him, these gangsters instructively parodied establishment attitudes. 'To me, the key phrase in the story is that whenever they wanted to kill somebody it was always a matter of policy. Before pulling the trigger, they told him: "Just business. Nothing personal." When I read that, McNamera, Johnson and Rusk flashed before my eyes.'

All right. Granted. Considerations of that kind had obviously played a part in previous career decisions – usually disastrously. But one must also suspect the quotation, since it was made after the film was released and parroted what quickly became one of the basic critical lines on the work.

One has to believe that other, more simple factors had induced him to make tests and take meetings. For one thing, the Don was obviously a great part, richer than anything Brando had done for years – the still, menacing, motivating center of a vast, dark epic. It was also one that would provide him with the opportunity to do what he had not done since playing Sakini in *Teahouse* – hide in plain sight. All the curious accents he had adopted in the intervening years, all the strange hair-dos and odd costumes he had worn, had never fully disguised him or his despised movie star persona, but this part would permit him to operate from deep cover. And while it would tax his talents, it would not unduly tax his time. For although it was a pivotal role, it was not a huge one, so his presence would not be required for the entire shooting schedule (this eventually stretched to almost ninety days). He could be in and out in a month or so, avoiding the boredom of a long shoot, and all that waiting around, which bores most actors, but which Brando particularly loathes.

169

Finally, however, it was Coppola's attitude toward the film, and toward the actor himself, that may have been, for Brando, the project's most encouraging aspects. Paramount had optioned Mario Puzo's book even before it was finished, mostly because his asking price was low, and thus easy to write off if the book flopped. No one had imagined, at the time, that it would become the mighty best-seller that it became, but even after it did, the studio saw *The Godfather* as a low-budget project – $2 million – partly because another Mafia story, *The Brotherhood*, had been one of the company's failures in 1968, partly because it had endured several other even more expensive flops like *Paint Your Wagon* and *Darling Lili*. It raised the budget slowly, almost grudgingly, but even though the book stayed on the charts for over a year, it remained cautious and, perhaps for that reason, had trouble finding a director. Arthur Penn, Peter Yates, Costa-Gavras and Richard Brooks, among others, turned it down for various reasons. It was Brooks who, having read Coppola's script for *Patton*, and admired it, recommended that Paramount talk to him about the project. It is probably true that most of these men, reading Puzo's first-draft script felt, as Coppola did initially, that it was a 'hunk of trash'.

Maybe it was. But the book on which it was based wasn't – not really. It may be slapdash stylistically and sensational in some of its incidents, but it has something most popular fiction does not have – conviction. There is energy and passion in the writing, and reading it, one feels the writer is working from inside the world he is portraying, from inside the skin of his principal characters. Maybe it is an illusion, but if so, it is wonderfully sustained. And the more he thought about it, the more Coppola apparently realized that if the same spirit was brought to filming the story, something wonderful could be made of it. And surely, as an Italian-American who not only cherished his heritage, but drew daily sustenance from it, he realized that he was the man to do it. For what Evans later said about Coppola is true: 'He knew the way these men . . . ate their food, kissed each other, talked. He knew the grit.'

In any case, as he worked on the script with Puzo, who was the first person to suggest Brando for Don Corleone, some of the more sensational aspects of the story were eliminated, and a wise decision was taken to concentrate on its crucial passage: the post-war moment when the Mafia began the process of corporatizing itself, finding large-scale fronts for its activities in the respectable community. Above all, the most interesting and surprising element in the book, its insistence on the depth and passion of family relationships among criminals, was clarified and dramatically sharpened, creating at least a superficial sympathy for them – especially, one must imagine, to a crowd eagerly looking for that quality and (not being literary critics) impervious to some of the larger ironies the film worked. It was this, as much as the fact that Coppola was a *paisano*, that disarmed Mafia objections to the project. (It is known, too, that producer Al Ruddy met with mob leaders and promised that the word 'Mafia' would never be spoken from the screen, and that helped, though Ruddy would later say it was an easy promise to make, because the word was never used in the shooting script.)

It was not, however, because Coppola appeared on Brando's doorstep with a sound adaptation of what had turned out, after all, to be a hot property that the actor committed so fully to the enterprise. It was because Coppola was what he was – a young (31), passionate, knowledgeable and articulate film-maker who had paid his dues. He had written screenplays and he had already directed all kinds of movies: a B horror picture (*Dementia 13*), a Sixties youth comedy (*You're a Big Boy Now*), a 'personal statement' (*The Rain People*), and even a Fred Astaire musical (*Finian's Rainbow*). All of them had been messy and talented – qualities Brando could relate to. He could also relate to a man who was trying to do what Brando now had to do – escape the Hollywood fringe, get into the mainstream. Above all, he could relate to a spirit that was not cynical, that harbored serious ambitions not merely for himself, but for the medium, since Coppola intended to use whatever funds accrued from *The Godfather* for more idealistic venturings (which he actually did, with financially catastrophic results). Coppola, like Brando, was a seeker after truth, a man who looked as if he would patiently indulge a fellow pilgrim with whatever time and attention he needed to find his way (which also proved to be true).

And so a deal was at last struck. Brando received a small cash advance and 1.5 per cent of the gross, capped at $1.5 million. (It is said that after the picture was released Evans offered to raise the cap if Brando would permit a news magazine to do a cover story on him, which he refused at an eventual cost of who knows how many millions.) The cash was less than half what Coppola was making, and his percentage was lower, too, but it really didn't matter, since no one at this point believed the picture would be more than a routine commercial success – if that. The important thing was that in production both men remained true to the unspoken bargain they had struck. Coppola got the performance he needed, disciplined and brilliant; Brando got the conditions he required to give that performance.

Or as the director later put it: 'Before we started, I thought of him as this strange, moody Titan. But he turned out to be very simple, very direct. . . . He's very tactile, he likes to touch you. He likes to be dealt with honestly, likes to feel he's listened to and told "No" when his idea is stupid, "Yes" when it's good. . . . I avoided intellectual discussion, and tried to make him feel he wasn't going to be taken advantage of.'

His strategy worked. And the fact that in pre-production Coppola kept fighting to give the picture the qualities it needed was not lost on Brando either. The director persisted in the struggle for the cast he wanted, and he forced the budget up over $6 million, assuring that it would be done on location in New York and with handsomely detailed period flavor. He agreed to a 53-day shooting schedule, knowing full well that he would require all the days his original schedule had called for. He took the chance that once the studio had committed funds it would accept his overages and neither fire him nor shut the production down. For his part, Brando was helpful in unexpected ways. When the studio found Al Pacino's screen test too reserved and balked at casting him, Brando called Evans and told him the role of Michael, the son who takes over the Corleone empire when the Don is incapacitated, required 'a brooder', because that would give the actor playing him room to develop a character. His intervention was probably instrumental in assuring Pacino the role. Later, when the studio disliked Coppola's dailies after a few days of shooting, Brando let it be known that if the director were fired he would leave also.

But perhaps his most important off-screen contribution was as role model and inspiration for the young cast and its young director. Sure, he sometimes did not report for work on Monday, and he sometimes changed his lines (and – beginnings of a new, not entirely agreeable habit – often had his words written out on cue cards, or even on his fellow-players' persons), but he enjoyed playing morale-builder and mentor, as *The Godfather*'s godfather.

'Mooning' was the production's great running gag. The guys – notably James Caan, Robert Duvall and Brando – were always dropping their pants and flashing their buns in the hopes of startling one another and shocking innocent bystanders. They would hang their behinds out of car windows, expose them in front of female extras, and most especially when they thought one of their own number was taking himself or his work too seriously. Sounds childish, if not downright distasteful, but this was the kind of set Brando loved. For japeries aside, it was also a place where actors could be as serious as they liked, so long as sobriety did not shade over into pretentiousness. It was, as well, a place where people could work freely, challenge one another without raising tension or tempers. To put it simply, something of the best spirit of American male adolescence was represented on this set, and Brando warmed to it.

There was one last struggle with the studio over the film's length, which was close to three hours, but Coppola and Ruddy prevailed, with Evans admitting that the longer version actually played faster than the truncated one. The kind of observations which greater length permitted – of behavioral detail, of setting – were in fact vital to the movie's success. It is perhaps not too much to say that they were its true subject. But in any case, they gave *The Godfather* its air of sobriety and veracity and, despite its many bloody doings and undoings, made it impossible for people to think of it as just a rattling good yarn, which at its simplest level it surely was.

If the contrast between the sometimes comic, sometimes almost sentimental presentation of the Corleone family's life away from their 'business' and the operatically staged violence (and paranoia) of their lives on the job is the most important of the contrasts the film offers, it is not the only one. The use of light provides another. The light in the family scenes is warm and sunny, and so is the light when they go forth to conduct their murderous affairs. But when they are in conference, scheming, cinematographer Gordon Willis's palette is dark, his tones burnished. You think of corporate boardrooms, and you are not wrong to do so.

Character contrast is important, too. Don Corleone has three sons, each of whom represents an aspect of his own nature. Sonny (James Caan) is hot-blooded – a womanizer, a comedian, and openly, eagerly violent. Michael (Al Pacino) is, indeed, a brooder, an educated man, avatar of his father's hopes for respectability, and yet an icy figure who has been warmed by only one thing, family loyalty. He sets it above all else, including his own best interests and softer needs. And he will enforce it at gunpoint. A third brother, Fredo (the late John Cazale) represents all the impulses the other men of the family suppress; he is soft, lazy, unmoved by passionate belief. In his good-natured need to be liked he is something of an unacknowledged burden to the rest of them. In short, there is an insinuating typicality about the Corleone family, and it works steadily throughout the picture to disarm our moral defenses. We know what they do is ultimately evil, socially costly in incalculable amounts. But diet, taste in clothes and interior design aside, they are in some respects so like us, or at least so like people we know, that it takes an effort of will to deplore them.

But that puts the point too mildly. Actually, we envy them. Their milieu, and the low melodramatic conventions of the movie, permit them, encourages them, to act out emotions boldly, without the circumspection that bedevils us in life. As an extended family they are like the rest of us, at once treasuring and sustaining bonds of family tradition and also maddened by their inability to escape from them. But they were allowed to vent this range of emotions more boldly than we are, settle their disputes openly, without hypocrisy. It was the same way, only more so, in 'business'. The conventions prevailing in their line of work permit them, encourage them, to do what the rest of us only dream of doing – deal with their disputes and rivalries in a straightforward fashion, display their emotions fully, indeed, bloodily. There are, one feels, no ulcers in the executive ranks of the Mafia. And – obviously – no golden parachutes for disloyal or incompetent managers. At one level the film is, therefore, a relief from the prevailing pieties about both family and corporate life, a shrewd, joyful and finally anarchic penetration to the emotional heart of the frustrations that rule most American lives.

Because the movie was framed in a morality not at all customary in American films, the critical controversy that swirled about *The Godfather*, especially after it became not merely a runaway box office success but a touchstone event in the recent history of popular culture, was framed incorrectly. For example, Pauline Kael, one of the film's great champions, and eager to stress its instructional value, wrote: 'Organized crime is not a rejection of Americanism. It's what we fear Americanism to be. It's our nightmare of the American system.' But that's not quite right. At its most wicked, *The Godfather* proposes organized crime not as nightmare, but as ideal, a necessary break from legal and social restraint. You can't blink that away. The most you can impute to that strain in the picture is a high satirical impulse, so high that never by word, deed or twelve-frame cut does it announce such an intention.

In other words, the 'morality' of *The Godfather* consisted of forcing us nervously to chortle our recognition of archetypal emotions and acknowledge thereby our dark wish that the blunt ways the Corleones dealt with them were permitted us, too. That is to say, it put us in touch with feelings we were almost never allowed to bring to the surface, and were encouraged by our pious public life to pretend never occurred to us – in 1972, after all, sanctimonious Richard Nixon, a Don Corleone without the courage of his evil convictions, was in the White House. One could go still further, perhaps, to the other end of the political spectrum, and propose the possibility that in the Corleones we saw that freedom, that ability to take fate into their own hands, which, applied to a world stage, might long since have ended the anguish of Vietnam.

At the time, though, the picture's opponents were content to tax it for its failures (as they saw it) of conventional morality. Here is John Simon: 'Missing is the banality of evil: the cheap, ugly, petty racketeering that is the mainstay of organized crime and that neither the script of Mario Puzo nor the direction of Francis Ford Coppola could have made glamorous or palatable.' Mostly, one wishes to add, because that was not their subject. It is Martin Scorsese's subject, almost two decades later, in *Good Fellas*. In any case, one must ask, is there not sufficient 'banality' in the capacity of the Corleones to sit down to a huge Italian feast, with the entire family gathered warmly about, immediately before or after executing a contract on some enemy? Consider only the famous cross-cut sequence in which, while they attend an elaborate wedding, Michael Corleone's soldiers fan out across the underworld, executing all their opponents, consolidating his position.

Andrew Sarris got closer to *The Godfather*'s true intention: 'The irony is not that the Corleone family is a microcosm of America, but rather that it is a typical American family beset by the destructively acquisitive individualism that is tearing America apart.' But then, unaccountably (or accountably, if you imagine that there is more of critical politics than of acute observation in some reviewing – a deliberate desire to get out of step with the majority) he goes off in this direction: 'It is an idea that Chaplin developed so much more profoundly in *Monsieur Verdoux*: that if war, in Clausewitz's phrase, is the logical extension of diplomacy, then murder is the logical extension of business.'

This is a whopper possibly worth probing. Chaplin's retelling of the Bluebeard myth, pallid, self-referential and self-pitying, concludes with a straight-to-camera lecture, hysterical, intellectually banal and dramatically miscalculated (it goes on for something like five minutes), in which the star nails home the point Sarris quotes. Compare that to the death of Don Corleone. It comes as he plays in the garden with a grandchild. He cuts an ogre's teeth out of an orange rind, puts them in his mouth and is silently, lumberingly, humorously chasing the giggling child around when a heart attack fells him. This business was Brando's invention – he had amused his own children with the orange trick. But it has, like so much of the film, that astonishing rightness of effect that cannot arise entirely out of conscious calculation, that comes only when artists achieve an unconscious harmony with their material. Here a man who has ruled his world through fear at last acknowledges, self-satirizingly, that he knows what he has been and implies as well that his carefully cultivated air of monstrousness was, among other things, a strategy, a put-on useful in a business that he like many another businessman may have conceived of as – yes – a game. Does this moment sentimentalize the Don? Yes. Does it also create the most chilling of all his resonances? Yes, again. And does it make precisely, vividly, subtly, the linkage which Sarris thought understressed in the film. Yes, once more – with feeling.

Curiously (because most actors, and especially this actor, usually cannot analyze why a role went well for them), Brando came closer to the truth about his success, and by extension the success of the movie, than any of the reviewers. A few years later, reminiscing with uncharacteristic geniality about *The Godfather*, Brando dismissed his accomplishment as an accident: 'What the hell did I know about a 65-year-old Italian who smokes twisted goat shit cigars?' But then he added: 'I'll tell you the real secret: the people who plonk down six bucks to see a fantasy on celluloid actually supply their own fantasy and do a helluva lot better . . . than I do. People lived the character of Don Corleone in their own mind's eye.'

In other words, he could only make a good (anyway, plausible) guess about a Mafioso's mannerisms, but he had been around the movie business (and around life) for a while, and so he knew something about the core psychology of the powerful, those aspects of it that are found everywhere in contemporary life. And that he could communicate in terms all of us could recognize and employ (as he suggests) in making our connections with his character specifically, *The Godfather* in general.

There is in his work a marvelous objectivity, a refusal to judge his character, that sets the tone of the picture, and permits us, finally, to read it in whatever spirit we choose. For what Brando gives us in the Don is a portrait of a man who has distilled his drive for power to its essence and is, of course, the more menacing by the carefully measured reserve with which he deploys the force of his will. He is all understatement; he makes people lean in to hear what he says in his thin, cracked, voice that is, strictly speaking, a shade older tonally than his years might dictate. And when people lean in, they usually bow their heads, assuming, perforce, an attitude of respect, obsequiousness. This effect is further reinforced by the dim light in which he is placed when he is conducting business. You have to strain your eyes as well as your ears to attend him.

Is he capable of kindness? Naturally – when it does not interfere with his larger interests. Is he sentimental about women and children? Certainly – most ambitious men are when they have a moment and the courtly emotions occur to them. Is he reluctant to acknowledge that there are people in the world who disagree with him, almost weary when he is forced to exert himself against their rebelliousness? Of course – strife is bad for business, bad for a CEO's digestion.

The unstated wit of this performance is breathtaking. Brando's Don is in every respect a recognizable man – full of contradictions, full of muted, antithetical emotions which are only resolved by his drive for power. And so, while a part of our mind recognizes him as evil incarnate, another part of it must admire both his directness of intention and his delicate in-direction of language when he quietly rasps what became the movie's catch phrase, and one which has passed permanently into the language: 'Make him an offer he can't refuse.' Some part of us quite simply wants to be him, to exercise power untrammeled by the niceties – and of course the weaknesses – that fasten us 'round.

It is perhaps needless to add that Brando, no less than the movie, was subjected to willful critical misunderstanding, born of the desire to rein in popular enthusiasm for the work rather than impose morally correct attitudes on a wildly enthusiastic mass audience. Here is Simon again, accusing him of 'hamming things up by sheer underacting' – an oxymoron of astonishing wrong-headedness. It was not quite as amazing, though, as Sarris's assertion this was 'a role Lee J. Cobb could have played in his sleep without special make-up'. Yes, let's have evil power thump and crash about, so everyone recognizes it and draws the right, comfortable, distancing conclusions from monstrousness made clearly visible. Better still, let's revisit the classic gangster movie and revel once again in its clichés.

But, of course, such criticism is as irrelevant as it is risible. A more typical review, by *Newsweek*'s Paul D. Zimmerman, got much closer both to the truth of the performance and the truth of our response to it: 'There is no longer any need to talk tragically of Marlon Brando's career. His stormy two-decade odyssey through films good and bad, but rarely big enough to house his prodigious talents, has ended in triumph.' Especially for those of us who had long since struck what Sarris shrewdly called our 'Faustian' bargain with the actor, this performance could not be looked upon as anything but a long-delayed fulfillment. For the first time he was doing what we had imagined he would be doing at this age (since we had also imagined for him the kind of coherent development that we fondly anticipated for our-selves): accomplishing singular work in a context that was fully worthy of that work.

It is impossible to say whether Brando took his tone from the film or vice versa, but there is a remarkable seamlessness in the fit of character to con-text. It is equally futile to try to determine whether it was word of this per-formance or word of the film's richness of color and sheer narrative power, or the hope that it would at last reveal the secrets of the underworld (so glamorous in their mystery), that powered it commercially. What is certain is that *The Godfather* was an instant success and went on to become the mightiest hit of its day, grossing some $81 million in North America in its first year of release, 1972. That was more than three times what the next most successful film took in that year, and it was $31.5 million more than *Love Story*, then its nearest rival on the list of all-time box office champions, had taken in. Eventually the picture grossed some $150 million, worldwide, which does not count huge television and video cassette sales. It is not too much to say that *The Godfather* initiated the modern definition of the term 'blockbuster', which thereafter could not be reasonably applied to any film taking in less than $100 million domestically.

For Brando, the irony must have been delicious: fourteen consecutive flops, the longest dry spell any major movie star has ever endured, and now, overnight, he had the biggest hit since *Gone With the Wind*. But there is no hint that he savored it. What we may somewhat more safely speculate is that it energized him, renewed his self-confidence. Around this time he granted an interview in which he allowed – and, for a man who had so often expressed his contempt for his profession, it was a major allowance – that acting, on a certain routine, 'let's pretend' level, was 'a perfectly reasonable way to make a living. You're not stealing money, and you're entertaining people.' He implied that if he could have been that kind of an actor he might have led a contented life. But, of course, he was not. He was the kind of actor, he insisted, who could not help but 'upset' himself in certain roles, had to dive down deep within himself and examine the junk and offal buried there; and that, he said, had grown increasingly difficult for him. It was on this occasion that he expressed the thoughts that, I think, bear repetition. 'There comes a time in one's life when you don't want to do it anymore.

His performance in *The Godfather* cannot be dismissed as merely technical acting. But it clearly derives from observation and imagination, not from self-exploration or self-revelation, and so represents the glorious culmination of his effort, almost two decades long, to become the new Paul Muni, hiding out behind accents and make-up and avoiding the dark depths he alluded to – depths he had not, in fact, fully penetrated since *On the Waterfront*. But even before its release he knew – could not help but know – that his work in *The Godfather* was extraordinary; and felt – could not help but feel – energy, conviction flowing back into him. Possibly, just possibly, he was ready for one more dive into the blackness.

And, coincidentally, along came Bernardo Bertolucci, acclaimed director of *The Conformist* among other serious and ambitious works, offering him the opportunity to take a voyage to the bottom of the sea under something like ideal circumstances. He came under good auspices, as the friend of Christian Marquand, who was then living with Dominique Sanda, *The*

Conformist's star who was then committed to appear with Jean-Louis Trintignant (who was – further, odder coincidence – Marquand's brother-in-law) in the project the director was now offering to Brando, *Last Tango in Paris*. There has never been a satisfactory explanation of why the Sanda-Trintignant pairing was abandoned, but one must suspect that once Bertolucci met Brando (*emozionato* was the director's word for his feelings – 'scared and excited'), poor Trintignant, such a cool, 'intellectual' actor, didn't have a chance to keep his role.

And Brando did not have a chance to escape it. Here is Bertolucci's recollection of their first meeting: 'For the first fifteen minutes he didn't say a word; he only looked at me. Then he asked me to talk about him. I was very embarrassed but I got around it. I didn't talk about him, but about the character I had in mind for the film, how I saw him in the role.' But soon monologue turned to dialogue, and Bertolucci began interviewing Brando, 'using the material that came out to construct or perfect the story in my mind. He listened carefully, and then he said "yes" right away, without asking to read the script.'

A good thing, too. For Bertolucci, who had once won an Italian literary prize for a book of youthful poems, had come to believe 'literature was the past I had to overcome and contradict with something. That something was cinema. I try to write the scenarios of my films as best I can to negate them, dissolve them with the camera.' In other words, the likelihood is that little, if anything, was at this point committed to paper. Perhaps something got down a little later, when Bertolucci visited Los Angeles for two weeks for further conversations with Brando.

Or perhaps not. For by this time he must have known that the appeal of the project for Brando lay in its lack of pre-ordained structure, the opportunities it offered him not merely to improvise a character, but to let his own character interpenetrate a screen character so no one could tell where the one left off and the other began. Bertolucci said at the time that he liked to create characters based 'on what the actors are in themselves', instead of asking them 'to interpret something pre-existent'. He felt Brando's training as an actor made him an ideal candidate 'to superimpose himself upon the character in the film'.

We cannot imagine Brando relishing the idea of using *Last Tango in Paris* as an autobiographical platform. On the other hand, his entire history in the movies spoke of his impatience with following a script as written. And his more recent history announced an increasing reluctance to learn lines in any but the most approximate ways. Bertolucci's methods would at least free him from his recent dependence on cue cards. After all the high-toned blather about the brilliance of Bertolucci's radical new working methods, it *is* something of a comedown to suggest that he gathered in his most famous recruit because these methods suggested to Brando a practical solution to a very practical issue. Yet the thought is inescapable.

So is the notion that, however sketchy, the tale Bertolucci told Brando at their meetings must have contained a powerful hint of the erotic elements that made *Last Tango in Paris* the sensation it became when it was released, and that this was, at least, not uninteresting to Brando. Conventional love scenes did not, as a rule, turn him on. But as early as *Streetcar* and as late as *The Nightcomers*, we have observed that the admixture of sex and violence (even if the violence is, as it is here, more psychological than physical) does stir something in him. In the event, of course, it delivered even more than Bertolucci promised.

Finally, though, it may be that Bertolucci's personality was the most important element in recruiting Brando to this project. He is, by all accounts, the most seductive of directors. At the time, Chris Mankiewicz, the American writer-producer, who is also the son of Joseph L. Mankiewicz, was occasionally on the set and later told a reporter, 'Bernardo is the kind of man you work for out of love rather than fear or just for the job.' Almost two decades later, after working with Bertolucci on *The Sheltering Sky*, Debra Winger was saying virtually the same thing: 'To meet Bernardo is to love him. Then to work with him is to really love him deeply. . . . You can just feel him saying, "Just go and do it, baby, I'm right here helping you."'

So it was, certainly, with Brando. In their pre-production meetings and on the set Bertolucci was ever the soft-spoken, youthful collaborator with his star, creating an ambiance which Mankiewicz described as charming Brando in such a way that 'he was not aware of being charmed'. The film's production manager described Bertolucci's technique as *violentandolo dolcemente* – gentle rape. The director himself put it otherwise: he understood Brando to be 'a hunter of instinct . . . he isn't capable of rationalizing.' And so, from the start, 'my rapport with him was solely emotional.' As work proceeded, the picture became, in Bertolucci's words 'a kind of psychological adventure', and one that engaged the star's attention more deeply than anything he had done in years. Even his dresser noticed: 'Something's going on here; he's taking this seriously.' An attempt by Anna Kashfi to spirit their son Christian away from his father's custody (he was found in Mexico) required a flying trip home by Brando in the middle of the shoot, but even that could not interrupt his concentration.

As time went on, Bertolucci and Brando required less and less in the way of verbal exchange in order to do their work, and when it was finished Bertolucci would remember 'the glances that Brando would send me. His look was full of meanings, as though he wanted to say: "Is it worth doing all this? Being actors, wanting success, performing, putting our hearts into it?" I think that it is . . . even if one must always be aware that each thing is immediately consumed, that it is already over when it has scarcely begun.'

One thinks: not so fast, Bernardo. Pauline Kael may now regret announcing that the date *Last Tango in Paris* premiered at the New York Film Festival, October 14, 1972, 'should become a landmark in movie history comparable to May 29, 1913 – the night *Le Sacre du Printemps* [*The Rite of Spring*] was first performed – in music history.' The film now seems more of a curiosity than a precursor to anything very much. On the other hand, it did not evanesce with anything like the immediacy Bertolucci imagined it would. It caused a gorgeous ruckus: banning in Bertolucci's native Italy, the threat of consorship everywhere, twitterings in the fashionable quarters of all the world's cultural capitals.

A simple recital of the story as it finally evolved explains only the least interesting aspects of this stir. It opens with a man named Paul and a woman named Jeanne (played by the unknown Maria Schneider) meeting in an apartment which both are thinking of renting. Having checked it out, but before they have even introduced themselves, he falls upon her and she, in the modern manner, accepts him for a quick, brutal fuck. Thereafter, they continue meeting in the apartment for increasingly vivid fornications. Isolated, the domineering male and the submissive female are freed from all conventional restraint – it's the classic porn device – and the intensity and daring of their sexual feats escalate. Value-free, history-free, future-free, Paul and Jeanne furnish the apartment only with a bed, a plain table and chairs, lust and memory. For these rooms are an existentialist symbol as well as a pornographic device – a central void in the universe, to be filled in the absence of God (or whatever) with autobiography as well as sex.

Between these encounters we learn that she is involved with a young film-maker, who is recording their relationship (he will eventually propose marriage) and her biography for a documentary. He wishes to impose the spurious order of art on life. It is also revealed that the Brando character's wife has recently committed suicide, and that this has summoned both reminiscence and remorse on his part – along with the need for the affectless sanctuary the apartment and the girl afford.

Eventually there is a somewhat banal role reversal. After dancing their 'last tango' in an elegantly decadent ballroom, he proposes a conventional

living arrangement to her. But she has by this time decided that she has explored to the full the de Sadian paradox which holds that in sexual slavery
lies sexual freedom, got all the good she can out of the degradation he has
imposed on her. He follows her to the home she shares with her parents to
plead his case still further, but when he violates that bourgeois sanctuary
she kills him with her father's army revolver. The film closes with her rehearsing her story for the police: he was a total stranger, he broke in and
tried to rape me, etc.

Rather obviously, this movie could – and did – support a wide range of
interpretations, or perhaps one should say over-interpretations. Alberto
Moravia, for example, offered a Freudian one: Eros (the little world of the
apartment) versus Thanatos (the great world outside), with the former
offering man's only means of reaching 'complete expression . . . total recovery of reality' in a 'mortuary' society. Others put a Marxist spin on the
film for it offers a rather obvious critique of bourgeois values. Both
Wagner and Verdi were evoked by other critics in attempts to suggest the
picture's emotional tonalities. And the artist Francis Bacon, whose pictures were used as backgrounds for the main titles, and who was frequently
mentioned by Bertolucci in interviews, came up often ('psycho-sexual pain
. . . within the enclosure of the contemporary world.' to quote one critic).

This is an awful lot of weight for a slender, if elegantly made, film to
carry. One feels that much of it was imposed on the film by the understandable desire to defend it from the censors by finding its redeeming social
value. Confronting the picture now, after the passage of almost two
decades, one also feels a powerful desire to skip all that. Its abiding interest
is as elegant erotica, as a significant moment in its star's career and as a
social phenomenon of its moment. Having said that, one feels a powerful
desire to pass a few compliments to cinematographer Vittorio Storaro for
the fluidity of movement he placed at the disposal of his endlessly improvising director and for the wintry late afternoon light in which he
bathed (and aestheticized) that apartment; to make approving mention of
the 'uterine' color scheme devised for it by art director Maria Paolo Maino,
and to pass out of these rarified realms.

But one cannot always move as quickly as one would like. The efforts to
locate *Last Tango in Paris* within the landscape of traditional modernist
culture require some comment, if only because they miss its essence as an
experience. This is not to say that Bertolucci, for all his anti-literary pro-
testations, was unaware of his work's possible cultural resonances. He is a
self-conscious artist, and the critical edifices constructed on the film have a
basis in his aspirations. But the fact is that the film as it finally evolved is,

intellectually speaking, strictly soft-core. It is a consequential act not in the intellectual or artistic history of our age, but in its celebrity drama.

In order to have taken up the Big Themes which Bertolucci clearly wanted to examine, the film would have needed to maintain what we must presume was its original dramatic focus, as a story of male and female equals who, as they fall into a romantic turmoil resonant with philosophical implications – can be seen as 'universals'. To have accomplished this, the movie would have had to be cast quite differently, very possibly with unknowns or little knowns (Trintignant and Sanda, for example) or, failing that, with stars of roughly the same magnitude. In other words, once Brando had been cast, what was required was someone whose significance in our fantasy lives was equal to his. Bertolucci seems to have recognized this, for an effort was made to sign Catherine Deneuve. She had a following, and *Belle de Jour* had recently imprinted her cool capacity to portray the darker enigmas of female sexuality on everyone's mind. But being prettily tied up and lightly flogged in a Bunuel dream sequence is one thing; enduring the earthier, more realistic humiliations Bertolucci had in mind, quite another. She passed, as did some other stars of comparable stature. Bertolucci began interviewing unknowns.

Once that decision was taken, his film could not be what he had envisioned initially. For *Last Tango in Paris* needed to be a duet sung by equals. Only if that balance of forces is achieved can we begin to ignore a great personality, working in a dominant role, performing unprecedented public acts, and fully attend to the other matters the movie wants to take up. In other words, this movie should not be an aria, forcing all of our attention on a single figure, summoning up all the feelings and fantasies we have built up about him over the years.

But once Bertolucci decided to go with Schneider (who got the job by unashamedly stripping for the camera in a test) the picture became Brando's. For even though Schneider was a game, lively and pretty young woman, the best she can do in this context is play accompaniment to a recitalist in full song. The differences in their age and experience assured that no matter what the actors did, we would read Brando somewhat paternalistically. And though by all accounts he was very sweet and comforting to an inexperienced actress taking on a role that would tax the resources of a much more experienced performer, the fact remains that he was the star, drawing not only most of our attention but also most of the bedazzled Bertolucci's attention on the set. In modern film we determine a film's power center by observing not only who has the most lines, but also who has to take off the fewest clothes. On both counts Brando is the winner here.

The Rite of Spring, indeed! The thing is the star vehicle to end all star vehicles. And that's precisely why Norman Mailer, in his famous essay on the film, registered only half-ironic disappointment in the film's sex. It may be well faked, and not without its ability to turn us on, but it is, nevertheless, quite visibly faked. As a result, it is, in his view, curiously disappointing. He wrote, 'Brando's cock up Schneider's real vagina would have brought the history of the cinema one huge march closer to the ultimate experience it has promised since its inception (which is to embody life).' Bertolucci, it would seem, understood this point. 'Bernardo wanted me to fuck Maria . . . on screen,' Brando said later. 'I told him, "That's impossible. If that happens, our sex organs become the centerpiece of the film." He never did agree with me.'

Both were right, of course – Brando more simply so. It may be that Bertolucci held the Mailerian view, and wanted, at last, to push the cinema on to that destiny in perfect realism that they were not alone in imagining for it. But it may also be that he sensed a disappointing incongruity between the sex he was filming and the talk he was filming. In the latter sequences, we feel, no niceties have been allowed to intervene; Brando, in particular, gives the impression that he has been allowed to say anything that comes into his head, or anything that came into it during rehearsals and was saved for the takes.

This material is of two distinct kinds. The first is pure autobiography, a rehearsal of the character's history from childhood to the present. It is full of snips and snaps and puppy dog's tails that remind us of things we seem to remember hearing about the actor as well as oblique references to his film roles – an exquisite blending of private and public history. Here we witness Kowalski-Malloy-Brando arrived at the mid-life crisis, and speaking its concluding unscientific postscript. It is actually plausible to imagine the fictional components of that construct winding up in Paris as a kept man, trying desperately to imagine how, exactly, he had come to that curious pass. And it is more than possible to imagine, from what we know of the star's private conversational style, that he is speaking from the heart of his private darkness, giving us authentic insight into the life in which we had taken such an avid interest these two decades, this life we thought we had shared.

The versimilitude of this dialogue is further reinforced by Brando's behavior. We have long since observed that the effort not to appear as himself in public is, perhaps, the major theme of his career – all those accents and make-ups and so on. Now, forced to appear, as it were, in his own skin, he is bereft of his usual disguises. And Bertolucci makes capital of Brando's frantic borrowings to escape not from nakedness, but from naked confession. If the actor wants to drop into an English accent or adopt the mannerisms of a bouncy adolescent, he lets him. Brando can mumble his lines or stumble on them, he can strike poses or he can sulk. Best of all, he can indulge his free-associational humor, which leads him inevitably toward the sexual and scatological. And the more he tries not to be Brando, the more he is Brando – in one sense at least. For the essence of his art has always derived from the tension between his impulse to truth and his instinct to hide.

And so, autobiography and behavior combine to guarantee – or create the illusion of guaranteeing – the truth of the second major portion of his dialogue, the sexual fantasies, which up to a point his partner must act out for him. And if, whether fantasized or acted out, these disgust, so be it. All right, he seems to say, you wanted the truth about me. Well, here it is, go gag on it. When Brando buggers Schneider's chic, saucy, *cultured* little bourgeois ass, he is buggering everything that has bugged him, all those middle class importunings, all those demands for discipline, responsibility and, while you're at it, how about a *Hamlet*? When he forces her to explore his own fundament, the while describing his fancy of her copulation with a dying pig, he is saying something about the fate he would like to visit on all who have tried to probe him for his secrets these many years. In these moments, we are all Blanches to his time-warped Stanley, allowing ourselves to be reamed breathless by his contempt.

Mailer: 'The crowd's joy is that a national celebrity is being obscene on screen. To measure the media magnetism of such an act, ask yourself how many hundreds of miles you might drive to hear Richard Nixon speak a line like: "We're just taking a flying fuck at a rolling doughnut" or "I went to the University of Congo; studied whale pronging." Only liberal unregenerates would be so progressive as to say they would not drive a mile. No, one could start mass migrations . . .'

It is surreal, says Mailer, adding that surrealism has become the objective correlative of our time. 'A private glimpse of the great becomes the alchemy of the media, the fool's gold of the century of communication.' But it is the essence of the novelist's argument that, interesting as this may be, it represents a sell-out of a sort, a realization that the audience will be satisfied by something less than the honesty of full sexual disclosure. It is enough for them to glimpse a celebrity's 'kinks' offering 'sympathetic vibration to their kinks'. A truly great artist, Mailer seems to suggest, would not be content with this teasing, would (as teenagers of his generation used to say) 'go all the way'.

This radically redefines the whole notion of 'heroic' acting, of course.

But in very Sixties (and quite primitive) terms. It also does not credit Brando for being what he now was – a veteran actor and a veteran public figure, capable of judging his effects quite closely. As the film defined itself existentially, we must at least grant the possibility that its star, seeing that he had the screen essentially to himself, and had a director who would not deny him anything, chose not to settle for the more obvious forms of self-exposure, sensing that they could only distract from the kinds that really interested him, and that he could even appear 'tasteful' in his refusals.

So he got on with the business that he most cared about. Which was, of course, copping a plea for himself, for all the years people kept telling him he had wasted (and which even he knew had not fulfilled his promise). Paul is not – or not certainly – Brando, but he is an uncanny parallel: a gorgeous, not too well educated, but naturally gifted man, if we are to judge by his reminiscent monologues; and a man widely disapproved of by nice, middle-class people; and thus forced to live on life's less serious margin; and endlessly distracted by sex; and, finally, a kept man, not permitted to fulfill himself (what Paul's dead wife was to him, the movies were to Brando in this scheme).

Are we reading too much into his work? No more than Mailer, surely, and we at least have many eyewitness accounts of Brando's increasing malleability as shooting proceeded, an unwonted desire for hard, charged-up work. This was 'Building a Character' in ways far more satisfying than Stanislavski ever dreamed.

Was it 'heroic' work? Arguably, yes, in that it betokened a very original awareness of the crossroads where personality and performance meet and an energetic effort to communicate this radical perception. And less arguably so if we recall Brando's reluctance to 'upset' himself by plunging into his own depths in pursuit of emotional truth.

Was it honest work? I think so, in that Brando saw these depths as polluted. What had once been a pure and authentic spirit – that of an idealistic artist, as he perhaps saw it, certainly an uncorrupted invididualist – now carried the poisons of fame in his system. It was this bile that he spewed forth here, under the not entirely erroneous assumption that we, the audience, were as much responsible for its creation as he was and deserved a sample of its bitter taste. And so what we had was the first (and so far only) performance in which the *fact* of the star's stardom – not just the idea of stardom, which we sometimes get in movies about movies and the theater – was the subject of the starring role.

In the formal sense, this probably was not really acting, but it was an astonishing act of self-assertion. For Brando had taken it all – his

During a break from filming *The Young Lions*.

Rehearsing with Anna Magnani for
The Fugitive Kind.

Brando directing *One-eyed Jacks*.

PREVIOUS PAGE As Major Lloyd Gruver in *Sayonara*.

James Dean visiting on set.

With his new love Tarita on the *Bounty* set.

On location in Tahiti, Marlon photographing Tarita.

Brando in *The Ugly American*.

Brando appearing on David Susskind's *Open End* in April 1963.

David Niven, Shirley Jones and Brando relax on the set of *Bedtime Story*.

Brando is abused when he attends a demonstration against a housing
development that refused to sell homes to black Americans.

(Left to right) Charlton Heston, Harry Belafonte, James Baldwin and Marlon
Brando after a race demonstration in Washington (1963).

As Sheriff Calder in *The Chase*.

As Matt Fletcher in *The Appaloosa*.

Charles Chaplin directs Brando and Sophia Loren in
The Countess from Hong Kong.

John Houston on set with Brando for *Reflections in a Golden Eye*.

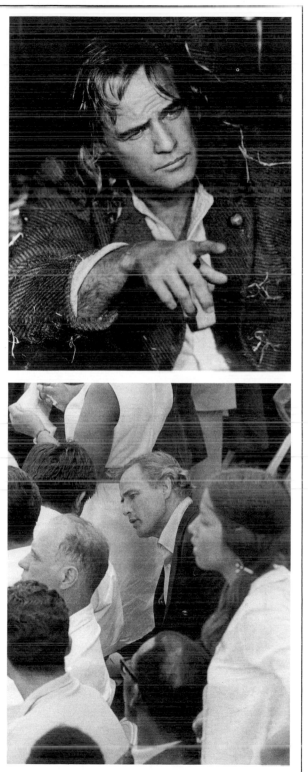

As Peter Quint in
The Nightcomers.

At the Poor
People's March 1969.

(Left to right) James Caan, Brando, Al Pacino and John Cazale
in *The Godfather*.

With Francis Ford Coppola.

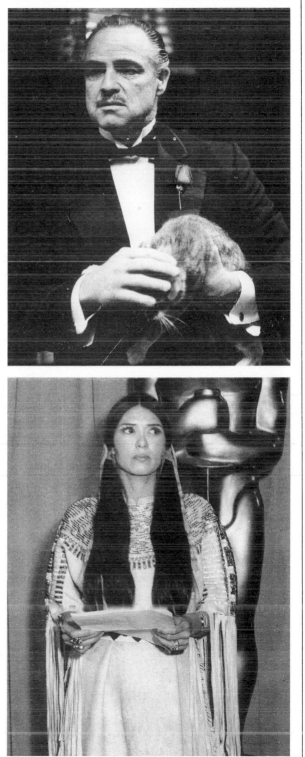

As Don Vito Corleone
in *The Godfather*.

Sasheen Littlefeather reads
Brando's reasons
for refusing an Oscar at the
Academy Awards ceremony.

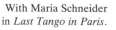
With Maria Schneider
in *Last Tango in Paris*.

Bernardo Bertolucci with
Brando and Schneider.

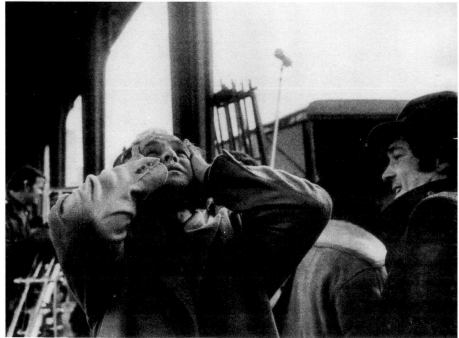
Seeking inspiration on the set of *Last Tango* with Bertolucci.

Jack Nicholson with Brando in *The Missouri Breaks*.

As Lee Clayton in *The Missouri Breaks*.

As Colonel Kurtz in *Apocalypse Now*.

Addressing a rally after American Indians completed their 'Longest Walk' in 1978.

Listening in court as his son is held without bail.

With his son Christian on his release from jail in August 1990.

OVERLEAF Brando restyles his Godfather role as Carmine Sabatini in *The Freshman*.

conceptions and misconceptions of himself, our conceptions and misconceptions about the same subject – and made a role of the mess. And we are not talking here about a few scribbled rewrites on the set, designed to match image and skills more closely to the demands of the writers' blueprint. No, we are talking about an organic symbiosis: something that does not, I think, exist in nature but can perhaps be used as a term of description in the unnatural world of celebrity. Brando, especially toward the end of the film, when he puts on his fallen angel mask, begs for a tragic interpretation of his efforts. And one feels like conceding it to him, if only for his death scene. Shot by his lover, done in, that is, by the bourgoisie, Paul reels backward out of her parents' overstuffed living-room on to a balcony and, before plunging from it to his death, pauses to remove his gum and stick it to the railing. We can imagine no other actor in the history of the movies, possibly in the history of the world, imagining that gesture, let alone playing it. Compared to it, his 'real' cock up Maria Schneider's 'real' vegina is nothing – the easy stuff, as any actor but few literary gentlemen would know.

If life were artfully organized, like a good novel, or even a good screenplay, this narrative could now come to a close, and on a triumphant note as well. For whatever one thought of the film as a whole, Brando had for the first time linked himself with an alternative school of film-making, one that proceeded in a way that was exactly the opposite of Hollywood's and, in this period when the unplanned was much admired had taken the dangerous art of improvisation further than it had ever gone before – making up not just an isolated scene or two, but an entire character, an entire movie while he was on his feet. This was the kind of daring his talent and his spirit had promised from the start. So it seemed a culmination and a fulfillment. And his energy and commitment to the processes of this film seemed to suggest renewel, a re-engagement with a best, lost self now just slightly adapted to meet new conditions, new ways of doing. All of this was recognized when – sensationally – *Last Tango in Paris* went forth into the world. Whatever its intrinsic values, the picture was blessed with high good fortune in its release. For it was a consumation devoutly wished for by the cell leaders of the Sexual Revolution. Fueled by the not entirely correct belief that The Pill liberated humankind from the practical consequences of promiscuity, and by pent-up resentment against the goody goody blandness with which Fifties popular culture had treated human sexuality, it also derived some energy from the posturings of the decade's self-proclaimed political revolutionaries. What its leaders had been missing was a popular cultural object (in particular a film, for this was also a decade in which the literary-intellectual community and its middlebrow hangers-on also discovered that movies were an 'art form' as they patronizingly phrased it) that openly, graphically portrayed heterosexual coupling in an unmistakably artful context.

For the truth was that throughout the Sixties and early Seventies movies ran well behind the nation's fantasies in conjuring up all the delicious possibilities of sex. *I Am Curious – Yellow* just didn't do the job. Neither did The New Wave. In this period, at a screening of a soft porn film for which its producers harbored delusions of artist grandeur, I remember encountering a journalist who was devoting many years to an epic taxonomy of the sexual revolution and was locally famous for his public discussions of the kinks he had twisted himself into in pursuit of first-hand reportage. 'What do you think?' he inquired hopefully of me. 'Will we ever have a really good erotic movie? You know, with good camera work and lighting?'

I thought at the time that his questions had a curious kind of innocence about them – implying that if a porn movie could be made to look like a regular movie, look, that is, as if it had not been shot in a Havana brothel or a Southern California motel room it would disarm, possibly even delude, moralists into accepting its hateful premises. (We were then a few years from *The Devil in Miss Jones* and other technically well-made hard core items, which had their enthusiastic champions in sexually radical intellectual circles, but didn't fool many fundamentalists.)

But I must also confess that some part of me sympathized with my friend. We were respectably (and in my case faithfully) married men with young daughters in the Sixties. Yet we were also horny children of the Fifties – he of repressive Catholic background, I of repressed WASP upbringing, both possessed of the secret (in his case not so secret) thought that the movies, like life itself, ought to offer us something richer, more adventuresome than they did when they explored the realm of the senses. Around this time another friend of mine looked up at me over the rim of his scotch and soda and inquired: 'Did you ever think you'd live to see the day when you would walk down Fifth Avenue on a summer afternoon and see *nipples*?'

No, I didn't. And the fashion for bralessness was only a hint of what was inchoately stirring everywhere – feminism, gay rights, nude encounter groups, sex clubs, large matters and little what-have-yous, but all reflective of general, and long denied, yearnings to act out freely at least some aspects of our sexual natures, or failing that to speak of them without hypocrisy. Whatever failures Brando had endured, and would endure, in finding metaphors through which to assert his political radicalism, *Last Tango in*

Paris gave him the opportunity to assert, at last, his sexual radicalism. And that, I think, reflects a general truth. Most of us did not find a way of surfacing our unspoken political radicalism, that contempt for the superficiality and irrelevance of American political life, during the short-lived and vulgarly stated 'revolution' of this time. But many of us did ultimately find ways of bringing our sexual radicalism to the surface, and many lives were indeed changed, for better or for worse, by that process.

I make no large claims for *Last Tango* in this regard. It is, at best, an artifact of an interesting passage in our lives. But in terms of its public life, that is to say in the sub-critical discussion it engendered among people who never saw it or saw it only superficially because it became a phenomenon, it was the movie my friend had hopefully inquired after. For it did undeniably contain the pornographic device we have already observed (the isolated room, where the world and its moral conventions cannot intrude) and, in its early passages, it had an undeniable pornographic structure, with each new sexual encounter more outrageous than the last. And these were redeemed (or at least rendered defensable) by the obvious seriousness with which *Last Tango* developed the issues its sexual encounters so vividly introduced. Sight unseen this was a movie to be cherished by everyone harboring the belief that a good society was one that confronted sexuality openly, freely and by all of us who loathed the paltering censorship that had for so many decades been imposed on the movies, primarily by Catholics working in the American film industry's back channels. As the picture prepared to open, an 'us against them' alignment developed and none of 'us' was going to deny the film, or even develop a subtle analysis of it, lest we be mistaken for one of 'them'.

They, of course, played into our hands, as they so often do. For *Last Tango* was more or less simultaneously banned in Italy and booked as the closing night attraction at the New York Film Festival in 1972. Italian law forbade the movie's export until its case was fully adjudicated, but after well publicized negotiations, the picture was allowed out of the country – under armed guard – for its single festival showing. The screening became the hottest ticket in town. And then Kael got *The New Yorker* to break with custom and permit her to review the film, even though it would be months before it could possibly play the theatres.

Her wildly enthusiastic notice increased the anticipatory buzz about the movie, and after it had been freed for export by the Italians the X rating given to it by the Motion Picture Association's code administrators guaranteed a pre-release media frenzy. More importantly, when the pictures finally opened in early 1973 it assured that everyone who was anyone (or

189

aspired to be) would make the pilgrimage to the handful of theatres where it was playing. For we were all desperate to see a movie that had apparently achieved that 'ultimate experience' the cinema had promised 'Since its inception' – a perfect blend of the sexually lubricious with the aesthetically aspiring. You just had to have had an opinion – and an early (and favorable) one at that – about *Last Tango in Paris*. And that assured its profitability. As for Brando, he had now enjoyed, within months, a personal triumph in the largest commercial success and the largest *succès d'estime* anyone could remember. His come-back was as remarkable as his failure had been and, before that, his annunciation had been. He was, of course, nominated for the Academy Award for his performance in *The Godfather*, and he quickly became both the betting and the sentimental favorite to win. Inside the industry and beyond there was a desire to commemorate his achievement, and Hollywood also wanted to send him a signal: 'Come back, all is forgiven.'

Before the awards ceremony, on 27 March, there was much speculation as to whether he would or would not appear. But no one, except producer Howard Koch and some of the show's other personnel, expected anything like what happened when his name was read out as winner of the Oscar for best actor. They were aware that Brando was not in his seat when showtime arrived, and they noticed his stand-in, a young woman calling herself Sasheen Littlefeather (real name, Maria Cruz; sometime occupation, Miss American Vampire of 1976), arriving late for the show (she had been delayed as Brando drafted and re-drafted his statement). You could hardly miss her: she was dressed in full tribal regalia. Catching her in the lobby, Koch inquired after her intentions. She showed him Brando's 400-word screed. Too long, said Koch. I'll give you two minutes, and if you're not done you'll be escorted from the stage.

In the event, she actually performed well, considering the boos and catcalls that occasionally interrupted her. She improvised a shortened version of the piece, speaking of the historic injustices visited upon the Indians, and of their inaccurate portrayal on the screen. She concluded gracefully: 'I beg at this time that I have not intruded upon this evening, and that we will, in the future, meet with love and understanding in our hearts. Thank you on behalf of Marlon Brando.' There was no applause.

Off-stage, in the press room, she read Brando's entire statement, which concluded: 'I, as a member in this profession, do not feel that I can as a citizen of the United States accept an award here tonight. I think awards in this country at this time are inappropriate to be received or given until the condition of the American Indian is drastically altered. If we are not our brother's keeper, at least let us not be his executioner.'

Most of those who immediately commented expressed outrage, though Michael Caine took the cooly reasonable view that if a man feels he has to speak his piece he ought to have nerve enough to do it himself. Presenting the best picture prize, an equally cool Clint Eastwood wondered if perhaps he should dedicate it to 'all the cowboys shot in John Ford westerns over the years.'

Since Brando was a founder and heavy financial backer of the new and militant American Indian Movement (AIM), no one questioned the authenticity of Brando's feelings on this matter. And there was precedent for rejecting an Oscar: George C. Scott had done the same thing the year before. But he had done so for what most people judged to be a better reason, because it was a specifically professional one – he didn't believe in competition between artists, particularly elective competition. No such logical connection between belief and action could be attributed to Brando, and in the end few took him seriously. A search for deeper motives was immediately launched.

At the time the standard Hollywood wisdom held that he was getting his own back at everyone who had ignored or patronized or rejected him over these many difficult years. But in the light of his subsequent history, one has to think there was more to the matter than that. One cannot escape this thought: having proved, if not beyond doubt, then to his own satisfaction, that his mature skills – and nerve – were the equal of his youthful ones, he was, in effect, announcing his retirement as – shall we say? 'a contender'. But not – and here, as we shall see, a certain confusion arose – as an occasionally working actor.

He stayed away from movies for three years after winning his Oscar, and this period was the height of his dedication to AIM. Perhaps as a result of his recent professional success, perhaps because of the economic security it provided him, perhaps because he felt a need to justify his Oscar night gesture, he took positions that were much more overtly radical than they had been in the past. He was present when participants in the violence at Wounded Knee were brought to trial, and at the Menominee Uprising, where protest also turned to violence. He subsequently went bail for AIM leaders charged with violent crimes, and tried to help others to avoid arrest. He was moved to tears when invited to participate in tribal ceremonies, and moved to another kind of sorrow when some Indians dismissed him as a publicity-seeking actor. (It is said that in Menominee some tribe members, emulating the famous *Godfather* sequence, placed a severed horse's head in his sleeping-bag.)

Eventually (and roughly coincident with his first reappearance on the screen) his public activism on behalf of this cause dwindled, though he has never ceased trying to interest Hollywood in a movie about American Indian history; he has claimed he can't count the number of scripts he has written. That return to the screen had about it a certain promise both for him (above and beyond his million dollar salary) and for audiences, since his co-star and his director on *The Missouri Breaks* represented the kind of company everyone thought he should be keeping.

This western united him with his Mulholland Drive neighbor, Jack Nicholson, who was an admirer ('He gave us our freedom,' he once said, speaking as an actor, of course), and it reunited him with Arthur Penn, who believed in giving performers the liberty to improvise as a matter of principle, not as an excuse for laziness. Moreover, the script, by the then promising novelist, Thomas McGuane, seemed to offer not just possibilities for this kind of playfulness, but to demand them. For McGuane had to leave the country to work on another project before he could do any extended revisions on his first draft (which both stars and the dirctor had individually rejected; it was the idea of working together that finally secured all their commitments). But then, suddenly, the start day was upon them all and no one had done any hard work on the script. As Penn put it, 'We were out there tap dancing for our lives . . . making up the movie as we went along.'

McGuane's story contained a very nice ironic reversal. A band of horse rustlers (led by Nicholson) takes a little spread in Montana to serve as a base for their operations, and the local cattle baron brings in a 'regulator' to drive them out. But as he settles down on the land, and falls in love with the rancher's daughter (nicely played by Kathleen Lloyd) Nicholson reverts to his boyhood identity as a peaceable farmer. On the other hand, Brando's lawman is a schizophrenic growing madder and more murderous by the moment. Movies with less interesting premises than that have been welcomed critically. So have many movies with less interesting performances than this one.

Brando thought it was 'a steal. For the first twenty pages of the script, I'm the character everyone's talking about – he's coming, he's coming. On page 21, I arrive. I can do anything, move like an eel dipped in vaseline. I'm here, I'm there, I'm all over the place. . . . Poor Jack Nicholson, he's right in there at the center, cranking the whole thing out.' As far as it goes, that's a fair summary of the role. But there's more to it. He and Penn agreed that the character, as originally written, had no psychological spine. 'I don't know who this guy is,' Brando complained. 'So in our discussion,'

Penn would later recall, 'we decided, "Well, wait a minute – let's turn this apparent deficit into an asset."'

Which is why, friends, Brando enters the film hanging upside down from his saddle, wearing white fringed buckskin and talking in an Irish accent. Later he dresses as a preacher talking in a fluting English manner. And still later he turns up in dress and poke bonnet, acting like your basic Middle-western granny. The last, in particular, is one of those on-set brainstorms that works – not least because the star improvised a hilarious monologue involving his horse and his mule and their impolite contention for a carrot. Truth to tell, it's Brando's best comic performance, and, inspired by him, Nicholson gets in some good licks, too.

Penn recalled one little nothing of a scene, in which Brando menaces Nicholson as he hoes his garden. 'Once they got going, I couldn't leave the scene. I just stayed there and let them play off one another . . . and I thought, "I don't care what the content of the scene is, you gotta watch these people do it." And that was the pleasure of that movie. Now, admittedly, if you want a simple, clear, coherent narrative, *Missouri Breaks* ain't it.'

Apparently people did. The outrage of disappointed expectations greeted it. Serious reviewers often couched their disapproval on near-to-moral grounds: they just couldn't believe these three heavyweights had 'indulged' themselves in such a loosy-goosy way. But what really got to the critics was that this playfulness violated the sober generic conventions of the western form. Actually, it went further than that, joyously and un-selfconsciously converting itself into another genre entirely. *The Missouri Breaks* may play weirdly as a western, but it makes perfect sense as a horror picture. Think of the prairie as a big haunted house. Then think of Brando as a monster haunting it, popping out of the shadows periodically to bump off one of the innocents who have invaded his domain. It not only achieves coherence when viewed in this light, it is hugely enjoyable.

But however much fun Brando had making the film – and he actually stayed beyond his contractually stipulated time, for no extra fee (as he had done at the end of *The Godfather*) in order to finish the job properly – the reception accorded it was all too familiar. It was, like his Sixties films, a commercial failure, and one that raised all the old, boring questions about what he thought he was doing, all the old boring clichés about how he was wasting himself. It would be too much to say that its reception disappointed him – receptions interested him less than ever, if that is possible. But the fact is that after this film he never acted again. Not really. Not in the sense that *The Godfather* and *Last Tango* had seemed to promise.

From the release of *The Missouri Breaks* in 1976, through *The Freshman* fourteen years later, he would work in a total of just five movies and one television program. In only two – possibly three – of them was his role central to the narrative; in none of them was it long or in any way taxing. Save the most recent of them, these are appearances, guest star shots, not performances. They engage neither the actor's emotions, nor the audience's. Confronting them, this phrase occurs: 'left over life to kill'. And in fact, one would rather not confront them, would have preferred to fade out on *Last Tango in Paris*. The main group of these films were made between 1978 and 1980. For the record they are:

Superman (1978). Brando played Jor-El, the father of the eponymous hero in the film's prologue. On the planet Krypton, populated by an advanced civilization, he's the wisest of its many wise men, and has snow-white hair as befits his status. When the planet starts to blow up he rockets his son into space, aiming him in the general direction of Earth. It is the sort of job Orson Welles was always doing in those days for a lot less money.

Roots: The New Generation (1979). Apparently impressed with the moral seriousness of the phenomenally successful original mini-series, he volunteered for this sequel. 'I'm no snob about television,' he said. 'I think more important things should be done with TV, since it reaches a mass audience.' Indeed, Brando proposed that it should become the serious medium, and leave 'frivolity' to the movie houses. His cameo was as George Lincoln Rockwell, founder of the American Neo-Nazi party. He won an Emmy for it.

Apocalypse Now (1979). He was back working for Coppola, in a movie that was everything *The Godfather* was not: narratively and thematically muddled, ineffeciently produced, crazily over-budget (you cannot improvise an epic, as D. W. Griffith was the first, but not the last, to discover). In this resetting of *Heart of Darkness* in Vietnam, Brando played Kurtz, the chap who has gone native somewhere up-river. Dressed in black, with his head shaved, he is photographed only in heavy shadow, apparently to disguise his girth. He and Coppola, with whom he 'collaborated' on the script for his scenes (eyewitnesses recall the actor hanging from palm trees tossing coconuts at the director during their 'conferences'), turn an enigmatic figure into an incomprehensible one.

The Formula (1980). This time he is only semi-bald, but he wears a hearing aid (actually it is radio receiver, picking up his lines as broadcast to him by an assistant director), and talks in a good-ole-boy accent. He is a powerful industrialist, managing a murderous conspiracy designed to keep a chemical substitute for oil from coming to market. His interpretation of this figure is as a foxy old gent, and that robs him – and the film – of menace. His co-star, playing the detective on his trail, is the only other man to reject an Academy Award, which turned out to be about the only thing Brando and George C. Scott had in common.

A pattern is evident here: Brando would idle professionally until he needed some money, then take whatever job seemed to offer the best pay for the least amount of work and, afterward, withdraw again. It would be pleasant to see it as embrace of the dispassionate professionalism he had once described – not stealing, but entertaining. Yet the work did not measure up even to that modest standard. For it was edged by contempt for both his craft and his public.

Now even the pretense of memorizing lines was abandoned, and so was the pretense of keeping up appearances. For *Last Tango* he had achieved the look of a noble ruin; in his subsequent films he appears in what became his permanent make-up, his final disguise, which is that of a hugely fat man. He also made sure the public knew what he was making – sometimes as much as $2 million for a few days' work. Occasionally he tried to turn that into a form of social criticism: 'What kind of society overpays its actors and neglects its underprivileged?' But what it read as was detestation for self and others: 'Look how much I'm making; look how little I'm doing.' It was not until 1980 that he more or less owned up to what he was doing. 'I'm not an actor and haven't been for years,' he finally admitted. 'I'm a human being hopefully a concerned and somewhat intelligent one – who occasionally acts.'

By that time, Gary Carey, one of his biographers, estimated that in his last four appearances, totaling well under an hour of screen time, he had made $10 million. And now, for almost a decade, he could afford to disappear from the screen, from public life, entirely. It became news – actual reportable news – when he was spotted in a restaurant. No one knows how he passed his time, and he resented it when people inquired. He said they had it backwards. Work was 'time out' for him, not vice vesa. It was what most people would consider idleness that was 'real'.

The truth is that he didn't do anything consequential. He was like an old gentleman retired from corporate life, filling his direction-less days as best he could. He added to his family (counting adoptees, he now has nine children). He read a lot, and never lightly. The easily impressionable said that he was continuing to search for the meaning of life. He put it more modestly: 'I've sort of lived a contemplative life, trying to figure out what it is I would like to do. I never really knew.' He also said he wrote a bit. He traveled a bit, too, mostly back and forth to his island, where he puttered inconclusively with various visionary schemes for tropical agriculture. He called his friends all over the world, at all hours of the day and night. And he ate. People found him curled up in bed with full gallons of ice cream. Others reported midnight Big Mac attacks. Thinking about him in his mansion, one began to think of Norma Desmond in hers.

In the late summer of 1989 a trailer for *The Dry White Season*, his first film in eight years, was shown in a crowded theater. One of his close-ups flashed on the screen. A gasp went up, so shocking was his appearance – grotesquely wrinkled and flabby. The little performance, as an idealist-cynical lawyer with pip-pip Oxbridge accent fighting apartheid laws in South Africa, was fine – he had two nice scenes. He went on Connie Chung's television show to denounce the producers for failing, he said, to make contributions they had promised they would make to various organizations opposing the South African regime. Ever hopeful of his favor, ever guilty about its own bad behavior in the past, Hollywood gave him another Academy Award nomination.

The following summer there was *The Freshman*. It was a sweet little farce, about an innocent college boy (Matthew Broderick) who falls in with the Mafia. Broderick and the rest of the young cast found him avuncular and supportive and anxious that his reputation not overwhelm them. Brando is reprising Don Corleone – same accent, but funny. People keep mentioning this uncanny resemblance, and when he overhears them he glares at them. It is a good running gag. And this is a good running performance, his first since *The Missouri Breaks*. He has a lovely moment when he visits the boy in his dorm room and awkwardly tries to articulate his affection for him. It is another of his singular, treasurable moments – pure behavioral magic. That moment is so truthful, and so startling in its casual context, that it makes you mist up, for it reminds you of your own failures to communicate across the generational line. And it reminds you that when we came in Brando was the young man sitting on the other side of that line, asking for understanding and not quite receiving it. To put it simply, it is richer in resonances than its creator could possibly know.

Eileen Heckart, a thoughtful and serious actress of Brando's generation, once said that 'anyone' could become a technically proficient actor, but added, 'The difference between anyone and a great actor is made up of those moments . . . in which they kindle a spark – something that makes a moment so real that what they are doing becomes great acting.'

She, of course, chose Brando to exemplify her meaning. Most actors do. Anne Jackson called him 'the daddy of them all. He dares and defies, and I love him for it.' A character man named Paul Benedict, who contributed a marvelous comic turn to *The Freshman* (He's the pompous and mean-spirited teacher of film theory) put it yet more simply: 'To those of us who came up in the Fifties, he's the man. He's the god.' Not long after he spoke, *Life* magazine devoted a special issue to the hundred most influential Americans of the century. Brando was the only actor who appeared in it, precisely because everyone its editors and reporters talked to, everyone who knows anything at all about acting, insisted that, evade though he will responsibility for a talent he cannot take credit for, he cannot evade history. 'He gave us our freedom. . . .' Yes. The freedom to imagine ourselves and our place in the world in a new way.

One wonders: does it drive him crazy, this determined refusal of others to accept him on his own discounted terms? One thinks of two other actors, each in his way Brando's peer. The first is John Barrymore, he whose name was so frequently evoked when Brando was coming up. The parallels between their late lives seem more vivid than whatever parallels may have existed between their early lives – the self parodies their audiences witnessed, the pervasive sense of waste that their supporters feel in contemplating their overall records. Two or three things Edmund Wilson wrote about Barrymore seem apposite to Brando 'He tried hard to find some role in life itself that he could count on and that would express him' and 'whenever, through exercise of will, he had achieved a high point of intensity by imposing on life his personal dream the role always failed and let him down with a crash'. Wilson speculated that Barrymore, as well as his brother Lionel and his sister Ethel, failed of fulfillment because 'they never had the actor's vocation.' Wilson adds: 'You see it very clearly if you compare them with their uncle, John Drew, who, glass of fashion and mold of form though he was, took the theater with professional seriousness, and even in his later years, at his blindest and most arthritic, kept his cast and himself up to scratch with the rigor of an old general at maneuvers.'

It is saving, this sense of vocation, and the professionalism that derives from it. It is where, at last, 'meaning' is to be found, if by that word we signify something modest – in the case of actors the search for truthful behavior, authentic emotion and the means of vividly imparting them to an audience, assuring them that they are not alone in their feelings, that what they experience in their privacy is shared by others. By making these matters public art comforts (and sometimes discomfits), but above all makes connections, assuages our loneliness – and perhaps the artist's as well. It is not nothing to have a gift for such work, and it is not nothing to exercise it with care and sobriety. And to look upon it as a calling and respond to that calling with passion. It is a completely honorable way to fill one's days – and one's thoughts.

Lacking a calling, all the Barrymores drifted into addiction. Lacking a calling, Brando drifted into self-absorption. And then into the self-contempt that analogizes so well with John Barrymore's. Curious, it is not, that two actors who are among the greatest members of their profession that America has produced in this century, were accidental actors, men for whom acting was not a cherished dream they could not help but embrace, but merely a way of escaping inconsequence, something to do until they could discover what they really wanted to do. Which, in turn, became a bad dream in which the dreamer desperately twists and turns trying to elude the demon of his own talent and the demon of (to him) false acclaim.

Here another acting name intrudes on one's thoughts. Paul Newman is almost exactly Brando's age, and he is everything Brando is not. He is fit and attractive. He has endured personal tragedy with dignity and courage. He continues to find serious work that engages and challenges him. He has also found causes that elicit his concern and he is practical-minded and effective on their behalf. He has, as well, found a way to remain present in the world, and at the same time to maintain his privacy. To put it simply, he has been a responsible artist and a responsible man, and so far as a stranger can tell, he leads a life of contentment and coherence, befitting a man who has worked seriously to develop the character he lives and the characters he plays.

It may be true that there are fewer 'moments' in his career, fewer of those seismic shocks of recognition where the actor brings us face to face with some truth we all acknowledge and share, but have not previously seen represented on the screen or stage. But the kind of epiphanies we are talking about are not created out of moral imperatives – hard work and a good life have nothing to do with their making. They are, as Brando's frantic desire to dismiss praise of them acknowledges, accidents of a sort – the products, perhaps, of genes and instincts and opportunity interacting unpredictably; the products, possibly of that thing people like to call genius, for which, as Laurence Olivier once remarked, the theatre has no room, because it is too troubling.

Troubling especially to those who possess and are possessed by it. How do you base a life on something that strikes you out of nowhere, is summoned up, usually, without conscious effort on your part? By putting yourself in places where the lightning seems most likely to strike. But how hard that is to do, especially when you think of that gift as not valuable or consequential in a world that appears to be lost in desperate agony; especially when you were taught long ago to consider yourself unworthy of special praise, and a highly unlikely receptacle for special endowments. One thinks – only half comically – that here is one final point of reference between Marlon Brando and the rest of us. One thinks that perhaps, in his sleepless early morning hours, he, too, wishes he were Paul Newman. Wishes, that is to say, that he did not have to waste the gains he considers ill-gotten on a stunned and reclusive search for coherence.

Of that, we cannot speak. Indeed, all we can confidently speak of in contemplating this life are our own memories of it. We may treasure, as he does not, the moments he gave us, at the same time speculating about the ones he didn't give us, out of spite or goofiness or whatever has moved him to not move us. Looking at him now, one can't help recalling the illimitable promise of his youth and perhaps of our own, and the inevitable confusions and compromises life imposes on us, the inevitable follies we impose on ourselves. Of the many illusions celebrity foists upon us the illusion of coherence, the sense that there are privileged people in the world who somehow know what they are doing in ways that we do not, is the largest, and possibly the most dangerous. But Marlon Brando has kept faith with incoherence. Whatever he has done and not done, no actor in his life and his work has more consistently kept us in touch with the erratic – that which is unpredictable and dangerous in ourselves and in the world. We continue to wish him well, some of us, for in so doing, we wish ourselves well, too. Wish ourselves, that is, that most elusive of miracles, the miracle of self-understanding.

BAD TIMES

'**A**s his lawyer addressed a throng of reporters gathered outside the courthouse under drizzling gray skies, the thirty-two-year-old freelance welder slipped quietly away in a chauffeur-driven black Mercedes-Benz.' This paragraph of routine reportorial prose has about it an uncommon resonance. Quite simply describing Christian Brando's exit from the courthouse on January 4, 1991, after his lawyers had succeeded in getting the original charge brought against him in the killing of Dag Drollet – first degree murder – reduced to voluntary manslaughter, to which he had just pleaded guilty, it also seemed to compress in a few words almost everything it is essential to know about him.

The disposition of the criminal act which is the only significant occurrance in his life is, as the victim's father, Jacques pointed out elsewhere in the article, the kind of outcome that well-connected young men, whose parents are willing to spare no legal expense, can usually look forward to in matters of this kind. Indeed, it was the consumation his team of lawyers had been trying to achieve since his arraignment in the early summer of 1990. Moreover, there is a poignance in the story's close juxtaposition of the young Brando's humble (and, to any parent harboring aspirations for his child, disappointing) occupation and the grand means by which he was transported to and from his day in court. Symbolically that juxtaposition suggests the vast range of confusions that must in some way brought him at last to this crime and the punishment attendant upon it.

It has never been my intention to write at length about Christian Brando and the events of May 16, 1990. Or to speculate about what occurred in his father's house when, in his sister Cheyenne's presence, he angrily confronted Drollet about the beatings she is supposed to have told her halfbrother her lover administered to her. For the record it must be noted that the girl, who is the daughter of Marlon Brando's third wife, Tarita (to whom he is still married, though he recently fathered a child, his ninth, with another woman) was twenty years old at the time, and was said to have told investigators that the killing was not accidental, but premeditated (at least for a matter of hours). It also has to be noted that Cheyenne subsequently fled to Tahiti, from which place it was impossible to extradite her and where – misery piled upon misery – she is said to have twice attempted suicide, leaving her in no condition to testify in a reliable fashion in her brother's case. It was, obviously, their inability to place her on the witness stand that led the prosecutors to at last accept Christian's plea to a lesser crime.

A little more than a month later, after a sentencing hearing that required a few more days of the court's (and the press's) time, Christian Brando received a sentence somewhat longer than a court-appointed social worker had recommended, somewhat shorter than his prosecutors had demanded: ten years – with possibility of parole in about half that time a distinct possibility. The young Brando bore himself with dignity and with obvious regret during this final ordeal, and evidence was introduced to show that he had been successfully treated for his addictions and that he was now a faithful member of Alcoholics Anonymous. The social worker's report, however, indicated that his addictions had caused him some permanent impairment of his faculties.

There, with the facts that became generally known in the months between Christian Brando's crime and its legal disposition one must leave this matter. Or so it seems to me. I do not believe that the sins of a father are necessarily visited on his children. Nor do I believe that a stranger can gain useful insight into a father's character by examining and speculating on a troubled son's and daughter's actions. Some dubious reportorial work along these lines has, of course, already appeared – and more will doubtless follow. Based on interviews with fringe figures – both in the life of Hollywood and in the lives of the Brando clan – what has so far been published offers the predictable pop narrative of offspring alternately ignored and indulged by a prominent and distracted father. In portraying Christian Brando this material mentions drugs, alcohol and an incapacity for stable relationships; a brief, checkered academic record; dashed hopes for an acting career; a work life consisting solely of odd menial jobs. These reports also portray Cheyenne in distressing terms; erratic, emotionally unstable, highly manipulative in her dealings with her family, with a particularly strong hold over Christian.

This is familiar stuff – not in its specific details, but in its general tenor. The supermarket tabloids, not to mention several decades of ghosted autobiographies by the troubled offspring of the rich and famous, have taught us not to be surprised by their miserable and often melodramatic doings. In this milieu, unhappy families seem to be all alike, and the progeny of the happy families do not attract the attention of the grocery store press, or feel compelled to write vengeful memoirs. One also notices in the journalism and in conversations about the Brando case, a certain grim and perhaps unworthy satisfaction about it – an implication that a comeuppance has been achieved. And that, too – psychobabble posing as social and moral comment – is something I want to avoid.

But as this chapter in the life of Marlon Brando moved toward its conclusion at the same time this book moved toward completion and then into the publishing process, one aspect of the former more and more insistently seemed to require some consideration in the latter; that was Marlon Brando's public response to the tragedy besetting his family. It was at apparent odds with the patterns of public behavior he had long since established. Yet it was not entirely out of character, either. Or so it seemed to someone who was then in the process of trying to make what sense he could out of this life.

One of the detectives summoned to the scene on the night Dag Drollett was killed has reported an interview with Brando that was both tearful and soulful. Questioning the actor in his bedroom, the policeman found himself being questioned about his own religious beliefs, his children and his relationships with them. Brando spoke about the difficulties of providing moral education for one's offspring, insisted that he had tried as best he could to do so while implying, according to the officer, that if he had it to do over – whether he was speaking of his life in general, or his relationship with his children specifically is not clear – he would manage things differently. The detective, more voluble than most members of his profession, described Brando as humble, almost meek, a tired and beaten man who seemed older than his years.

He continued to project this air in his appearances at various pre-trial hearings in his son's case. On these occasions, for the first time in his life, he did nothing to avoid the press. Quite the opposite. In the summer and fall of 1990, Los Angeles television stations ran lengthy excerpts from Brando's exchanges with the reportorial wolfpacks gathered outside the courthouse. It has been reported that on some of these occasions he spoke with the press for as much as forty-five minutes.

His basic line, quite naturally, was that he believed his son's story. Yes, the young man had suffered drug and alcohol problems, but, Brando insisted, he was innocent of any crime other than carelessness in this instance. 'He has never lied to me,' Brando kept repeating. He also implied, not implausibly, that his own fame was affecting his son's fate. The District Attorney's office, he said, was turning the case into 'a zoo and animal show' suggesting, not erroneously, that if Christian had been the son of some anonymous figure, he would have had a much better chance of achieving a negotiated settlement of the case against him. He also noted, with equal accuracy, that there would have been no more than brief, routine press coverage of this case were he not the father of the accused.

He was, however, careful not to criticize the press. 'You've taken shots at me,' he said on one occasion. 'Often I've deserved them. It's been part of the game.' But, he went on to say, his children were not famous in their own right, and therefore, in all justice, should not be included in the game. He more than once permitted tears to flow when the newspeople inquired with seeming sympathy about how he and the rest of the family were bearing up.

The victim's father, Jacques Drollet was not sympathetic to this performance. 'Brando is an actor and even in his private life he is always acting. He can cry and lie like a horse can run.' In anger and anguish, Drollet had arrived at a reading of Brando's character that the actor had long ago admitted ('I mean only forty per cent of what I say'). He had also somehow divined what few civilians, even film and theater critics, find difficult to believe, namely that crying on cue – which seems unimaginable to the none actor – is by general admission among themselves one of their easiest tricks, especially so for an actor trained in the tradition that informed Brando.

Drollet is obviously a shrewd man. For in the same brief quotation he also had this to say: 'I think he is making the whole case his own case.' This is precisely so. But for reasons perhaps less obvious than the victim's angry and anguished father could see.

Brando is, as all his attempts to grapple with complex or abstract issues show, a very simple man. His art, at its height, was concerned with the nuances of behavior and emotion, not of thought – no matter how many books he devoured (autodidacts are nearly always radical innocents). His view of the celebrity that so long ago caught him in its toils is as simple as his views about, say, geopolitics. It is, as we have seen, that it is embarrassing nonsense, this adulation of role players, imitators of life, mouthers of other people's words and ideas, receptacles of other people's fantasies. But so far as he could see – and he probably did not see far enough – the fact that he was famous and rather clumsily and excessively despised that condition harmed no one but himself. He seems not to have observed that it affected his children as they were growing up in a variety of ways that were hard to pinpoint and impossible to analyze or discuss.

Then in mid-May 1990 it was finally (and forcefully) borne in on him, in a very specific way, that his fame was now doing direct, quite calculable, harm to Christian in the ways we have heard him describe. And so Marlon Brando entered upon the remarkable course he pursued during the pre-trial months. His strategy was really quite transparent. He would give the press what it had for so many years lusted after – access to him. Or at least the appearance of access. He would patiently respond to its questions. He would reveal, appear to reveal, his emotions, which he presented in the most unambiguous readable terms – a father suffering and loyal and some-what pathetic, anyway meek and submissive, in an astonishing situation. The idea, very simply stated, was to deflect attention away from his son and on to himself.

That this was Brando's plan became particularly obvious in September, 1990, when he called Army Archard, the *Daily Variety* gossip columnist, and announced that he was going to write his autobiography. There was nothing he was unwilling to write about, he said, since he had 'no in-hibitions' and was, at last, eager to 'set the record straight' after so many decades in which he had been misrepresented by other writers. This was, of course, even more remarkable than his talking politely to the press, and it caused the predictable diversionary flurry. It was reported that a first bid for the book of $2 million was summarily rejected, and that other publish-ers would be invited to see an outline, talk to Brando's representative (his old friend and sometime director, George England), perhaps even meet with the would-be author, who insisted he required neither agent nor ghostwriter to bring the project to fruition.

Brando eventually did sign with a publisher, though by the time he did so, it seems likely that his needs and motives had changed. In his initial strategy, however, one perceived a search for simple justice – or, anyway, a desire, as he saw it, to rebalance its tilted scales. So much attention was being focused on Christian's case only because he was his father's son. Why not, therefore, encourage that attention to shift where it really wanted to be – on the father, on his responses to the situation? It was not hard to manage, not for a man practiced since childhood in the art of deflecting attention away from embarrassing kin and on to himself. And if, in the course of absorbing the media attention he could make a plea for fair treatment for his son, if he could turn him into the innocent victim of his father's fame it would surely do no harm to the son's cause. This, too, suited Brando's character, for as we know the defense of individuals, of whole classes of people he conceives to be innocently victimized, has been a lifelong habit. Indeed, the thought occurs that perhaps it was only now, in these melodramatic circumstances, the he finally saw Christian as a victim of his progenitor's celebrity, though in fact he had certainly been that – whatever else he had been – since childhood.

Certainly that was the tenor of Marlon Brando's remarkable appearance on the witness stand at Christian's pre-sentencing hearing. Television cameras were permitted in the courtroom and very extensive excerpts from it were broadcast. It was a saddening thing. First of all, there was his physical presence. Recent films, not to mention newspaper photos, had prepared us for the grotesquely swollen body, but not quite for its defeated carriage. Or for his manner of speaking. The mumbled tones were near to self-parody, and the hesitations between sentences and paragraphs made one think that possibly the man had suffered a mild stroke.

Then there was his singular manner. For despite the formality of the setting, his aim was to establish an air of rueful intimacy with his audience. He was like a father discussing 'kids' with some other veteran of the parental wars late at night as the Cognac went round, accepting his errors of commissions and (particularly) omission as he accepted responsibility for his son's messed up life, in particular rehearsing the terrible turmoils of his split with Anna Kashfi, and their impact on Christian in his formative years. At the same time – again there was a typicality about him – he took what pride he could in his son's good qualities – his honesty, his struggles to escape addiction and to make some kind of life for himself free of his father's fame and wealth. Finally, and most movingly, he described asking police officers to open the body bag in which Dag Drollet's body was being taken from the scene of the crime, and kissing the young man – whom he said he had grown to love – farewell. He also apologized (in French) to the Drollet family, who were in court.

With all this he succeeded in establishing the genuineness of his own emotions and in establishing the idea that, except for the deadly outburst against Dag Drollet, Christian was not so very different from the troubled and indulged offspring of other upper-middle class children of divorce, deeply disturbed by the warfare between their parents, and as a consequence over-indulged as they grow up and then over-subsidized as they endlessly prolong the search to 'find themselves' in young adult life.

Listening to him, a person who has acquired a certain knowledge about Marlon Brando's personal history could not help but reflect on how the actor's own young manhood might have influenced his relationship with his son. After all, he had scarcely been a model of bourgeois propriety, even after he has achieved his astonishing early success. Nor had his own family provided him with a example of functional stability. Reluctantly, one came also to the topic he had forbidden himself: Brando's endless pursuit of darkly exotic women, women as far removed in appearance and manner from his mother as it was possible to be (of which Anna Kashfi, deracinated and profoundly troubled was paradigmatic) and his inability to establish with any of them anything approaching a comfortable, 'normal' life which would be nurturing to a growing child.

Listening to him, watching him, this simple thought occured: the man was never given the chance, or took the chance, to get his feet under him, never had that period of time which, say, the college years or the long, lean years when one struggles to establish a career (and there is lots of time, when the phone is not ringing, for fruitful self-examination) provide the rest of us to get to know ourselves. He lurched from unstable adolescence to destabilising fame, to unhinging failures to despairing cynicism, with only a relatively few moments of professional gratification (which, comparatively speaking, seemed paltry) to sustain him.

Many agreed with the elder Drollet: his appearances, informal and formal, on his son's behalf seemed to be yet another performance. Perhaps in some sense they were. Perhaps they were no more than canny impersonations of the other middle class parents he had heard trying to puzzle out their messed up kinds. In other words, it is possible to read all this cynically.

But as it happens, I do not. It is one of the most obvious things about this life: Marlon Brando is never more childlike and transparent than when he is affecting cynicism or when he is trying to behave in a calculating fashion. Put ons are within his natural range as an actor, but cunning is not. It seems to me he did not play his chosen role in this instance very subtly. Yet it also seems to me that his inauthenticity betokened a larger authenticity – a desperation and a grief that he has not yet come to terms with, and may never come to terms with.

It may well be that his autobiography, even if it first occured to him as a diversionary tactic, but which he finally contracted for in the weeks after Christian's final court appearance, may have been transformed, in his mind, into just such a final effort to come to terms with the chaos of his runaway life. I hope so. At the outset of this book I suggested that the tragedy Marlon Brando has lately endured is something with which anyone – especially any parent, trying to imagine his or her reactions if his or her child fell into trouble as terrible as this man's son has – can identify and sympathize.

But now that this drama has fully played out one can say that it has changed the nature of our relationship with him. Until now, most of what we have known about him as a mature public figure outside of his roles and most of what we have heard about him as a private person has seemed too exotic, too *sui generis* if you will, to provoke such feelings. When we were all young together he more or less accidentally, through his work, gave shape and form to what we were pleased to think was rebelliousness, but was actually a desire to make a separate peace with the world we never made. Now that we are all older he quite accidentally, through this crisis in his life, gives, so it seems to me, shape and form to age's natural desire to achieve a separate peace with the world we have had quite enough of, thank you. And to the knowledge, which we all try desperately to deny, that somehow circumstances will always somehow contrive to deny us that peace. If he can deal with all that in his writing he might yet achieve what he sometimes, momentarily, achieved in his work as an actor – an imitation of life breathtaking in its perfection, its sense of truth unmediated by artifice.

Probably he will not accomplish this. What writer ever does? But the effort if honorably undertaken and sustained is worth undertaking and it is appropriately undertaken at this moment.

In some curious and cruel way, this story has come full circle. We would have preferred, surely, to see Marlon Brando perform *Lear* on a stage somewhere, or on the screen, cast, not cast up, in this role, rehearsed in it, not improvising it for the hand-held cameras of the newsmen. And one cannot help but wonder if, at last, he might secretly share that preference. For disciplined, concentrated professional engagement, that saving quality that Marlon Brando discovered as a young actor, and then abandoned (or squandered) in his later years, might have consoled those years (as it did Olivier's for instance), might even has provided an example of function for his seemingly disfunctional family. Perhaps his plunge into what 'the abyss' of the self, conducted in private, can at last provide him what he never found in the more public profession that found him and in which he only occasionally found himself – a sense of coherence, a sense of an ending.

About these mysteries we cannot speak with any confidence. But this final irony must be recorded. The fame that has so plagued him and, as he conceived it, damaged and finally threatened his son is not unjustified – whatever he may think. To be sure, most of the reporters who pressed around him had only the slightest knowledge of the work by which he initially achieved the prominence they were now obliged by their trade to exploit. To be sure, most of their readers had even less sense of what his career had meant to the history of his art, the history of the media in which he had practiced it. To them he was in the famous phrase, well known primarily for being well-known. But here at the end it seems necessary to reiterate this simple fact: the force of his public personality and his work, however incomplete has left it, however often he has denigrated it, has in itself and in its influence, permanently altered the way we perceive and judge the actor's art.

He may register contempt for that achievement and indifference to that measure of immortality he has gained through it. But deny it though he will, we cannot and should not. If, perhaps, we wanted more of him, if, perhaps, he might have given more, he yet did enough to change permanently the way his profession represents ourselves to ourselves. Caught up as we have been of late in the short run of scandal, we need to remind ourselves that Marlon Brando is also caught up more gratefully and more permanently in the longer run of at least two generation's memories, and that these memories are not entirely inconsequential; the impact of his personality and the aesthetic values he represented to some degree altered our understanding of ourselves and our world. We also need to remind ourselves that he is caught up as well in the still longer run of history and that it, like this book, is likely to judge his place in the life of his times to be significant, even in some measure shaping. To think otherwise is to surrender this life and therefore some portion of our own lives, to the meanest impulse of our age, which is to trivialize all that is not instantly and comfortably comprehensible.

Acknowledgements and Bibliographical Note

Some of the factual matter in this book is based on previously unpublished material. An American publication, which prefers anonymity, gathered a great deal of first rate reporting about Marlon Brando through the years and very kindly permitted me access to its files. They contained no startling or scandalous revelations, but there was much there that, for various reasons – among them, doubtless, space limitations – was not immediately usable journalistically, but was invaluable to someone trying to put this career into longer perspective. Brando, for example, offered interesting insights about his own work in a time when he was somewhat more accessible to reporters, and the recollections of his formative years, made by family, friends and early theatrical colleagues when their memories were undimmed by the passage of time, seemed to me fresher and more richly detailed than what they have said more recently or written in their autobiographies. In any case, I am pleased to acknowledge my debt to the owners of material that has greatly enriched this book. I am equally grateful to three of Brando's directors, Elia Kazan, Joseph L. Mankiewicz and Arthur Penn, for their memories of working with him, which they offered me in the course of more wide-ranging interviews, conducted in aid of a different project, in 1990.

The bibliography that follows records my most important debts to printed sources. Place of publication is New York, unless otherwise noted.

Adler, Renata, *Toward a Radical Middle: 14 Pieces of Reporting and Criticism*. Random House, 1969.

Bosworth, Patricia, *Montgomery Clift*. Harcourt, Brace, Jovanovich, 1978.

Callow, Simon, *Charles Laughton*. Grove Press, 1987.

Capote, Truman, *The Selected Writings of Truman Capote*. ('The Duke in His Domain'). Random House, 1963.

Cary, Gary, *Marlon Brando: The Only Contender*. London: Robson Books, Ltd., 1985.

Ciment, Michael (ed.), *An American Odyssey: Elia Kazan*. London: Bloomsbury Publishing, 1988.

Cole, Lester, *Hollywood Red*. Palo Alto: Ramparts Press, 1981.

Cowie, Peter, *Coppola: A Biography*. Charles Schribner's Sons, 1990.

Dmytryk, Edward, *It's A Hell of Life But Not a Bad Living*. Times Books, 1978.

Downing, David, *Marlon Brando*. Stein & Day, 1984.

Farber, Manny, *Negative Space*. Prager Publishers, 1971.

Fiore, Carlo, *Bud: The Brando I Knew*. Delacorte Press, 1974.

Geist, Kenneth L, *Pictures Will Talk: The Life and Films of Joseph L. Mankiewicz*. Charles Scribner's Sons, 1978.

Gill, Brendan, *Tallulah*. Holt, Rinehart & Winston, 1972.

Hirsch, Foster, *A Method to Their Madness: The History of the Actors Studio*. W. W. Norton & Co., 1984.

Higham, Charles, *Brando: The Unauthorized Biography*. NAL Books, 1987.

Houseman, John, *Front and Center*. Simon & Schuster, 1979.

Huston, John, *An Open Book*. Alfred A. Knopf, 1980.

Jordan, René, *Marlon Brando*. Galahad Books, 1973.

Kael, Pauline, *Deeper Into Movies*. Boston: Atlantic-Little, Brown, 1973.

Kael, Pauline, *Reeling*. Boston: Atlantic-Little, Brown, 1976.

Kashfi, Anna & E. P. Stein, *Brando For Breakfast*. Crown Publishers, 1979.

Kazan, Elia, *A Life*. Alfred A. Knopf, 1988.

Kolker, Philip, *Bernardo Bertolucci*. Oxford University Press, 1985.

Koster, Henry (Interviewed by Irene Kahn Atkins) *Henry Koster*. Metuchen & London: Directors Guild of America and The Scarecrow Press, 1987.

Lewis, Robert, *Slings and Arrows: Theater in My Life*. Stein & Day, 1984.

Mailer, Norman, 'A Transit to Narcissus', *New York Review of Books*. May 17, 1973.

Mankiewicz, Joseph L, *More About All About Eve* (A Colloquy with Gary Cary). Random House, 1972.

Marill, Alvin H, *Samuel Goldwyn Presents*. A. S. Barnes & Co., 1976.

Nickens, Christopher, *Brando: A Biography in Pictures*. Garden City: Dolphin/ Doubleday, 1987.

Offen, Ron, *Brando*. Chicago: Henry Regnery, 1973.

Ray, Robert B, *A Certain Tendency of the Hollywood Cinema, 1930-1980*. Princeton: Princeton University Press, 1985.

Redfield, William, *Letters from an Actor*. The Viking Press, 1967.

Ross, Lillian & Helen, *The Player*. Limelight Editions, 1984. (Reprint of 1962 edition.)

Sarris, Andrew, *Confessions of a Cultist: On the Cinema, 1955-1969*. Simon & Schuster, 1970.

Sarris, Andrew, *Politics and the Cinema*. Columbia University Press, 1978.

Schnayerson, Michael, *Irwin Shaw: A Biography*. G. P. Putnam's Sons, 1989.

Selznick, Irene Mayer, *A Private View*. Alfred A. Knopf, 1983.

Shivers, Alfred S, *The Life of Maxwell Anderson*. Stein & Day, 1983.

Simon, John, *Reverse Angle*. Clarkson N. Potter, 1982.

Thomas, Tony, *The Films of Marlon Brando*. Citadel Press, 1973.

Walker, Alexander, *Vivien: A Life of Vivien Leigh*. Grove-Weidenfeld, 1987.

Warshow, Robert, *The Immediate Experience*. Garden City: Doubleday & Co., 1962.

Wilson, Edmund, *Classics and Commercials: A Literary Chronicle of the Forties* ('The Life and Times of John Barrymore'). Farrar, Straus & Co., 1950.

Acknowledgements of Photographs

The following illustrations appear by the kind permission of:

Aquarius 72; Associated Press 68, 69; Cecil Beaton/Sotheby's 33; The Kobal Collection 20, 22, 23, 24, 25, 26, 29, 30, 31, 32, 34, 35, 36, 37, 39, 40, 42, 43, 45, 46, 47, 50, 52, 53, 54, 55, 57, 58, 60, 64, 65, 66, 70, 71, 73, 74, 76, 77, 78, 80, 81, 82, 83, 84, 85, 89; Lou Valentino 1, 3, 4, 6, 8, 11; New York Public Library 14; NY Public Library/Theatre Collection 17, 18, 19; NY Public Library/Vandamm Collection 15, 16; Pictorial Parade, 2, 5, 7, 9, 12, 13, 27, 28, 41, 44, 51, 59, 61, 62, 63, 67, 75, 79; UPI/Bettmann 38, 49, 56, 86, 87, 88.

The publishers acknowledge with thanks the cooperation of the following film producers and distributors whose publicity photographs appear in this book:

Allran; Les Artistes Associés; Columbia; Charles Feldman; Goetz Pictures; Samuel Goldwyn; Elliott Kastner; Elia Kazan; Stanley Kramer; MGM; Omni Zoctrope; Paramount; PEA; Pennebaker; Scimitar; Seven Arts; Sam Spiegel; Tri-Star; 20th Century-Fox; United Artists; Warner Bros.

FILMOGRAPHY

THE MEN
Director: Fred Zinnemann
Screenplay: Carl Foreman
Photography: Robert de Grasse
Cast: Marlon Brando, Teresa
Wright, Everett Sloane, Jack
Webb, Howard St John
Running time: 85 mins
Released: 1950
Produced by Stanley Kramer

A STREETCAR NAMED
DESIRE
Director: Elia Kazan
Screenplay: Tennessee
Williams, from
his play
Photography: Harry Stradling
Cast: Vivien Leigh, Marlon
Brando, Kim Hunter, Karl
Malden
Running time: 122 mins
Released: 1951
Produced by Charles K
Feldman/Elia Kazan

VIVA ZAPATA
Director: Elia Kazan
Screenplay: John Steinback
Photography: Joe MacDonald
Cast: Marlon Brando, Jean
Peters, Joseph Wiseman,
Anthony Quinn, Arnold Moss,
Margo, Frank Silvera.
Running time: 113 mins
Released: 1952
Produced by 20th Century Fox

JULIUS CAESAR
Director: Joseph L Mankiewicz
Screenplay: Joseph L
Mankiewicz, from the play by
William Shakespeare
Photography: Joseph
Ruttenberg
Cast: John Gielgud, James
Mason, Marlon Brando, Greer
Garson, Deborah Kerr, Louis
Calhern, Edmond O'Brien,
George Macready, Michael
Pate, John Hoyt, Alan Napier
Running time: 121 mins
Released: 1953
Produced by MGM

THE WILD ONE
Director: Laslo Benedek
Screenplay: John Paxton, from
the story The Cyclist's Raid by

Frank Rooney.
Photography: Hal Mohr
Cast: Marlon Brando, Lee
Marvin, Mary Murphy, Robert
Keith, Jay C Flippen
Running time: 79 mins
Released: 1954
Produced by Columbia/Stanley
Kramer

ON THE WATERFRONT
Director: Elia Kazan
Screenplay: Budd Schulberg
Photography: Boris Kaufman
Cast: Marlon Brando, Eva
Marie Saint, Lee J Cobb, Rod
Steiger, Karl Malden, Pat
Henning, Leif Erickson, James
Westerfield, John Hamilton
Running time: 108 mins
Released: 1954
Produced by Columbia/Sam
Spiegel

DESIREE
Director: Henry Koster
Screenplay: Daniel Taradash,
from the novel by Annemarie
Selinko
Photography: Milton Krasner
Cast: Jean Simmons, Marlon
Brando, Merle Oberon,
Michael Rennie, Cameron
Mitchell, Elizabeth Sellars,
Cathleen Neshitt, Isobel Elsom
Running time: 110 mins
Released: 1954
Produced by 20th Century Fox

GUYS AND DOLLS
Director: Joseph L Mankiewicz
Screenplay: Joseph L.
Mankiewicz, from the musical
by Jo Swerling and Abe
Burrows
Photography: Oliver Smith
Cast: Frank Sinatra, Marlon
Brando, Jean Simmons, Vivian
Blaine, Stubby Kaye, B S
Pully, Robert Keith, Sheldon
Leonard, George E Stone
Running time: 149 mins
Released: 1955
Produced by Samuel Goldwyn

THE TEAHOUSE OF THE
AUGUST MOON
Director: Daniel Mann

Screenplay: John Patrick, from
his play
Photography: John Alton
Cast: Marlon Brando, Glenn
Ford, Eddie Albert, Paul Ford,
Michiko Kyo, Henry Morgan
Running time: 123 mins
Released: 1956
Produced by MGM

SAYONARA
Director: Joshua Logan
Screenplay: Paul Osborn, from
the novel by James A Michener
Photography: Ellsworth
Fredericks
Cast: Marlon Brando, Miyoshi
Umeki, Miiko Taka, Red
Buttons, Ricardo Montalban,
Patricia Owens, Kent Smith,
Martha Scott, James Garner
Running time: 147 mins
Released: 1957
Produced by Goetz Pictures-
Pennebaker

THE YOUNG LIONS
Director: Edward Dmytryk
Screenplay: Edward Anhalt,
from the novel by Irwin Shaw
Photography: Joe MacDonald
Cast: Marlon Brando,
Montgomery Clift, Dean
Martin, Hope Lange, Barbara
Rush, May Britt, Maximilian
Schell, Lee Van Cleef
Running time: 167 mins
Released: 1958
Produced by 20th Century Fox

THE FUGITIVE KIND
Director: Sidney Lumet
Screenplay: Tennessee Williams
and Meade Roberts, from the
play by Tennessee Williams
Photography: Boris Kaufman
Cast: Marlon Brando, Anna
Magnani
Running time: 119 mins
Released: 1960
Produced by United Artists/
Martin Jurow/Richard A
Shepherd/Pennebaker

ONE EYED JACKS
Director: Marlon Brando
Screenplay: Guy Trooper and
Calder Willingham, from the
novel 'The Authentic Death of

Hendry Jones' by Charles
Neider
Photography: Charles Lang
Cast: Marlon Brando, Karl
Malden, Pina Pellicier, Katy
Jurado, Slim Pickens, Ben
Johnson, Timothy Carey,
Elisha Cook Jnr
Running time: 141 mins
Released: 1961
Produced by Paramount/
Pennebaker

MUTINY ON THE BOUNTY
Director: Lewis Milestone
Screenplay: Charles Lederer
Photography: Robert Surtees
Cast: Trevor Howard, Marlon
Brando, Richard Harris, Hugh
Griffith, Tarita, Richard
Haydn, Percy Herbert, Duncan
Lamont, Gordon Jackson,
Chips Rafferty, Noel Purcell
Running time: 185 mins
Released: 1962
Produced by MGM/Arcola

THE UGLY AMERICAN
Director: George Englund
Screenplay: Stewart Stern. from
the novel by William J Lederer
and Eugene Burdick
Photography: Clifford Stine
Cast: Marlon Brando, Eiji
Okada, Sandra Church, Pat
Hingle, Arthur Hill, Jocelyn
Brando, Kukrit Pramoj
Running time: 120 mins
Released: 1963
Produced by Universal
International/George Englund

BEDTIME STORY
Director: Ralph Levy
Screenplay: Stanley Shapiro
and Paul Henning
Photography: Clifford Stine
Cast: David Niven, Marlon
Brando, Shirley Jones, Dody
Goodman, Aram Stephen,
Marie Widnsor
Running time: 99 mins
Released: 1964
Produced by Universal-
International/Lankershim/
Pennebaker

**THE SABOTEUR, CODE
NAME "MORITURI"**
Director: Bernhard Wicki
Screenplay: Daniel Taradash,
from the novel by Werner
Jeorg Kosa
Photography: Conrad Hall
Cast: Yul Brynner, Marlon

Brando, Trevor Howard, Janet
Maslin
Running time: 122 mins
Released: 1965
Produced by 20th Century Fox/
Arcola/Colony

THE CHASE
Director: Arthur Penn
Screenplay: Lillian Hellman,
from the novel by Horton
Foote
Photography: Joseph La Shelle
Cast: Marlon Brando, Jane
Fonda, Robert Redford, Angie
Dickinson, Janice Rule, James
Fox, Robert Duvall, E G
Marshall, Miriam Hopkins,
Henry Hull
Running time: 135 mins
Released: 1966
Produced by Columbia/Sam
Spiegel

**THE APPALOOSA (aka
SOUTHWEST TO SONORA)**
Director: Sidney J Furie
Screenplay: James Bridges and
Roland Kibbee, from the novel
by Robert MacLeod
Photography: Russell Metty
Cast: Marlon Brando,
Anjanette Comer, John Saxon,
Rafael Campos, Frank Silvera
Running time: 99 mins
Released: 1966
Produced by Universal

**A COUNTESS FROM HONG
KONG**
Director: Charles Chaplin
Screenplay: Charles Chaplin
Photography: Arthur Ibbetson
Cast: Marlon Brando, Sophia
Loren, Patrick Cargill,
Margaret Rutherford, Charles
Chaplin, Sydney Chaplin,
Oliver Johnston, John Paul
Running time: 120 mins
Released: 1967
Produced by Universal

**REFLECTIONS IN A
GOLDEN EYE**
Director: John Huston
Screenplay: Chapman Mortimer
and Gladys Hill, from the novel
by Carson McCullers
Photography: Aldo Tonti
Cast: Marlon Brando,
Elizabeth Taylor, Brian Keith,
Julie Harris, Robert Forster,
Zorro David
Running time: 108 mins
Released: 1967
Produced by Warner Seven Arts

CANDY
Director: Christian Marquand
Screenplay: Buck Henry, from
the novel by Terry Southern
Photography: Giuseppe
Rotunno
Cast: Ewa Aulin, Richard
Burton, Marlon Brando, James
Coburn, Walter Matthau,
Charles Aznavour, John
Huston, Elsa Martinelli, Ringo
Starr, John Astin
Running time: 124 mins
Released: 1968
Produced by Selmur/Dear/
Corona

QUEIMADA (aka BURN!)
Director: Gillo Pontecorvo
Screenplay: Franco Solinas and
Giorgio Arlorio
Photography: Marcello Gatti
Cast: Marlon Brando, Renato
Salvatori, Norman Hill,
Evaristo Marquez
Running time: 132 mins
Released: 1968
Produced by PEA/PPA

**THE NIGHT OF THE
FOLLOWING DAY**
Director: Hubert Cornfield
Screenplay: Hubert Cornfield &
Robert Phippeny, from the
novel 'The Snatchers' by Lionel
White
Photography: Willy Kurant
Cast: Marlon Brando, Richard
Boone, Rita Moreno, Pamela
Franklin, Jess Hahn
Running time: 100 mins
Released: 1969
Produced by Universal/Gina

THE NIGHTCOMERS
Director: Michael Winner
Screenplay: Michael Hastings
Photography: Robert Paynter
Cast: Marlon Brando,
Stephanie Beacham, Thora
Hird, Harry Andrews, Verna
Harvey, Christopher Ellis,
Anna Palk
Running time: 96 mins
Released: 1971
Produced by Scimitar/Kastner-
Kanter-Ladd

THE GODFATHER
Director: Francis Ford Coppola
Screenplay: Francis Ford
Coppola and Mario Puzo, from
the novel by Mario Puzo
Photography: Gordon Willis
Cast: Marlon Brando, Al
Pacino, Robert Duvall, James

Caan, Richard Castellano, Diane Keaton, Talia Shire, Richard Conte, John Marley, Sterling Hayden, John Cazale
Running time: 175 mins
Released: 1971
Produced by Paramount/Alfran

LAST TANGO IN PARIS
Director: Bernardo Bertolucci
Screenplay: Bernardo Bertolucci and Franco Arcalli
Photography: Vittorio Storaro
Cast: Marlon Brando, Maria Schneider, Jean-Pierre Léaud
Running time: 129 mins
Released: 1972
Produced by Lews Artistes Associés/PEA/United Artists

THE MISSOURI BREAKS
Director: Arthur Penn
Screenplay: Thomas McGuane
Photography: Michael Butler
Cast: Marlon Brando, Jack Nicholson, Randy Quaid, Kathleen Lloyd, Frederick Forrest, Harry Dean Stanton, John McLian, John P Ryan, Richard Bradford
Running time: 126 mins
Released: 1976
Produced by United Artists/Elliott Kastner

SUPERMAN
Director: Richard Donner
Screenplay: Mario Puzo, David Newman, Robert Benton and Leslie Newman
Photography: Geoffrey Unsworth
Cast: Christopher Reeve, Marlon Brando, Margot Kidder, Jackie Cooper, Glenn Ford, Phyllis Thaxter, Trevor Howard, Gene Hackman, Ned Beatty, Susannah York, Valerie Perrine
Running time: 142 mins
Released: 1978
Produced by Warner/Alexander Salkind

ROOTS: THE NEW GENERATIONS*
Director: John Erman, Charles S Dubin, George Stanford Brown and Lloyd Richards
Screenplay: Ernest Kinoy, Sidney A Glass, Thad Mumford, Daniel Wilcox, John McGreevey
Photography: Joseph M Wilcots
Cast: James Earl Jones, George Stanford, Olivia de Havilland,

Henry Fonda, Greg Morris, Richard Thomas, Dorian Harewood, Ruby Dee, Ossie Davis, George Voskovec, John Rubinstein, Pam Grier, Percy Rodrigues, Beah Richards, Robert Culp, Paul Winfield, Dina Merrill, Brock Peters, Andy Griffith, Marlon Brando, Michael Constantine, Damon Evans, Avon Long, Fay Hauser
Running time: 6×96 mins
Released: 1979
Produced by ABC/David Wolper

APOCALYPSE NOW
Director: Francis Coppola
Screenplay: John Milius and Francis Coppola
Photography: Vittorio Storaro
Cast: Martin Sheen, Robert Duvall, Frederic Forrest, Marlon Brando, Sam Bottoms, Denis Hopper, Harrison Ford, Albert Hall, Larry Fishburne, Scott Glenn
Running time: 153 mins
Released: 1979
Produced by Omni/Zoetrope

THE FORMULA
Director: John G Avildsen
Screenplay: Steven Shagan, from his novel
Photography: James Crabe
Cast: George C Scott, Marlon Brando, Marthe Keller, John Gielgud, Beatrice Straight, Richard Lynch
Running time: 117 mins
Released: 1980
Produced by MGM/CIP

A DRY WHITE SEASON
Director: Euzhan Palcy
Screenplay: Colin Welland and Euzhan Palcy, from the novel by André Brink
Photography: Kevin Pike and Pierre-William Glenn
Cast: Donald Sutherland, Janet Suzman, Zakes Mokae, Jürgen Prochnow, Susan Sarandon, Marlon Brando, Winston Ntshona, Thoko Ntshinga
Running time: 107 mins
Released: 1989
Produced by MGM

THE FRESHMAN
Director: Andrew Bergman
Screenplay: Andrew Bergman
Photography: William A Fraker
Cast: Marlon Brando, Matthew Broderick, Bruno Kirby,

Penelope Ann Miller, Frank Whaley, Jon Polito, Paul Benedict, Maximilian Schell
Running time: 102 mins
Released: 1990
Produced by Tri-Star/Lobell-Bergman

*Made for television

PLAYS

I REMEMBER MAMA
(1944)
Writer: John Van Druten, from the novel "Mama's Bank Account" by Kathryn Forbes
Director: John Van Druten
Cast: Joan Tetzel, Mady Christians, Richard Bishop, Carolyn Hummel, Frances Heflin, Oswald Marshall, Marlon Brando

TRUCKLINE CAFE (1946)
Writer: Maxwell Anderson
Director: Harold Clurman
Cast: Frank Overton, Ralph Theadore, John Sweet, Kevin McCarthy, June Walker, Karl Malden, Ann Shepherd, Marlon Brando

CANDIDA (1946)
Writer: George Bernard Shaw
Director: Guthrie McClintic
Cast: Mildred Natwick, Wesley Addy, Olivier Cliff, Cedric Hardwicke, Katharine Cornell, Marlon Brando

A FLAG IS BORN (1946)
Writer: Ben Hecht
Director: Luther Adler
Cast: Qyentin Reynolds, Paul Muni, Celia Adler, Marlon Brando, Mario Berini, George David Baxter

THE EAGLE HAS TWO HEADS (1946)
Writer: Jean Cocteau
Cast: Tallulah Bankhead, Marlon Brando (fired after first night)

A STREETCAR NAMED DESIRE (1947)
Writer: Tennessee Williams
Director: Elia Kazan
Cast: Jessica Tandy, Marlon Brando, Kim Hunter, Karl Malden

INDEX